Quick Degunking Sheet!

The Degunking 12-Step Program

Here's the basic 12-step process you should follow to degunk your Microsoft Office setup:

1. Make sure that the version of Office you are using is the one that optimally suits your needs and that you've properly installed the software while limiting the introduction of as much gunk as possible (Chapter 3).

2. Organize your Office-related files and folders (Chapter 4).

3. Perform a set of cleanup and configuration tasks that make all the Office applications work better (Chapter 5).

4. Fully degunk and optimize Word (Chapter 6).

5. Fully degunk and optimize Excel (Chapter 7).

6. Fully degunk and optimize PowerPoint (Chapter 8).

7. Fully degunk and optimize Outlook (Chapter 9).

8. Use Office interoperability features to enhance your productivity (Chapter 10).

9. Implement key security best practices to keep personal and private information safe in shared documents and protect your PC from virus infection (Chapter 11).

10. Set up a backup schedule and create restore points so that you can successfully recover from application failures or calamities of nature (Chapter 12).

11. Perform a set of tasks to troubleshoot application crashes, repair broken installations, recover corrupted templates and prevent them in the future (Chapter 13).

12. Make the most of third-party add-ins and tools to increase the usefulness of Office (Appendix A).

Degunking with Time Limitations

The 12-step process is simple and straightforward. You'll get the maximum benefit out of the program if you perform each step in the order given, although that requires a bit of time. Even when you have time limitations, you can still gain benefits from degunking Office. Use spare moments throughout your day to nibble away at the clutter that's gunking up your system. Following are suggestions of how to degunk when your time is limited.

Ten-Minute Degunking

If you have just a short amount of time available or you're able to degunk while you wait on hold on the telephone, for instance, you should concentrate on high-priority degunking tasks, such as backing up your data and optimizing the space on your PC to help Office run more smoothly.

1. Back up your Office files and Outlook data by using the Backup utility or by manually copying specific folders to removable media (pages 299 and 301).

2. Run Disk Cleanup to optimize hard disk performance and remove excess gunk (page 39).

3. Run Disk Defragmenter to consolidate free space on your hard disk (page 70).

4. Run your antivirus software and any appropriate installed add-ins to scan for macro viruses and other bugs (page 287).

Thirty-Minute Degunking

When you have a bit more time, you can focus on getting organized by removing the excess gunk from your folder system and the default storage locations for Office files. We recommend completing the 10-minute degunking tasks as well as these:

1. Make a pass through the My Documents folder to be sure that it is properly organized with useful subfolders and that old and tired files are removed (page 53).

2. Move any Office files that remain in the root directory (usually C:) to appropriate subfolders you create in My Documents (page 54).

3. Clean up shared folders (page 54).

4. Search for and destroy any temporary files lingering on your system (page 56).

5. Empty the Recycle Bin (page 70).

6. Visit **http://office.microsoft.com/en-us/officeupdate/default.aspx** and download any free Office updates that you need (page 327).

One-Hour Degunking

When you have a whole hour to spend degunking, you can go a little deeper. Because Outlook is such an important application—it handles your daily communication and helps keep you on schedule—and it can get gunked up quickly, use this hour to focus on degunking it. Revisit any task from the 10- and 30-minute degunking sessions that might need repeating, such as deleting temporary file gunk, and then move on to degunking Outlook:

1. Sort your Inbox (and any other mail folders you might have) by sender or by date, and then remove blocks of e-mails that you no longer need (page 197).

2. Sort your mail folders by message size, and then delete 20—or more!—of the oldest or largest messages and attachments (page 60).

3. Examine the messages in your Inbox and then create subfolders that enable you to sort and store incoming mail quickly (page 197).

4. Configure the AutoArchive settings on each mail folder to optimize Outlook performance (page 198).

5. Configure the Rules Wizard to sort your mail automatically (page 213).

6. Set up a junk e-mail filter to get rid of annoying spam (page 215).

7. Organize your contacts by sorting them in last-name-first order (page 201).

8. Use color-coding in your calendars and tasks lists to stay organized (page 202).

9. Empty the Deleted Items folder (page 221).

Three-Hour Degunking

You can optimize Office overall when you have a large chunk of time available. Repeat any steps from the shorter degunking sessions that help you keep your folder system clean, and then jump into optimizing the common features of the Office applications:

1. In each Office application, clear out the unused commands that are gunking up your menus (page 86).

2. In each Office application, customize your toolbars so that commonly used commands are at your fingertips (page 89).

3. In each Office application, set up the default view to decrease the amount of time you have to spend setting up your workspace each time you open a new file (page 75).

4. Customize the keyboard shortcuts so that you can perform common activities, such as selecting and formatting objects, with a simple keystroke (page 96).

5. Set the AutoRecover interval in each application (pages 110, 150, 174, 208).

6. Customize the printer tray assignment and reverse the print order (page 100).

7. Make a macro-free copy of your custom templates (page 292).

Half-Day Degunking

When you have a half-day to degunk Office, you can get into customizing the functionality of each Office application. Perform the three-hour degunking tasks, and then focus on optimizing each application in turn:

1. In Word, focus on the following tasks:
   √ Change the default margins for all new documents (page 116).
   √ Add frequently used words and phrases to the AutoCorrect list (page 121).
   √ Develop styles for commonly used text formatting combinations (page 126).
   √ Make a backup copy of the Normal.dot template (page 77).
   √ Create templates to standardize new documents and save yourself formatting time (page 131).

2. In Excel, focus on the following tasks:
   √ Change the default number of sheets in a workbook (page 142).
   √ Create styles for commonly used cell formatting combinations (page 146).
   √ Enable word wrapping in cells (page 147).
   √ Customize cell selection behavior (page 149).
   √ Design a default workbook and worksheet template to speed new workbook creation (page 162).

3. In PowerPoint, focus on the following tasks:
   √ Turn off fast saves (page 169).
   √ Reduce the number of undos available (page 173).
   √ Turn off automatic formatting of inserted objects (page 175).
   √ Disable background printing (page 176).

    √   Customize design templates so frequently used slide layouts are easily accessible (page 185).

4. In Outlook, focus on the following tasks:

    √   Review your Inbox and remove old and unneeded items (page 197).

    √   Customize the formatting for new messages (page 209).

    √   Select the default folder Outlook opens in (page 212).

    √   Set the Deleted Items folder to empty automatically (page 221).

    √   Compress your archived folders (page 62).

Spare Moment Degunking

You can put your unclaimed moments throughout the day to good degunking use. While you're waiting for meeting participants to arrive, when you're on hold, or even when you're waiting for the coffee to finish brewing, complete one or two of the following quick Office degunking tips:

1. Delete five large e-mail attachments (page 60).

2. Eliminate a swath of old e-mail messages (page 60).

3. Empty the Deleted Items folder in Outlook (page 221).

4. Color-code the tasks on your to do list (page 202).

5. Search for and remove old temporary files (page 56).

6. Trash vacant user accounts (page 59).

7. Find old or redundant ZIP files and eliminate them (page 54).

8. Scan the My Documents folder and delete any unneeded files that reside there (page 53).

9. Make a pass through the folders you've created to hold your Office files, deleting unused folders and old files as you go (page 52).

10. Examine the names of your folders and files to be sure they are meaningful and descriptive. Rename items that are obscure (page 66).

11. Compress folders that contain information you want to keep but don't access very often (page 297).

12. Run Disk Cleanup (page 39).

13. Empty the Recycle Bin (page 69).

14. Back up your data manually or by using the Backup utility (pages 299 and 301).

15. Add a recurring task to your Task list to remind you to back up your Office data (page 301).

16. Defragment your hard disk (page 70).

17. Pick a menu in any Office application and customize it (page 88).

18. Add a frequently used command to a toolbar (page 89).

19. Set the AutoRecover interval in each of the applications (pages 110, 150, 174, 208).

20. Search the Internet for an add-in that can automate an Office degunking task (Appendix A).

DEGUNKING™ MICROSOFT® OFFICE

Wayne Palaia
Christina Palaia

PARAGLYPH™
PRESS

President
Keith Weiskamp

Editor-at-Large
Jeff Duntemann

Vice President, Sales, Marketing, and Distribution
Steve Sayre

Vice President, International Sales and Marketing
Cynthia Caldwell

Production Manager
Kim Eoff

Cover Designers
Kris Sotelo

Degunking™ Microsoft Office

Limits of Liability and Disclaimer of Warranty

Trademarks

Paraglyph Press, Inc.
4015 N. 78th Street, #115
Scottsdale, Arizona 85251
Phone: 602-749-8787
www.paraglyphpress.com

Paraglyph Press ISBN: 1-932111-95-6

Printed in the United States of America
10 9 8 7 6 5 4 3 2 1

PARAGLYPH
PRESS

The Paraglyph Mission

This book you've purchased is a collaborative creation involving the work of many hands, from authors to editors to designers and to technical reviewers. At Paraglyph Press, we like to think that everything we create, develop, and publish is the result of one form creating another. And as this cycle continues on, we believe that your suggestions, ideas, feedback, and comments on how you've used our books are important parts of the process for us and our authors.

We've created Paraglyph Press with the sole mission of producing and publishing books that make a difference. The last thing we all need is yet another tech book on the same tired, old topic. So we ask our authors and all of the many creative hands who touch our publications to do a little extra, dig a little deeper, think a little harder, and create a better book. The founders of Paraglyph are dedicated to finding the best authors, developing the best books, and helping you find the solutions you need.

As you use this book, please take a moment to drop us a line at **feedback@paraglyphpress.com** and let us know how we are doing—and how we can keep producing and publishing the kinds of books that you can't live without.

Sincerely,

Keith Weiskamp & Jeff Duntemann
Paraglyph Press Founders
4015 N. 78th Street, #115
Scottsdale, Arizona 85251
email: **feedback@paraglyphpress.com**
Web: **www.paraglyphpress.com**

Recently Published by Paraglyph Press:

Degunking Your PC
*By Joli Ballew
and Jeff Duntemann*

Degunking eBay
By Greg Holden

Degunking Your Email, Spam, and Viruses
By Jeff Duntemann

Degunking Windows
*By Joli Ballew
and Jeff Duntemann*

Degunking Your Mac
By Joli Ballew

Game Coding Complete, Second Edition
By Mike McShaffry

Small Websites, Great Results
By Doug Addison

**A Theory of Fun
For Game Design**
By Raph Koster

Perl Core Language Little Black Book, Second Edition
By Steven Holzner

3D Game-Based Filmmaking: The Art of Machinima
By Paul Marino

**Windows XP Professional: The Ultimate User's Guide,
Second Edition**
By Joli Ballew

Jeff Duntemann's Wi-Fi Guide, Second Edition
By Jeff Duntemann

Visual Basic .NET Core Language Little Black Book
By Steven Holzner

The SQL Server 2000 Book
*By Anthony Sequeira
and Brian Alderman*

To my family: No author had more love and support.
—Wayne

To Mom, for planting the seeds; to Dad, for providing the tools;
to Gram, for sharing her wisdom; and, of course,
to Dan, for taking such good care.
—Chris

About the Authors

Wayne Palaia has worked for the federal government as a computer scientist for 15 years, developing and maintaining software systems and specializing in real-time operations. Wayne administered the integration and deployment of more than 250 microcomputers to remote locations and designed the logistics support program for that system. He has used Microsoft Office for nearly 10 years to develop and maintain detailed technical documentation (user guides, handbooks, and developer documentation) and SQL client/server information systems using Microsoft Access and Oracle. He maintains a medium-sized office network and uses Office to develop Web sites, electronic books, and context-sensitive help systems for radar specialists.

Christina Palaia has been a freelance technical editor of computer-related books for nine years. She edits and develops certification exam manuscripts as well as general trade books and college textbooks on a variety of topics, including information technology and computer science. Christina has contributed to several Facts on File publications and developed a user manual for a customized software application for a national nonprofit organization. She is a partner in an editorial services business that serves major multinational publishing houses as well as small imprints and independent authors.

Acknowledgments

Thanks to Keith Weiskamp and the Paraglyph team. Special thanks to Christina, my coauthor and teammate, for all the late-night research and rewrites; the project could not have been done without her.
—Wayne Palaia

A book is the culmination of effort of many people, and we couldn't have had a more dedicated or supportive team. A big thank you goes to Wayne—the project wouldn't have come together without his technical knowledge. Thanks to Keith Weiskamp for giving us this opportunity and for keeping us focused. And to the rest of the Paraglyph crew, including Steve Sayre, Cynthia Caldwell, Judy Flynn, Kim Eoff, and Niki D'Andrea—your hard work is very much appreciated. Special thanks to Dan Young for providing the index when he could have been snowboarding instead! I simply could not have done this without Dan's constant support and encouragement.
—Christina Palaia

Contents at a Glance

Contents

Chapter 9
Degunking Microsoft Outlook 195

Chapter 12
Backing Up and Restoring Office 291

Chapter 13
Fixing Things That Break in Office 321

Introduction

At long last, you feel like a bonafide member of the twenty-first century, hip with the latest technology. Your new PC has the latest edition of Microsoft Office installed on it or you're about to install an upgrade and you've discovered you can use the Office applications to do amazing things. Who would have thought you could design the company letterhead by yourself with the help of Microsoft Word? And did you ever imagine you'd so easily be able to keep in touch with all your college buddies using that fabulous tool, electronic mail?

You've probably had a lot of fun experimenting with all the different things you can do with Office at home and at work. You've created spreadsheets in Excel to track the progress of each project you're involved with at work. You've compiled a slide show photo tour of your latest vacation. And you've discovered how to use the stationery feature in Outlook to add some pizzazz to your e-mail messages.

But lately, things have been going wrong. At home you can't find where on your PC you saved an important document you've been working on. At work, your company's main client is demanding that all vendors, including your organization, update to the latest version of Office, and you're nervous that your existing project files will suffer in the conversion process. Not to mention the application crashes you've been experiencing! It might seem that you can't have Word open for more than a couple of hours before something causes it to rudely abandon your work and close down. You start wondering, what's going on with Office that it's become so flakey lately?

Quite simply, Office has become gunked up. Fortunately, we'll show you in this book how to get everything in shipshape again using simple methods that involve just a little time, some dedication, and practically no expense.

Gunk is a by-product of the Office applications you use; it's like that nasty film of pink mold that creeps out of the corners of the shower when you're not paying attention. Electronic gunk has the same opportunistic nature, and if you ignore it, it can end up messing with you 'till you're ready to take a magnet to your hard disk and start anew. We definitely do not recommend approaching your PC with any sort of magnet, no matter how badly your software is behaving. In *Degunking Microsoft Office* we aim to show you the simple steps you can take to keep Office running on your PC in a smooth and efficient manner.

Office is an amazing product. The technology built into each of the core Office applications, which include Word, Excel, PowerPoint, and Outlook, enables you to use the software to create documents and files with minimal understanding of how they will be structured and stored. It's often a very good thing to let Office do the organizational work for you so that you can focus on the creative stuff. But an occasional tweak and a regular maintenance plan, which we'll present in this book, can mean all the difference between having a completely gunked system (and the inherent lost efficiency and frustration that go with it), and having a system that continues to boost your Office productivity.

TIP: With the latest rollout of Microsoft Office, called the Office 2003 Editions, Microsoft has changed the name. Over the years, the software has progressed from a simple suite of productivity applications into an integrated system that includes not only the four familiar Office applications—Word, Excel, PowerPoint, and Outlook—but also a host of additional applications, services, servers, and other tools to boost your productivity. The Microsoft Office System now includes myriad products, but at the center remain those four familiar applications. In Degunking Microsoft Office, we concentrate mainly on showing you how to degunk these four applications because they are common to each of the Office 2003 Editions and earlier versions of Office. For more on version and edition information, see the section entitled "A Note on Office Versions" later in this introduction and also Chapter 3, "Performing a Gunk-Free Installation or Upgrade."

As you've probably experienced, Microsoft has cleverly transformed many of the tasks you might perform in a traditional paper-based office environment—managing correspondence, tracking expenses, creating presentations, transferring and sharing information—into the electronic sphere so that you can now perform these functions and many more almost intuitively and with ease. Microsoft Word, Excel, PowerPoint, and Outlook give you maximum flexibility to be creative while you accomplish a variety of activities and develop various documents—from business and personal letters to electronic mail messages and newsletters, from accounting spreadsheets to electronic slideshows, at home and at work.

There is a drawback to the wide-ranging capabilities of Office, though. The inclusion of so much functionality into Office applications makes the applications cluttered and more difficult to use. Microsoft wants Office to be able to do so much for us that inevitably some inefficiencies are coded into the Office apps. For instance, Word can be considered a quasi–desktop publishing tool. It enables average and skilled users to create fairly complicated documents that include inline graphics, special formatting, and intricate layout, but it offers nowhere near the functionality an expensive specialized desktop publishing application can supply.

Nevertheless, we don't mind tolerating these inefficiencies and deficiencies in Office applications because the software so generously enables us to accomplish so many tasks with relative ease and professional-quality results. It also saves us the expense of purchasing and learning to use gaggles of specialty programs that likely supply almost too much functionality for our everyday needs. Using Office is like grabbing the screwdriver from the kitchen junk drawer and using it to scrape paint off the windowpanes, loosen the soil for the tomato transplants, hammer in the shelf bracket, and poke a hole in the condensed milk can. A razor blade, a spade, a hammer, and a can opener might all be better-qualified tools for each situation, but the screwdriver is handy and works sufficiently well in each case. Periodically, we simply have to wipe off the screwdriver shaft and tighten on the handle to keep it in working order, and it's the same for Office: the simple degunking tasks we introduce in this book enable you to keep it streamlined and handy.

Why You Need This Book

Keeping Office in prime condition takes a bit of effort on your part—but the payoff is well worth the energy expended. You must wisely use the resources available to you to maintain a gunk-free environment. We aim to help you trim the so-called fat from your installation of Office, no matter which edition you use or where and how you use it, including in a small office/home office (SOHO) environment, or in a corporate or academic setting. By the time you read the last page of *Degunking Microsoft Office*, you'll be as skilled a GunkBuster as ever stepped up to a keyboard. Although we can't cover every possible type of implementation of Office, we do provide many examples—we want to clue you in on how Office works so that later you can intuitively degunk based on the details of your situation, as well as your understanding of the Office innards.

First, you need to recognize that gunk in Office is the result of two things. Innate Office functionality is so intricate that it eventually globs up into gunk after routine use. The second cause of gunk is how you work within the Office environment. If you learned how to use Office applications by clicking toolbar buttons to see what would happen or you've become accustomed to doing things in Office a certain way using the Office defaults, you might not be using Office to its ultimate potential and you might be a bit disorganized in your methodology, both of which lead to gunk. In addition, if you don't have a regular Office maintenance plan in place, you are inadvertently enabling gunk to infiltrate your system.

Degunking Microsoft Office can be your trail guide on the path to gunk eradication. Using the simple degunking methods we explain application by application, how you can save yourself heaps of time and frustration. Here are a few things we'll show you how to do to maintain a gunk-free Office:

√ Set up a "housekeeping" regimen to scour your file system periodically to free it of gunk.

√ Perform an installation of any Office version with a minimum of gunk buildup.

√ Upgrade from a previous version of Office in an organized fashion that keeps your files safe.

√ Organize your file system so that important documents are at your fingertips and you keep a handle on how Office saves your stuff.

√ Understand the functionality of each Office application and how you can clean out and prevent gunk buildup as you use it.

√ Repair problems that result from built-in Office functionality and keep you from operating in a clutter-free environment.

√ Implement a security system that keeps your PC and the Office-related files on it safe and sound.

√ Understand how you can back up your Office files and restore lost data after a catastrophe.

√ Use degunking methods to troubleshoot problems you experience in Office.

√ Use add-ins and third-party tools to enhance the Office applications.

How to Use This Book

In the first part, we explain how and why Office can possibly get so mucked up. We then take you through the procedures of installing a fresh edition of Office or upgrading from a previous version without allowing things to get icky right from the start. Then we show you how to organize your virtual office so that you can get on using the applications without losing data or functionality along the way.

In the second part of the book, we explain degunking methods specific to each core Office application. In the final part, we supply lots of useful information on how to keep Office free of gunk overall and implement safeguards that will keep you from jeopardizing or losing your data in any way.

A Note on Office Versions

The degunking methods in this book were written to work for Office 2000, Office XP, and the common features of the Office 2003 Editions, including Office Professional Edition 2003, Office Standard Edition 2003, Office Small Business Edition 2003, Office Student and Teacher Edition 2003, and Office Basic Edition 2003. You can also apply most of the degunking tips to earlier versions of the Microsoft Office suite.

The Degunking Mind-Set

The degunking mind-set is the concept of continually eliminating unnecessary and unwanted files while enhancing your implementation of the Office applications using built-in tools. Degunking is a method of not only optimizing the way Office works in your specific computing environment, but also optimizing how you work with Office in your specific environment.

When you've got a degunking mind-set, you will use the tips discussed in this book on an ongoing basis to ensure your important Office-related files are safe and organized. Keeping a gunk-free Office can bring you back to those days when you actually enjoyed spending hours using Office, and we think you'll experience a lot more satisfaction and a lot less aggravation when your environment is continuously degunked.

Why Is Office So Gunked Up?

Degunking Checklist:

√   Learn that purchasing a software or hardware upgrade isn't the solution to your problems with Microsoft Office.

√   Understand how Office gets gunked up through normal usage.

√   Find out how Office saves application files in various locations and how this contributes to gunk.

√   Understand how Office applications save files and how you can customize this process to suit your needs.

√   Discover what temporary files are and why they might stick around longer than necessary, creating gunk on your computer.

√   Find out why a typical install of Office isn't always your best option.

If you've picked up this book, most likely you think that something is wrong with your installation of Microsoft Office or that there is "a better way" to use it hovering just beyond your grasp. Perhaps Word has begun to lock up and crash so many times per day that you'd rather hire a ghostwriter to finish the family holiday newsletter. Maybe your boss is asking you to use some of Excel's more sophisticated functions, and you just can't get them to work or they cause your system to freeze up. PowerPoint is a major space hog and is crashing other applications. You can't seem to find the files you need because your filing system is a mess. Or maybe your Outlook Inbox fills up with so much junk e-mail that each day you must wade through at least 73 spam messages, including 42 ads hawking the latest pirated software.

Underneath all that gunk are the important documents that you really need, such as your daily portfolio update from your stockbroker and your bank statement. You might even feel that Office has somehow caused your slick, fast new PC to run sluggishly. You might wonder what's the use of having 2 gigahertz of processing power at your service if it's faster for you to create a brochure by cutting and gluing text and images by hand using an X-Acto knife. You might even be the sort of person who has nursed along an older PC, making sure there is just enough hard drive space to install the Office suite, but who now finds corrupted, useless copies of important documents and spreadsheets showing up in odd places in your file system, eating up your limited hard drive space. In a phrase, Office has become gunked up.

Don't Spend Money on Upgrades. Just Degunk!

Before you run out and buy a bigger, faster PC to run Office, or before you purchase a newer version of Office, we want to tell you that there *is* an easier way. This book will help you just clean up and degunk your current installation of Office rather than spend your hard-earned money on an expensive computer consultant or a needless hardware or software upgrade. Keep in mind that the Microsoft Office suite of programs is actually a set of integrated applications that is designed to enhance and improve your productivity. Office should help you work more quickly and efficiently, regardless of whether you run a home office, work in a networked corporate environment, use your PC at school, or simply use your PC at home to pay bills, track expenses, and send e-mail. We know that it's easy to lose sight of the potential productivity gains of Office when your PC crashes every couple of hours and you can never find the files you're looking for—so we'll help you out of this mess.

The four key programs that make up the integrated Office environment—Word, Excel, PowerPoint, and Outlook—are so sophisticated that you might not quite know how to get them working on your system to your optimal benefit. What you want to do is find important files easily, have backups at the ready in emergency situations, and enjoy smooth, crash-free performance, right?

But you have a million things clawing for your attention every day, and the last thing you need to do is become an expert on the inner workings of Office. The day you installed Office, you had the best of intentions: you were going to read the latest book on Office from cover to cover and learn all about it. We know—we made those promises, too. But you got so busy actually using the software that you found no time to study up on it.

We're here to help. Even if you don't know Office inside and out, *Degunking Microsoft Office* will help you get each application running quickly and keep it running so you can work most efficiently with this very complex piece of software.

What Is Gunk?

You should know that even in the best of times, regular use of the Office applications creates gunk, and that gunk accumulates over time. When we use the word *gunk,* we're talking about any problem that slows down your PC, decreases your productivity, creates delays in finding files, or causes your PC to freeze up or crash—basically, gunk is anything that gets in the way of using Office quickly and efficiently to get a job done! If you're like most people, you'll notice that after using Office for a while, you will begin to experience some performance problems. After a little more time, so much gunk will have accumulated that it causes you to lose important documents and makes others unrecoverable, adding unneeded stress to your already busy life.

Gunk is a natural by-product of application use. It mostly comes from how we use and organize our applications, although some gunk problems are related to how Office is programmed. Think of your PC as sort of like your house. When you first moved in, ideally you had a chance to clean the carpets and organize your stuff in each room so that you could find the things you need and have easy access to the items you use frequently. For the first month or so, your house appeared to stay perfectly orderly; everything had a place and everything was in its place. But after your vacation to Mexico and hitting a couple of garage sales, you found that you'd accumulated a lot of new stuff and didn't have the time or the right space to organize it neatly. Plus, the dust began to build up and the floors begged for scrubbing. In other words, gunk began to creep into your abode, and it continues to pile up, even as we speak. Unless you find time each week to toss junk mail, sweep the kitchen tile, and organize the closets and pantry, you'll be swimming in a morass of household gunk till it drives you to distraction and you feel you need to buy a new home and start over to regain your sanity.

It's inevitable that the same thing has probably already happened to your PC. If you use the Microsoft Windows operating system, normal daily use—combined with how Windows functions innately—creates gunk that you must be diligent in keeping at bay. *Degunking Windows* by Joli Ballew and Jeff Duntemann (Paraglyph Press, 2004) can help you optimize your Windows machine. On the other hand, if you have an Apple Macintosh, Joli Ballew's book *Degunking Your Mac* (Paraglyph Press, 2004) can help you keep the Mac OS running gunk-free. Here, in *Degunking Microsoft Office,* we want to show you how to keep the supremely useful Microsoft Office application suite from gunking up your PC.

We hope you feel better knowing that *you* didn't create all the gunk by yourself. But we have to tell you that although gunk occurs naturally as you use Office, it doesn't go away just by wishing. You need to implement a regular maintenance plan using the degunking tips we show you in this book to keep Office running quickly, efficiently, and without creating unnecessary gunk. Think of gunk as the layer of dust that clings to your TV and this book as the magnetized dust rag that swipes it away!

You can optimize the Office environment first by becoming clear on your expectations of each application's functionality and then by understanding how to implement and enable each application's feature options to satisfy your productivity requirements. The following sections explain in more detail some reasons why Office gets so gunked up. Throughout this book, we show you how to work with Office functionality to remove gunk and prevent future gunk buildup.

Understanding How You Got So Gunked Up

Now that you know what Office gunk is, it is important to review how most users end up amassing so much of it. This will help you get a better perspective on how the entire degunking process we're discussing works. In the following sections, we first explain how the Office Setup.exe program unintentionally creates gunk on your PC and then how the default Office file management system contributes to gunk accumulation. Next, we consider how temporary files and the Office upgrade process add to the clutter.

Setup.exe Saves Files—Everywhere!

The Office Setup.exe program is like the event coordinator who travels ahead to the concert location to set everything up for the star performers. When you run Setup on your PC (for instance, during an installation or upgrade), it goes in and arranges everything so that the Office applications can be installed properly. Setup performs installations and upgrades of the Office suite by examining your PC's current file system, or organizational structure, and then inserting or copying the application feature options files to subdirectories within your file system. These important files are stored in logical groupings, usually in separate folders off in a far corner of your file system and out of your way so that you don't mistakenly delete or write over them (see Figure 1-1). Setup then registers the application feature options in the Windows Registry, the place where your computer stores information about your files.

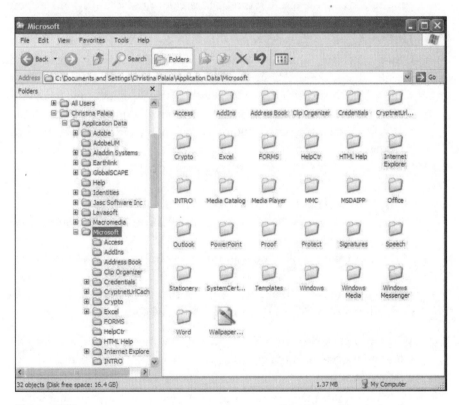

Figure 1-1

Office files are stored in a designated spot in your folder hierarchy.

However, as it prepares for the arrival of the star applications, Setup by default copies application program feature options files—some of which you will probably never use—to several locations in your file system in an attempt to anticipate how an average user will eventually use the applications. In trying to meet the needs of the average user, Office Setup creates an initial gob of gunk on your system.

Office's Unique File Management System

One of the most important things you can do to keep Office gunk free is to understand the Office file management scheme. *File management* is the way the computer system organizes and tracks files and documents. Office creates a sophisticated means of tracking and organizing your Office files and documents. However, this default file management system might not suit your situation to a T, and as a result, it can open the door to let gunk come skipping in.

Office Applications Store Files in Several Places

Office can create gunk right off the bat by storing application program files—the files that make the Office applications work—and files you've created in various locations on your PC. Office does this in an attempt to optimize its own performance, sticking together files it uses frequently for easy, quick access, and providing a simple file management system to help you store your documents in a logical manner. However, the default settings aren't always the best to keep your system from getting gunked up.

How Office Applications Save Files

When you know how the Office applications save the files you have created, you can begin to understand how to tweak that functionality to make your life easier. Let's briefly look at how an Office application such as Word saves a file. Keep in mind that this is also the procedure that Excel and PowerPoint use to save files—Outlook, though, is a whole other story and we'll explain how it stores files in Chapter 9, "Degunking Microsoft Outlook."

When you click Save or Save As on the File menu, Word basically follows a four-step process to initially save a document or to save changes made to an existing document:

1. Word creates a temporary file of the document you are working with. Say you are writing a short article and you save the document as Puppies.doc. When you select Save from the File menu, Word creates a temporary file as shown in Figure 1-2, naming it ~$xxxx.tmp, where xxxx is the last part of the original file's name.

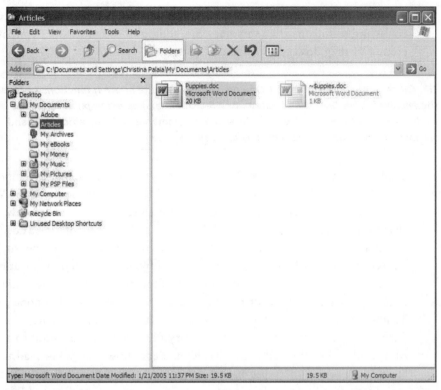

Figure 1-2
The temporary working file for Puppies.doc is created in the same folder as
the original.

2. Word then writes the changes you have made to Puppies.doc to the temporary file named ~$*xxxx*.tmp.

3. If the temporary file is successfully created, Word actually deletes the original
   version of Puppies.doc.

4. Word then renames the temporary file ~$*xxxx*.tmp to the same name as the
   original document; thus, ~$*xxxx*.tmp becomes Puppies.doc, and subse-
   quently when you open Puppies.doc, Word follows this same procedure to
   write changes to the latest saved version of Puppies.doc.

Office apps gain significant performance enhancements by placing the temporary file in the same directory as the saved file. By creating the temporary file in
the same directory as the original saved document file, Office can use the MS-
DOS MOVE command to quickly rename the temporary file as the saved
document when it gets to the fourth step in the file-save procedure. Otherwise,
if Office were to place the temporary file in another directory, it would have to
use the MS-DOS COPY command to move the temporary file from the other

directory to the location of the saved document, and then use the MOVE command to rename the temporary file, adding to the process a step that can eventually drag down performance.

TIP: *Office applications use MS-DOS commands for some internal functions because the Microsoft Disk Operating System, or MS-DOS, is a simple computer language that works directly at the machine level to execute commands quickly, efficiently, and without the overhead of the Windows operating system.*

When the four-step save operation completes without a hitch, the temporary file is "deleted" (actually renamed as the original file). If for some reason Word crashes before you have a chance to save and close a document properly, your changes are not saved to the original document and a version of the ~$*xxxx*.tmp file that was created lingers in your file system with a name such as ~WRL*xxxx*.tmp, where *xxxx* is a string of numbers calculated by the application using an internal algorithm. This type of temporary file is either a lifesaver or gunk, depending on your point of view (see the section "Temporary Files That Turn into Gunk" later in this chapter). If you need to recover data lost during an application crash, this temporary file is the one you want to access. Almost all of the other temp files are illegible, and those that can be read are just bits and pieces of your original document—nothing you can really recover useful information from. In Chapter 4, "Organizing Office-Related Files and Folders," we describe how you can clean up these lost souls and free your file system from temporary file gunk.

Where Office Documents Might Be Stored

Windows 95 introduced the capability of Windows applications, including the Office applications, to work with long 256-character file names with the standard Office file extensions (.doc, .xls, .ppt) appended to the end. We all know it's easier to remember a descriptive file name such as Jack's First Birthday Party Guest List.doc than it is to remember a cryptic 8-character file name such as Jck1bday.doc. When you save a file for the first time, Office examines the file extension at the end of the file's name (the last few letters after the rightmost dot, such as Spaceships.*doc,* Monthly Budget.*xls,* or Cancun Vacation.*ppt*) to help determine where that specific file can be stored by default. Office automatically will offer the My Documents folder and its default subfolders as the file save location for Office-related files.

Oftentimes, unless you have changed the default file save locations, you end up saving most document files to the C: drive (also called the root directory), to C:\Windows, or to the My Documents folder. Accumulating myriad files in the root directory or the Windows or My Documents folders quickly gunks up your PC and primes it for disorganization and possibly the loss of files. If you end up saving everything in My Documents, for instance, your work-related files will mix freely with your household management files, and soon you'll have to sort through heaps of file names in this bloated folder to find the one you want (see Figure 1-3). That's no fun—and that's why we show you later (in Chapter 4) how to implement a file-storage convention to keep things organized.

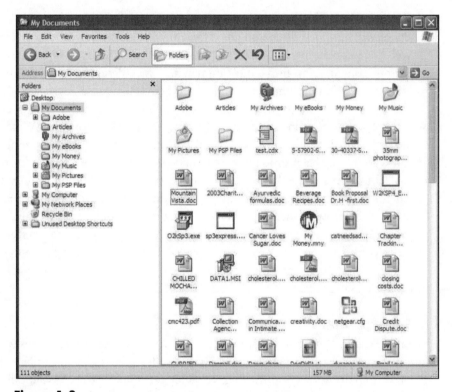

Figure 1-3

This is an example of what a cluttered folder can look like with lots of Office documents mixed with other file types.

Files Stored in the My Documents Folder

Here we should quickly explain how Office applications use the default working folder called My Documents. Even though you can store documents and files anywhere on your hard disk, to maintain a gunk-free installation, it is best practice to use a logical file-saving scheme that works well in your specific situation. When the Windows operating system began to enable multiple users with separate user IDs to share space on a single PC, it configured the My Documents folder as the default file location to which each user could save his or her Office-related files.

You can change this default file save location by renaming the My Documents folder or by moving this folder to another location on your hard disk. However, we suggest that you simply create subfolders within the My Documents folder and use them to group and organize your Office documents and files. Of course, this entails saving each document file with an easily recognizable name and storing it in a logically organized folder subsystem. We show you how to create a smart subfolder hierarchy in Chapter 4.

Saving Web Pages

There will be times when you are surfing the Internet and you come across a Web page containing information that you'd like to have on hand later. For example, one day you find a most informative page describing exactly how to grow prize-winning gigantic pumpkins. When you choose Save As from the File menu while the page is displayed on screen, your Web browser offers to save the Web page as an HTM or HTML file in—get this—the parent folder of the last *Office* document you had open! For instance, if earlier in the morning you were adding electronic images to a slide show you were creating for work in a subfolder named ABWA Presentation in your My Documents folder, later when you try to save the interesting pumpkin-growing Web page, your Web browser attempts to save it in the ABWA Presentation folder. If you're not paying attention and accept the default file save location, you might never find the information you saved about pumpkins. A lost or misplaced file like this can be considered gunk, and you'll need to tweak Office functionality just a bit to keep things organized.

Saving E-Mail Attachments

And speaking of information you receive online, if a trusted source sends you an e-mail message with an attachment and you want to save the attachment separately from the e-mail—something we highly recommend to keep Outlook free of gunk, as well as to protect the attached file by storing a permanent copy of it—Office offers to save it for you in several different places. In Outlook, if you right-click the attachment and choose Save As from the context menu that appears, Outlook by default offers to save the file in your My Documents folder. If you instead double-click the attachment, the Opening Mail Attachment dialog box (shown in Figure 1-4) appears, asking you whether you'd like to open the file or save it to your computer. If you choose Save, Outlook again offers the My Documents folder as the default save location. However, when you choose Open in the Opening Mail Attachment dialog box and then select Save As from the File menu in the open file, Office will try to save the file in a default location with the path name C:\Documents and Setting*username*\Local Settings\Temporary Internet

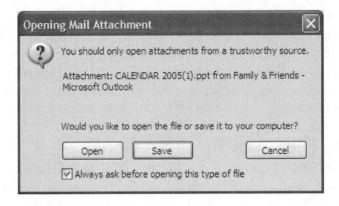

Figure 1-4
When you double-click an attachment, Outlook asks whether
you'd like to open or save the file.

Files*subdirectory name,* where *username* is the name of the logged-on user (you)
and *subdirectory name* is the name of the folder in the Temporary Internet Files
folder that will hold the file (see Figure 1-5). We wonder if you'd ever be able to
find that file again if you accepted the default file save location. If not, you've just
created more gunk!

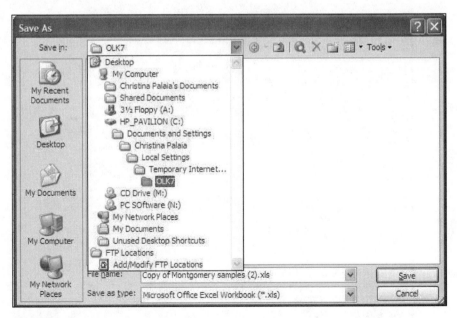

Figure 1-5
When you save an open attachment file, Outlook tries to save it in a somewhat
obscure location.

As mentioned, in Chapter 4 we show you exactly how to create a file management system that enables you to save Office files so that you can find them again quickly and easily, whether you've created them, downloaded them from the Web, or saved e-mail attachments to disk. In Chapter 5, "Degunking Office's Common Features," we show you how to tinker with the default file-save locations to suit your needs.

Temporary Files That Turn into Gunk

When you use Windows Explorer or choose Open from the File menu in an Office application, you might sometimes see document icons that look like they've been through the wash one too many times, like the ones shown in Figure 1-6. They may have strange and seemingly senseless file names attached to them. Don't worry—your PC hasn't been infected with a strange virus that causes it to spew out alien file names for ghostly documents. The faded icons represent temporary files that Office creates every time you open an existing

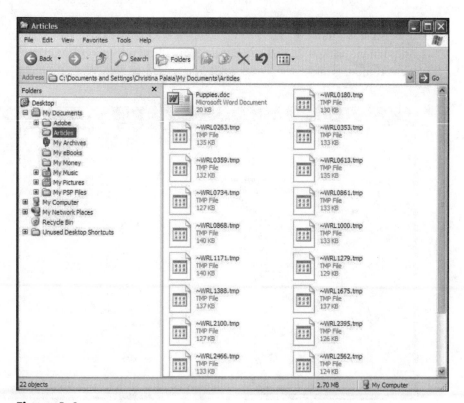

Figure 1-6

Temporary files linger long after they're useful if you're not vigilant.

document file to work with it (see the section "How Office Applications Save Files" earlier in this chapter for details on why and how temporary files are created); they are necessary for the proper operation of the Office apps. However, when temporary files stick around after you have closed the original document, they gunk up your system and must be dispatched with a firm hand.

As discussed previously, each time you open an existing Office file, Office creates a temporary or working copy of that file that enables Office to use memory resources efficiently while you work with the document. This also creates a type of safety net—the temporary file itself—if a crash (or other calamity) prevents you from saving and closing the document properly. Temporary files are stored in the same folder where the original file is located, and the file name usually begins with a tilde (~) and sometimes a dollar sign ($) followed by a few letters, numbers, and the .doc or .tmp file extension.

In normal circumstances, Office deletes the temporary file and writes all changes made to it to the original file when you close the document. But temporary files tend to linger long after they are welcome when for some reason Office exits irregularly from an editing session. So if you've suffered more than your fair share of system or application crashes or freeze-ups, you probably have a ton of temporary file gunk on your machine! In Chapter 3, "Performing a Gunk-Free Installation or Upgrade," we help you set up a cleanup procedure that deletes temp files when they are no longer useful and puts the polish back on your file system.

Upgrading through Several Versions of Office

It can be so exciting when you finally get your hands on the latest version of Office. All the performance enhancements and new features described in glowing detail on the bright-colored box can make your head swim with possibilities of how this version will finally fulfill all your productivity dreams. When you perform an upgrade, new features are added, new files are installed, previous-version files are uninstalled...and sometimes things don't transition to the new version in the same way the installation guide claims they will.

The good news is that most upgrades are performed by built-in wizards that leave you with just a few simple decisions to make. But because you might not be aware of all the optional features that exist for each Office application, at initial installation or when installing version upgrades, you might have allowed Setup.exe to perform a Typical install, which is the default installation type. A Typical install contributes to gunking up Office in two ways:

√   It automatically enables features that you will never use, thus wasting space and increasing the amount of clutter on your system.

√   It refrains from enabling feature options that can help you keep your system gunk-free.

Choosing to allow Setup to perform a Typical install might result at some point in lost legacy document files and lots of extra junk on your system. In other words, files from the version of Office that you were using previously that you need to keep handy get lost, and, as if this wasn't bad enough, unnecessary files are added to your PC. You might believe that your files are protected by backup archives or that they will be unaffected by Office Setup.exe. However, Setup frequently proves you wrong and document files are lost forever. See Chapter 3 to learn how to install or upgrade Office without sacrificing data safety.

Get Ready to Degunk!

As you can see, several factors can contribute to your gunk situation. By dedicating a relatively small amount of time to degunk your installation of Office according to the application-by-application plan we outline in this book, you will be handsomely rewarded with increased performance and a sense of serenity that comes from knowing your important data is protected from loss and within easy reach.

Degunking Your Office Setup

Degunking Checklist:

√ Make sure you understand that the best Office degunking payoff can be obtained by performing cleanup tasks in a specific order.

√ Learn how to spot Office-related gunk on your PC.

√ Understand the strategy behind degunking.

√ Know which questions to ask to get the best degunking results.

√ Learn the degunking 12-step program.

After reading Chapter 1, you should now have a good idea how Microsoft Office can get so gunked up. You might have gobs of temporary files on your hard drive, important Office documents scattered all over the place, e-mail attachments that you no longer need, and the Office apps configured so that they are really wasting your time. It's now time to start cleaning up so that you can become much more productive.

In this chapter, we'll start by introducing our Office degunking strategy. We'll introduce you to the important mind set that you'll want to adopt so that you can quickly improve the performance of Office. Our goal in this chapter is to get you started with the 12-step program that we've created specifically for this book. This program arranges the important degunking activities into a set of very do-able tasks. The best part is that even if you have limited time, you'll be able to prioritize and perform the important tasks that will greatly increase your productivity. You'll find that our 12-step strategy is a good way to get organized, and in this book you'll work through it chapter by chapter.

As you start degunking Office, the important thing to keep in mind is that you will likely get the best results by following the system that we present in this book. In particular, you should try to follow the tasks in the order that they are presented. For example, we'll start in Chapter 3, "Performing a Gunk-Free Installation or Upgrade," by showing you how to make sure that you are using the version of Office that best fits your needs and that the software is installed properly (with all of the gunk removed!). Then, we'll show you how to organize all of your Office-related files and folders and perform a set of cleanup tasks that relate to the four main Office applications: Word, Excel, PowerPoint, and Outlook. Finally, we'll begin degunking each of the Office apps, starting with Word. To better leverage the power of this degunking strategy, you'll want to perform the degunking tasks that impact *all* of the applications before you perform degunking tasks within a *single* app.

Learn to Spot Gunk

Perhaps you learned how to use the Office applications by clicking toolbar buttons to see what would happen. Or you've been using Office for so long now you've gotten used to doing things a certain way using the Office defaults. If you are extremely lucky, you've had some sort of formal training in how to use the Office applications. Even still, you might not be using Office to its ultimate potential, and you might still be a bit disorganized in your methodology—both of which lead to gunk accumulation.

First, you need to recognize that gunk in Office is the result of two things. Innate Office functionality sometimes creates clutter and redundancies; eventually the inner workings of Office glob up into gunk that you need to clear. The second gunk-generating issue is how you work within the Office environment. If you're still relying on your old habits, you're probably creating gunk in one of two ways: you're not taking advantage of the performance-enhancing features that are built into the applications which enable you to increase your efficiency, or you're allowing unused feature options to clutter up your PC. In addition, if you don't have a regular Office maintenance plan in place, you are inadvertently enabling gunk to infiltrate your system. In this book, we can help you eliminate gunk wherever it comes from.

The Strategy behind Degunking

The strategy and techniques that we'll be using to fully degunk Microsoft Office are based on how Office operates, including the following:

√   How Office stores certain types of files in specific folders (directories)

√   How Office configures your PC in different ways depending on the version of Office that you install

√   How Office applications share common features such as document formatting and printing capabilities

√   How Office applications such as Word use different types of file formats

√   How Office applications store and retrieve data on your computer

√   How Office's built-in tools, such as automatic document saving and recovery, can be used to protect your important data and recover it when things go wrong

√   How Office standardizes certain operations, such as document printing, across the different applications

√   How Office applies a number of critical default settings that control the behavior of its applications

√   How Office supports interoperability among Office applications as well as third-party software

√   How Office provides customizable application features that you can tweak to suit your situation

√   How Office automates certain features to save you time

To get good at cleaning up and optimizing Office, you'll need to understand the basics of how Office operates. For example, to get your files and folders well organized, you need to know how Office configures its applications to store and retrieve files on your hard drive. To get the most out of decluttering Outlook, for instance, you need to know where on your hard disk your e-mail messages are stored. To set up a maintenance procedure, you need to know how and where your important data is stored.

In this book, we focus on degunking the four core Office applications. Whereas Word, Excel, and PowerPoint share many features and functionality, Outlook operates quite a bit differently. In each chapter, we include some background information so you can begin to understand how the applications work behind the scenes. We want to clue you in to how Office works so that later you can begin to degunk effectively based on the details of your situation, as well as your understanding of the Office innards.

Keeping Office in prime condition takes a bit of effort on your part—but the payoff is well worth the energy expended. You have to use the available Office resources wisely to maintain a gunk-free environment. We aim to help you trim the so-called fat from your installation of Office, no matter which version you use or where and how you use it, including in a small office/home office (SOHO) environment or in a corporate or academic setting. By the time you read the last page of *Degunking Microsoft Office,* you'll be as skilled a GunkBuster as ever stepped up to a keyboard.

Important Questions to Ask Yourself

As you use Office on a regular basis, you need to ask yourself some of the following questions:

√   Does it seem that my Office applications have gotten so bloated that they take a very long time to load?

√   Do I really need all of the files and utilities that Office has installed on my PC?

√   Do I spend a lot of time searching for commands that are difficult to find in the application menus?

√   Do I feel overwhelmed because the Office applications provide so many options and features that I hardly ever use?

√   Do I find that running applications such as Word or Excel causes my PC to lock up too often?

√   How often do I look at my personal folders (My Documents and its subfolders) to view all of the files that I have been creating with Office?

√   When was the last time I cleaned up my e-mail folders in Outlook so that I didn't feel overwhelmed by all of the e-mail I've been collecting?

√   Do I have a backup system in place so that if my PC fails, I have a way to access copies of all of my Office documents?

√   Are the default settings that Office provides driving me crazy because I don't like them and I don't know how to change them?

√   Do I know exactly where to look to find the Office files that I want?

√   Do I have a security plan in place to protect my personal and private information when I share documents?

√   Do I have up-to-date virus-scanning software installed to protect my Office files and PC from being infected by computer viruses?

√   Do I have a good system in place to help me manage my e-mail?

Reviewing these questions helps you prepare to put a degunking strategy in place. You might have been thinking about these issues already, and you might have a number of your own that we haven't included here. Once you get more familiar with how Office works, you'll be able to see how our degunking 12-step program will help you save a lot of time and aggravation. Before you know it, you'll be free of all that clutter and unnecessary junk and you'll be much more productive with your work.

Proper Installation Is the Key

These days, myriad versions of Office are available—so how do you pick the one that suits you? The first step is to evaluate your needs and then match them to the version of Office that will best fit your expectations. After you have settled on a version to install or upgrade to, you need to do several things to prepare your PC for installation, including scanning your hard disk for viruses and malware, running the Disk Cleanup utility, and defragmenting your hard drive. Certain types of Office installations guarantee that you are adding unnecessary gunk to your PC, so we'll show you how to customize your installation so that only the applications and features you need and use are installed. After installation, you have just a few other tasks to complete to get Office in working order. Installing Office properly is the first step you can take to reduce gunk; starting with a "clean" installation puts you way ahead of the game.

File Management Basics

If you can't find the file or information you need when you need it, it might as well be nonexistent. Setting up an organized and efficient folder system to manage your Office-related files is critical to effective Office use. We'll show you how to de-clutter your root directory or the My Documents folder—or wherever you've been stuffing Office files—and then sort the remaining files you'd like to keep into a relevant subfolder system. Several handy techniques can be used to sift through your stored files to help separate what to keep from what to delete, including using the Windows Search feature, removing duplicate files, deleting vacant user accounts, and tossing temporary file leftovers.

While you're at it, we'll show you how to degunk your Outlook mail folders. You'll be amazed at the amount of space old e-mails and attachments consume, and you'll be better organized once all the waste is removed from Outlook.

You'll learn how to create useful subfolders and where to place them in the file hierarchy. Then, whenever you create or receive an Office file, you'll have an appropriate place to store it, whether you choose to organize your subfolder hierarchy by project, date, creator, client name, or some other categorizing detail. A place for everything, and everything in its place.

Making the Office Apps Perform Well Together

Office is an integrated environment in which the applications share common features and functionality. This is wonderful from a degunking standpoint because it enables you to use your knowledge of how any one application operates to get work done in any other app without having to learn too many new skills all at once. You can change a few settings here and there that will help all the Office apps work better for you, including customizing menus, toolbars, document views, and keyboard shortcuts. You'll also be able to degunk the printing process in each Office application.

Beyond this, Office applications are meant to work together to help you accomplish all that you need to do. For instance, here are just a few ways you can use the Office apps:

√   You can use Word as your e-mail editor in Outlook.

√   You can import Excel tables into Word documents.

√   You can copy text into and out of PowerPoint.

√   You can insert objects from one Office file into another.

√   You can use Office apps to reformat imported data.

√   You can link objects between Office documents.

Office is one of the most pervasive software packages today, and yet it also interoperates with other popular software systems. You should have no trouble exchanging files or data between Office apps as well as with users of other systems.

Getting the Gunk out of Word, Excel, PowerPoint, and Outlook

Although they are a part of the same software family, each Office application has its own unique personality (and settings), just like human siblings. In the second part of this book, we show you gunk removal techniques specific to each application. You'll find that in each application you can improve at least 10 things right away to see immediate results. And then we'll show you special features and functions in each app that enable you to take your degunking more in-depth.

Word is used primarily as a word processor, even though it is capable of so much more. To that end, you can take several steps toward making your inter-action with this application more efficient and productive, and the end result of your work more professional and organized. For instance, following are some of the Word gunk-busting techniques you'll learn:

√ How to put in place an automatic backup system to protect your files

√ How to use templates and styles to save time

√ How to apply formatting so that it's most effective

√ How to troubleshoot locked documents

Although Excel and PowerPoint don't accumulate quite as much junk as Word and Outlook do, you can still use specific techniques to degunk these two applications. Excel is perfect for storing and manipulating numerical data as well as for creating databases that can be linked to other Office documents. PowerPoint can be used to create slide shows complete with notes and a cohe-sive presentation style. For each of these apps, you'll learn how using templates can cut down on your formatting time, how you can choose alternative output methods such as printed pages or Web pages to present your finished product, and how customizing the default settings can make you more efficient.

Outlook is a notorious gunk magnet. Once you start poking around in various mail folders, you'll see how many unneeded messages and attachments you have hanging out cluttering up the place. It's easy to degunk Outlook, but it does take a bit of time and dedication. We'll show you many ways you can optimize Outlook, including these:

√ Cleaning up bloated mail folders and eliminating unessential attachments

√ Setting up an e-mail folder hierarchy to organize your incoming messages

√ Using rules to automatically sort e-mail

√ Reducing the amount of spam you receive

√ Degunking and customizing your calendar system

√ Organizing your contacts list so it's more easily accessible

The benefits of systematically degunking each Office application using the guidelines we present are worth the effort. You'll be able to find what you need when you want it, your days will be more organized, and you'll experience a lot less frustration while getting your work done more efficiently.

Fixing Things That Break in Office

Inevitably, there will come a day (if it hasn't arrived already) when something goes wrong with Office. Word crashes and you can't find the latest recover file, Excel mysteriously reorganizes the data in your worksheet, your PowerPoint slides don't look the way you originally formatted them, and it appears that all your Outlook e-mail folders are empty even though you know there are messages there somewhere. What a mess! This is when knowing a bit about how Office works comes in handy. We'll show you how to fix corrupted templates, reduce the number of application crashes you suffer through, and make repairs when Office messes up your data or settings.

Another important degunking strategy is preventative maintenance. To protect your data and prolong your sanity, you need to implement a backup and recovery plan so that when things go awry, you can gracefully resume normal operation. Office and the Microsoft Windows operating system supply built-in tools to help you protect your important files and settings, and we'll show you how to use them. This way, you can head off disaster before it strikes, and if something does break in Office, you'll know how to fix it.

Making Office More Secure

No matter how small your operation or how uninteresting you think your personal business is, there are people out there just waiting for the opportunity to harm your data, violate your privacy, or inconvenience you in some way. Less obviously, whenever you share Office files, you must always consider how you will protect them and ensure that personal and private data is not in plain view. Office applications are built to encourage collaboration among users. You do need to be aware of the threats to your data and your PC, and then take steps to reduce your risk. We'll show you how you can incorporate security practices into your everyday use of Office. We'll also share a handy checklist you can use to prepare your documents for review using Office's built-in features. And you'll learn how macro viruses propagate and how you can prevent them from infecting your Office documents and your PC.

Enhancing Office

We can't say enough about how useful Office is. The good news is that you can make it even better! Heaps of add-ins and third-party tools exist—even some you can download for free or for a nominal cost—that can enhance Office features and automate common tasks. We give you a quick review of the ones we find to be most useful.

The Degunking 12-Step Program

Here is the basic 12-step degunking program that you will be using in this book:

1. Make sure that the version of Office you are using is the one that optimally suits your needs and that you've properly installed the software while limiting the introduction of as much gunk as possible (Chapter 3).

2. Organize your Office-related files and folders (Chapter 4).

3. Perform a set of cleanup and configuration tasks that make all the Office applications work better (Chapter 5).

4. Fully degunk and optimize Word (Chapter 6).

5. Fully degunk and optimize Excel (Chapter 7).

6. Fully degunk and optimize PowerPoint (Chapter 8).

7. Fully degunk and optimize Outlook (Chapter 9).

8. Use Office interoperability features to enhance your productivity (Chapter 10).

9. Implement key security best practices to keep personal and private information safe in shared documents and protect your PC from virus infection (Chapter 11).

10. Set up a backup schedule and create restore points so that you can successfully recover from application failures or calamities of nature (Chapter 12).

11. Perform a set of tasks to troubleshoot application crashes, repair broken installations, recover corrupted templates and prevent them in the future (Chapter 13).

12. Make the most of third-party add-ins and tools to increase the usefulness of Office (Appendix A).

As you can see, this degunking strategy is logical and straightforward. You'll find each step easy to do, and you'll be surprised at how completing each one in order can make Office run better.

Summing Up

Now you've got a complete picture of the 12-step degunking strategy. It's pretty simple, right? With a little bit of time, some perseverance, and the plan outlined in this book, you can completely degunk and optimize Office so that it runs more smoothly and you work more efficiently.

Performing a Gunk-Free Installation or Upgrade

Degunking Checklist:

√ Choose the best version of Microsoft Office to install that fits your needs.

√ Uncover the issues you may encounter when using a PC with a pre-installed Office software suite.

√ Decide whether to upgrade or completely reinstall Office.

√ Prepare for your new installation by making sure your PC has adequate system requirements to handle Office effectively.

√ Clean up your Windows operating system before installing or upgrading your version of Office.

√ Consider performing a custom installation (instead of an automatic one) to ensure that you minimize the gunk that is installed on your PC.

√ Once you've installed a new version, decide whether to remove the old copy of Office from your PC.

√ Find out what to do after the installation.

Whether you are a new Microsoft Office user and wish to install a version of Office on your PC, or you've been using Office and you simply want to upgrade to a newer version, you should know a few things about how Office handles installations and upgrades. If you know how to choose exactly which version and options you need, you'll be all set to perform a clean install or upgrade—without losing files (or your sanity) in the process. If you want to learn where Office sticks stuff when it installs and how you can enable the options you want and get rid of the rest, read on! This chapter will help you get started with the degunking process.

We'll start by showing you how to select the version of Office you need. The different versions of Office that are available can make your head spin. And one of the reasons many users feel like they are working with a gunked-up version of Office is that they simply installed a version that doesn't quite fit their needs. Once you learn how to assess your needs, we'll take you through the process of either upgrading Office or doing a clean install. We'll use the Custom installation feature, and the end result is that you'll have a fully degunked version of Office installed on your PC, ready to go.

Choose the Office Edition You Need

We live in a world replete with options. Cash or credit? Paper or plastic? Pizza and a movie or dinner and dancing? The sheer number of choices confronting us can get really confusing and make us feel as if we are swimming in clutter. And with too many options, making a decision is really difficult. You might be wondering exactly which version of Office you really need. Should you purchase individual programs or the whole Microsoft Office System? You might even be stuck with the version of Microsoft Works that came pre-installed on your PC and you want to know if it is compatible with the Office editions currently available. If any of these questions concern you, we can help.

From talking to numerous Office users, we've found that the most frequently asked question they have is, "Which edition of Microsoft Office should I buy: Professional or Home Edition?" Another common question is, "I run my own business, but I am writing my master's thesis—do I want the Small Business Edition or the Student and Teacher Edition?" Just step inside a retail store that carries software and you'll see how confusing the options are. You might think that there are over 30 different versions of Office—Office for students, Office for business users, Office for professionals, Office for folks who flunked out of college, Office for men who spend too much time on the couch.

The initial Office purchase might seem expensive, so we want to help you make a good decision, one that you won't regret. Let's start by comparing the functionality offered in each of the different Office editions and then compare them to what is available in earlier versions of Office. As you read this, you'll need to think about how you will be using Office to match up your needs with the features available.

TIP: *In this chapter, we use the terms **version** and **edition** pretty much interchangeably. In fact, a **version** is a particular release of specific software, such as Office 95, Word 97, Excel 2002, or Office 2000. An **edition** refers to a particular bundle of software products within a version that includes a specific set of features and functionality—for instance, Office Small Business Edition or Office Standard Edition. But, hey, what's a little generalization for simplicity's sake among friends?*

Assessing Your Needs

Each version of Microsoft Office, from Office 95 to Office 2003, introduces new features and new technology; however, the basic functionality of the four core applications we talk about in this book are word processing (Word), spreadsheet creation and numerical manipulation (Excel), presentation creation and display (PowerPoint), and e-mail messaging and calendar keeping (Outlook).

A good place to start is to determine your needs by asking yourself the following questions:

√   Do I need to write letters, memos, and articles?

√   Do I need to create or maintain financial lists?

√   Do I need to develop or maintain a Web site?

√   Do I need to keep a calendar?

√   Do I need to edit graphics?

√   Do I need to develop or maintain slide show presentations?

√   Do I need to lay out brochures, newsletters, display advertisements, and similar documents?

√   Do I need an information database?

√   Do I need to surf the Internet?

√   Do I need to send and receive e-mail?

√   Do I need to keep track of contact information for colleagues and business partners?

Office Versions and Features

Microsoft offers several different flavors, or bundles, of the Office suite of products, including Office Professional Edition, Office Small Business Edition, Office Standard Edition, and Office Student and Teacher Edition (see Table 3-1 for a quick comparison of features and functionality). Once you are clear on how you intend to use Office, you can easily pick the edition that will satisfy your needs. Remember to allow for future eventualities—if you keep your checkbook by hand now, it's not inconceivable that once you install Office, you'll have Excel keeping up-to-the-minute tabs on your funds, as well as amortizing your mortgage, itemizing your deductions, and calculating your expense reports.

TIP: Microsoft Money (which might come pre-installed on your PC or at an additional cost) is a specialized application that specifically tracks your assets. You can download free Excel templates to perform similar tasks.

You can purchase each of the core Office applications (and quite a few of the extended Office System applications) as separate products. In the store, you'll notice at least another two display cases of single-application software boxes. But when you compare prices across that vast display, you'll see that the price break makes buying bundled suites of products more cost effective than it is to buy any two of the core Office applications individually. The primary reason you would opt to buy the Microsoft Office applications as a suite is lower cost.

Table 3-1   Comparing the Features in Office 2003 Editions

Application	Function	MS Office Professional Edition	MS Office Small Business Edition	MS Office Standard Edition	MS Office Premium Edition	MS Office Student and Teacher Edition
Word	Word processing	X	X	X	X	X
Excel	Spreadsheets	X	X	X	X	X
PowerPoint	Slide shows and graphics manipulation	X	X	X	X	X
Outlook	E-mail and calendaring		X	X	X	X
Outlook with Business Contact Manager	E-mail, calendaring, and contact management	X	X			

(continued)

Table 3-1   Comparing the Features in Office 2003 Editions *(continued)*

Application	Function	MS Office Professional Edition	MS Office Small Business Edition	MS Office Standard Edition	MS Office Premium Edition	MS Office Student and Teacher Edition
Access	Database creation	X			X	
PhotoDraw	Graphics editing				X	
Publisher	Desktop publishing	X	X		X	

Professional Edition 2003 also includes support for creating Extensible Markup Language (XML) documents in Word and Excel and for information rights management (IRM). The Student and Teacher Edition is for noncommercial use by—you guessed it—students and teachers. To help make it more easily available for educational purposes, it is sold at a substantial discount compared to Standard Edition, but that doesn't mean you should go hunting for your old, tattered college ID to get Office for cheap. And you won't be able to upgrade Student and Teacher Edition to a newer version later either.

GunkBuster's Notebook: Pre-installed Editions, Volume-License Editions, and Academic-License Editions

If you've recently bought a new PC, the question will be: Is the version of Office I have going to do the job for me? Luckily, Microsoft offers price discounts on upgrades as compared to new user pricing, making it especially tempting to run out and upgrade to a new edition rather than use an older version or Microsoft Works. The caveat to installing upgrade editions is that they require the original version to have been installed first, so don't lose or give away the install disk(s) for your older version if you're planning to upgrade. You might have a problem upgrading the Office version that came pre-installed on your new PC if it did not include an install disk because the upgrade version uses data files contained on the install disk and will discontinue the upgrade when it can't locate the proper files.

As you know, each installed copy of Microsoft software must be registered and licensed through Microsoft. If you work in a company that employs 121 people, each with their own copy of

Office on their PC or portable, each installation must, by right, be licensed. In this situation, your employer in all probability subscribes to the volume license program that Microsoft offers to ease the cost of licensing multiple seats, or installations of the software. For volume license users, Microsoft offers the Professional Enterprise Edition, which contains the same features and applications as Professional Edition with the exception that Outlook with the Business Contact Manager is available by request only and for an additional fee. Also available for volume buyers are Small Business Edition and Standard Edition.

In a different twist on volume licensing, Microsoft offers educators a special deal on licensing multiple copies of the Office product used throughout a school. These editions, including Professional Enterprise Edition and Standard Edition, are available to educational institutions through the Academic Volume Licensing program.

Upgrade Pre-2000 Office

If you currently have a version of Office installed on your PC, it might be a version or two behind the latest release. Earlier versions continue to do the job of basic document development and e-mail management and can enable you to accomplish your Office tasks without a lot of fuss or change. With a little luck, and a little degunking, we're hoping that you won't have to buy a new version of Office. We're sad to say, though, that if your version of Office is pre-2000, you should probably upgrade. A newer version will offer you the latest Microsoft technology. For instance, Office 2000 adds the feature of Web page (Hypertext Markup Language, or HTML) editing, Office XP adds smart tags, and Office 2003 adds XML tags (XML is a markup language for documents containing structured information).

Why Should You Upgrade?

Office 2003 offers much enhanced and additional functionality compared to earlier versions, but in a book about streamlining your installation and denying gunk a toehold in your file system, additional features do not necessarily translate into better functionality as far as we're concerned. In fact, the latest whiz-bang software gadget in an Office application can simply be considered gunk if you don't need it and don't use it.

If you are using an earlier version of Office, and it suits your needs just fine, you might not need to upgrade. Basic degunking—removing old files, organizing what you have, and optimizing the functionalities you do use—will probably be sufficient to improve your performance satisfactorily. Think twice before purchasing the latest version just because the software manufacturer makes you feel like you have to have the latest and greatest, when in reality you probably won't use any of the new features. Why go through the added expense and hassle of an upgrade if you've already got all you need?

Office 2003 Preview

Office 2003 is replete with added functionality that can improve your productivity, and it's a lot more stable and crashes less often than previous versions. Here, we highlight a few of the new and improved application features in the Office 2003 Editions, just so you can decide for yourself whether you really are missing out on the good stuff.

Office 2003: New Features

Office 2003 Editions are all about connections—connecting people to business processes, coworkers to one another, and customers to information. To that end, Office 2003 offers a new feature called Document Workspaces to facilitate collaboration by providing centralized sites that enable you and your coworkers to access shared files and exchange ideas quickly and conveniently. In Outlook 2003, coworkers can send files to team members as shared attachments; by sending files, coworkers create a Document Workspace, a virtual space where the team can meet and collaborate. From Word 2003, Excel 2003, and PowerPoint 2003, collaborators can check in at the Shared Workspace task pane to see whether updated files are available or whether other team members are online, among other things.

With the information rights management features, Office 2003 Editions also help you protect your documents and information from misappropriation and plagiarism. Each of the four core Office applications enables you to specify how recipients of your files can use the information, whether they can forward it, copy it, print it, or modify it. Essentially, you gain complete control over your intellectual property, and the restrictions and permissions stick with the documents regardless of where they end up.

Also included is a new feature called the Research and Reference task pane, which enables you to do research with dictionaries, thesauri, online sites, and the like while you're working in an application. Online services have been enhanced and expanded, as have the application Help features. New smart network detection features keep you insulated from poor network performance while you work, and Office 2003 Editions applications offer better file recovery options than previous versions. With the enhanced file format compatibility features, users of Office 97, Office 2000, Office XP, and Office 2003 Editions can share documents without a hitch.

Word 2003: New Features

Word 2003 has a new feature that enables you to lock down specified sections of Word documents so that unauthorized users cannot make editing changes. This is helpful when you are working on a team and you've created the perfect tagline for the advertising campaign and you want to keep your team leader, Bob, who thinks he's a superstar editor, from fiddling with or gunking up your work. Using the new formatting restrictions feature in Word 2003, you can also keep Bob from changing the text to all caps, bold, and underlined, as he is wont to do to get his point across. You know you don't keep people's attention for long by constantly shouting at them! Some of the Track Changes editing features have been updated and improved as well, and the Professional Edition of Word 2003 offers extensive controls to help you create XML documents and custom XML schemas.

Excel 2003: New Features

In Excel 2003, a new Reading Layout view is included to make sharing and reading Excel documents online a lot easier. Excel is now more closely integrated with Windows SharePoint Services and includes more advanced support for statistical functions. It also includes a visual mapping tool that enables you to import XML data into a spreadsheet easily.

PowerPoint 2003: New Features

PowerPoint includes a new feature that enables you to package a presentation to a CD. The presentation automatically begins when the CD is inserted into a CD drive. Now all you have to do is persuade your clients to insert the CD, and before they have a chance to forget about it (or you), your presentation will play back, with no fiddling on the viewer's part. Multimedia support has been expanded, and PowerPoint now recognizes more kinds of play formats.

Outlook 2003: New Features

Outlook 2003 enables you to share and synchronize your contact information with coworkers so that everyone is literally on the same page. It also enables you to share meeting information, such as agendas and lists of attendees, in a Meeting Workspace. Many of the calendaring features—including side-by-side calendars, event information, and meeting scheduling functionality—have been updated and improved. Outlook 2003 offers enhanced security features and junk mail filtering, as well as Desktop e-mail alerts. The latest edition also enables you to organize your e-mail messages by conversation, to flag messages by time or priority, and to search for and find particular messages, no matter which folder they are in.

Decide to Upgrade or Reinstall Office

Now that you have convinced yourself that you can't live without a newer version of Office, you have to determine whether you are going to upgrade your current version or do a completely new installation. One of the biggest factors to consider is cost. As mentioned earlier, Microsoft offers price breaks for continuing users who choose to upgrade from a previous version by purchasing the software specifically marked for upgrades. If you choose to splurge on a brand-spanking-new version, you'll probably pay full price, but at least you won't have the headache of trying to locate the older version's install disks amid the piles of software CDs and dust-encrusted floppies in your bottom desk drawer. You'll need the original installation disks or CD that came with your current version of Office to perform an upgrade. So, it's a trade-off, as usual, between cost and convenience.

Other important factors to consider in deciding whether to upgrade or reinstall are which version of Office you are currently using and which operating system is installed on your machine. Each dictates whether you can simply upgrade or whether you have to do a full install of Office; to upgrade Office on some computers, you may even have to install a newer operating system. For instance, if you are using Office 2000 or Office XP on a system running Windows 2000 or Windows XP or later, you can upgrade to Office 2003 with no problem. In fact, migration from Office 2000 or Office XP to the latest editions is relatively seamless because these three versions of Office use the same file formats, require no reboots during installation, and need not have their system files or Windows Installer files updated.

Office 2003 is built for complete *backward compatibility* with these two previous versions, meaning Office 2003 will support features and functionality of the earlier versions without batting an eye. However, if you are using an earlier version of Office or your PC runs any version of the Windows operating system earlier than Windows 2000, including Windows 95, Windows 98, Windows NT, or Windows Millennium Edition (heaven forbid!), most of which are built on Windows NT technology, you will have to perform a new installation of Office 2003 *as well as upgrade your operating system*. Although Windows NT is a stable operating system—meaning it causes you less gray hairs by reducing the number of system crashes and occurrences of file instability compared to, say, Windows Me—Microsoft will soon discontinue support for Windows NT and claims that the Windows 2000 and later operating systems provide enhanced stability and security features going forward.

TIP: *Degunking Windows* by Joli Ballew and Jeff Duntemann can help you with the basic process of upgrading or reinstalling a Windows operating system.

Remove the Old Version, or Just Install on Top?

Upgrading Office can be easier on your pocketbook than choosing to do a completely new installation. When performing an upgrade, Setup.exe expects to find a previous version of Office already installed on your PC and locates that previous installation. No previous installation, no upgrade. If you don't have the older version of Office installed, you must install it first: select Custom, and then select the minimum (one application) to complete the installation. Setup.exe will then notify you that this installation of the previous version must be uninstalled before the upgraded version can be installed. So, to upgrade, install Office, then uninstall Office, then install Office. Got it? Here, the trade-off is between install time versus cash: which is more valuable to you?

When upgrading a pre-existing installation, we want to *strongly* encourage you to back up all of your data files (including those with the .doc, .xls, .ppt, and .mdb file extensions), templates (including files with the .dot, .xlt, .pot, .mdz, .htm, and .xml file extensions), and Personal Folders (.pst) files onto removable media, or at least to another area on the hard drive. Setup.exe sometimes over-writes your data files, despite reassuring you during the installation process that your files are protected. Better safe than sorry, we always say.

For an Office XP installation (sorry, Office 2000 users), the Save My Settings Wizard stores information about program options and your preferences, custom templates and dictionaries, and AutoCorrect lists in a secure location on the Internet or in a file. By the way, you can also use the Save My Settings Wizard to restore settings to an Office XP installation (see Figure 3-1).

Prepare for the Installation

Even after all the hard decisions are made about which edition to pick and whether to perform an upgrade or a new install, don't take off your thinking cap just yet. You have a few more things to do before Office can be installed.

Make Sure Your Computer Meets the Requirements

The central processing unit (CPU), the brains of your PC, can perform calculations and manipulate data so quickly that it needs an area close at hand in which to store the functions and commands it uses most frequently. The random access

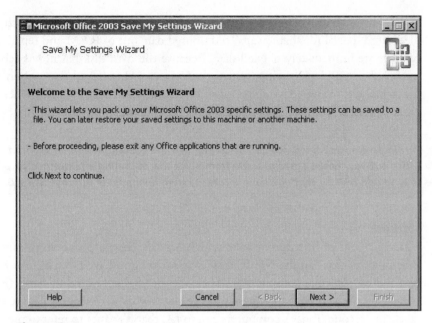

Figure 3-1
The Save My Settings Wizard stores your settings when you install Windows XP.

memory (RAM) modules or memory installed in your system provides the CPU with this temporary storage facility, speeding processing and CPU efficiency by keeping vital data nearby for convenient retrieval. Running applications installed on your system, plus the operating system processes, continually make demands on your installed RAM. These days, operating systems and applications seem to gobble up large chunks of RAM, not to mention hard disk space, with wild abandon. What hogs. But then again, newer PCs are built with tremendous amounts of processing power and storage, and so system capacity seems to keep roughly ahead of application demands.

Memory

The more RAM you can install in your system, the better the working performance of installed applications, including Office. Each edition of Microsoft Office 2003, for example, requires 128 megabytes (MB) of random access memory to run. Your operating system and any other installed applications that you run will also request RAM. So, if your system has 256 MB of memory or RAM available, you have just enough memory, for example, to run the Windows XP operating system (which also requires 128 MB of RAM) and Office 2003. Beware if you try to open any other application while you're using Office. As RAM fills up, the Windows operating system begins to use virtual memory to make up for the additional memory required. This process is called *paging* and is completed with what is called the *swap file,* or *page file,* which is a dedicated special file that "swaps" old unused data out of RAM and replaces it with more immediately needed data. Because the hard disk has now become involved in CPU processing, system performance slows. And then when the swap file gets swamped, you'll get disk errors and even worse performance, or your system will simply lock up and stare back at you, motionless.

TIP: The single greatest thing you can do to improve the overall performance of not only Office but your entire system, aside from somehow obtaining a faster micropro-cessor, is to add RAM so that you have a total system minimum of at least 512 MB.

Speed

And speaking of microprocessors, which are the central processing units on silicon chips that run the whole show, you're going to have to figure out how fast the one in your computer is. Processor speed is measured in hertz (Hz), which is a measure of the frequency of the chip's work cycles, equivalent to one cycle per second. Today's computers run so fast that it's easier to refer to proces-sor speed in units of megahertz (MHz), one million cycles per second, or giga-hertz (GHz), one billion cycles per second. To run Office 2003 Editions, you must have a PC with an Intel Pentium 233 MHz processor or faster. (Microsoft recommends installing Office on machines with at least a Pentium III chip.)

To find out what your system properties are, do the following:

1. Right-click the My Computer icon on your Desktop.
2. Select Properties from the context menu that appears. In the General tab, shown in Figure 3-2, you will see a succinct overview of your system capacities, including which operating system you are running, the name of the person the system is licensed to, the system manufacturer, the amount of RAM installed, and last but not least, the speed of the processor in megahertz or gigahertz.

Other System Requirements

Each Office 2003 Edition differs in how much hard disk space it will use, varying from 260 MB for the Standard and Student and Teacher Editions to 400 MB for Professional Edition, depending on the feature options selected. Your display monitor must also meet a minimum requirement of providing at least 800 by 600 dots per inch (dpi) resolution and must use the Super Video Graphics Array (SVGA) standard for color display so you can enjoy the full visual effects built into the applications. You need the finer resolution to better display details, and the larger the monitor (more display screen real estate), the higher the resolution you need to display objects on the entire monitor screen (edge to edge).

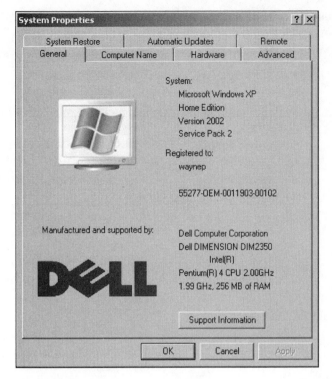

Figure 3-2
The General tab of the System Properties dialog box.

You also must have a CD-ROM or DVD-ROM drive. Table 3-2 summarizes the requirements your system must meet for a successful Office installation. Keep in mind that most computer stores sell systems that meet these minimum requirements, but just to be sure, verify the system specifications against the software requirements before you make your purchase.

Table 3-2   System Requirements for Office 2003 Editions and Previous Office Versions

Computer Component	Office Version	System Requirement
Processor speed	Previous Office versions (general)	Pentium processor, 75 MHz.
	Office 2003	Personal computer with an Intel Pentium 233 MHz or faster processor (Pentium III recommended); optional installation of Business Contact Manager for Outlook requires a 450 MHz or faster processor (Pentium III recommended).

(continued)

Table 3-2 System Requirements for Office 2003 Editions and Previous Office Versions *(continued)*

Computer Component	Office Version	System Requirement
Memory	Previous Office versions (general)	4 MB of RAM (Word, Excel, PowerPoint, Publisher),8 MB of RAM (Outlook, Access, FrontPage).
	Office 2003	128 MB of RAM or more; optional installation of Business Contact Manager for Outlook requires 256 MB of RAM.
Hard disk	Previous Office versions (general)	252 MB of available space, plus 182 MB for Publisher.
	Office 2003	400 MB of available space; optional installation files cache (recommended) requires an additional 200 MB of available space; optional installation of Business Contact Manager for Outlook requires an additional 190 MB of available hard-disk space.
Drive types	All versions	CD-ROM or DVD-ROM drive.
Display	All versions	Super VGA (800X600) or higher-resolution monitor.
Operating system	Previous Office versions (general)	Office 97 can be installed on computers running Windows 95, Windows NT Workstation 3.51 Service Pack 5, and later. Office 2000 can be installed on computers running Windows 2000, Windows XP, and later. Office XP can be installed on computers running Windows XP and later.
	Office 2003	Microsoft Windows 2000 with Service Pack 3 (SP3), Windows XP, and later.
Internet connection	All versions	Internet functionality requires dial-up or broadband Internet access.

Get Windows Ready Before Installing Office

You want to have a clean system prior to installing new software, such as Office, because your system is at its most vulnerable when installing applications and writing to the Registry. So, complete the following steps to tidy up before you introduce the new version of Office to your PC.

Virus Scan

Run your virus protection program, scanning on My Computer as shown in Figure 3-3, performing a memory scan as well as a full hard disk scan. Clean or quarantine any files identified as having a virus. The last thing you want is to have a virus corrupt your Office installation before you even get a chance to use it. A lingering bug can infect the Office program files and potentially crash your system. Always scan your system using an *up-to-date* antivirus program. Without an antivirus tool, you will never know whether your system is clean or contaminated. Tell-tale signs of possible infection include application and bootup sluggishness, excessive numbers of garbage files, corrupted files, and abnormal application and system behavior. You will need a tool to help you clean your system.

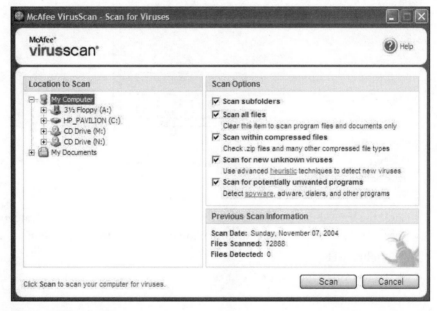

Figure 3-3

Prior to installation, scan your system using antivirus software to clear out corrupted or malicious files.

Disk Cleanup

Run Disk Cleanup to free up disk space by removing unneeded temporary files from the Internet or past downloads and removing files permanently from the Recycle Bin (see Figure 3-4). Start the Disk Cleanup utility by clicking Start, selecting Programs, Accessories, System Tools, and then clicking Disk Cleanup. The Recycle Bin and Temporary Files will usually be the areas with the most to clean up. Temporary Files contains the contents of the Windows Temp folder.

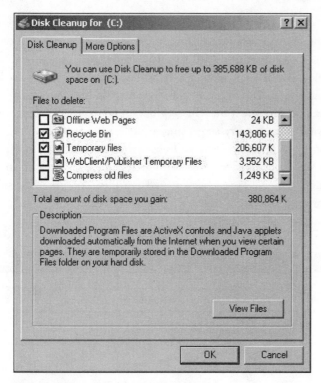

Figure 3-4

Use Disk Cleanup to free your hard drive of unnecessary gunk before installation.

Click the View Files button to see the specific files in the selected categories. Then place a check mark beside the following options to delete them:

√ Offline Web Pages

√ Downloaded Program Files

√ Old Chkdsk Files

√ Recycle Bin

√ Temporary Files

√ Temporary PC Health Files

GunkBuster's Notebook: Defragment Your Hard Drive!

Defragmenting and optimizing your hard drive can speed the installation process by placing your hard disk free space in contiguous order. File fragmentation is the consequence of file deletions and file saves. Imagine if you erased or deleted words from a page in this book, "gaps" or "holes" would appear on the page. Something similar happens during normal use of your PC. The operating system uses these "holes" by dividing a new file you want to save into smaller fragments and then saving these fragments all over your hard disk. The operating system makes the files appear whole when, in fact, they are not. Defragmenting your hard drive repositions the file fragments for more efficient retrieval, improving your system performance.

Disk defragmenting should be performed regularly so that when you ask your PC to locate the slide show you made out of your sister's vacation photos, the reader on the hard drive won't have to skip all over the place to locate all the bits of info it needs to display the slides as it would have to for a fragmented file. The Disk Defragmenter utility (see Figure 3-5) is a degunker's friend, enabling your computer to consolidate fragmented files and gain more efficient access to your folder system. Start Disk Defragmenter by clicking Start, selecting Programs, Accessories, System Tools, and then clicking Disk Defragmenter.

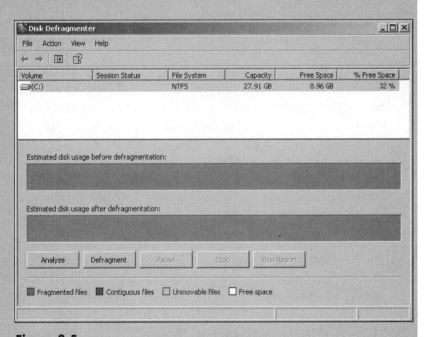

Figure 3-5
Disk Defragmenter consolidates hard disk free space and fragmented files.

Close All Programs and Reboot

Before performing the actual installation, you should close and shut down all other programs, specifically previously installed Office applications. If left running, those programs (shared files) might interfere with Office Setup or possibly corrupt the Office installation or the running program's open data files. Setup requires the Windows operating system to allocate memory to the installation process, and an open program can interfere with this allocation. Open programs also use memory resources, which might require Windows to use virtual memory to swap chunks of data in and out of RAM to the hard disk, slowing and maybe even corrupting the installation disk writes and the Registry updates. Save yourself the headaches and simply close down anything running on your PC when you're ready to install Office (or any other application). If you're worried about not being able to work while Setup runs, grab a latte and a muffin to keep your hands busy instead.

Perform a Custom Installation

Earlier in this chapter, you asked yourself a few questions about how you expect to use Office. Well, think back to the answers you came up with. Defining your requirements can assist you in selecting exactly which Microsoft Office features to install so you can keep your installation and later application use gunk free. After you insert the installation CD into your CD or DVD drive, the Setup Wizard starts and you are presented with a screen on which you can choose the type of installation you'd like to perform (see Figure 3-6). Yeah, it'd be nice to hit Automatic and go enjoy your muffin while Office does its thing. But, unfortunately, Automatic isn't one of the options on the Setup Wizard screen: Typical and Custom are. By selecting the Typical (Install Now) option, you direct Setup to copy nearly 260 MB of Office system files to your hard drive. Keep in mind, you might never use the application features that require these files, so you might have just allowed Setup to add a whole bunch of gunk to your hard drive.

When you select the Custom installation option, you can customize the Office installation, optimizing it and installing only the features you know you will actually use. If, in the future, you determine that you need additional features, you can install those options separately (just keep your installation CDs handy because you'll be prompted to use them if you want to add more features).

Using the Installation Discs

As you install Office, it makes a record of the CD-ROM or network installation you used to install Office feature options (version, edition, and install path). The Setup Wizard searches the prerecorded install path for the file called data1.msi

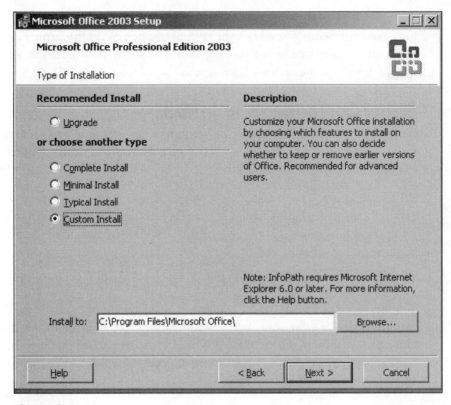

Figure 3-6
Choose the Custom option to streamline your installation.

from the Windows Registry. It is critical that you keep the installation CD-ROM disc(s) nearby because you will need them later when you upgrade or update your Office edition, modify feature options, or remove feature options.

Select an Installation Location

By default, the Setup Wizard installs Office programs to the C:\Program Files\Microsoft Office folder. It then creates an entire file system under the currently logged-on user's account ID at C:\Documents and Settings*username*\Local Settings\Application Data\Microsoft (where *username* is the name of the currently logged-on user) to store user-customized configuration settings.

Although it is possible, try *not* to change these default locations for system files. They are the standard and preferred locations and enable Microsoft update support (incident support, chargeable support, warranty support, and security update support) to proceed automatically. Should you change the location of these files, every upgrade, change, and so forth that you make will require you to redirect the Setup Wizard to your custom location. With the frequency that Microsoft releases updates, if you regularly check the Microsoft site for the same, this will become a huge time sink for you. Don't do it.

Select Components to Install

By keeping in mind the productivity requirements you previously identified for yourself, you can pretty easily select which individual feature components to install in a Custom installation.

When the Setup Wizard starts, most people simply select the Typical install option because they figure hard disk space is relatively cheap and they don't pay attention to how much space Office takes up. Besides, a customized installation might seem too complicated.

Wrong.

You should consider using the Custom installation option because it will help you avoid gunking up your system with features that you might never use. Upon presentation of the list of features available to install (see Figure 3-7), you can easily install all you will *use,* improving your hard disk usage and your awareness of the available features.

For instance, if you just need to develop administrative letters, memos, and faxes, during a Custom install you would disable Web page and reports options while enabling the address book feature. If you're a student, you would enable the Word More Templates and Macros options to have more available features for thesis and research papers.

If you plan to develop simple Web pages (HTML) using Word as your Web page editor, enable the Word Web Page Wizard install option. On the other hand, if you intend to seriously develop Web sites, use FrontPage as your Web page development environment (this is one of the extra applications that make up the Office System) and disable Word's Web Page Wizard. It's all about being smart about which features you decide to enable now and knowing that you can always reinsert the installation disc later and choose more options to install if you need them.

Install to Hard Disk, or Install on First Run?

Many of Office's features are set to install at first use. For example, the first time you attempt to use the Translation feature, Office will prompt you to insert the Office installation CD so it can download the proper application files to make Translation work (see Figure 3-8). Allowing Office to install features at first use, as opposed to installing features to hard disk, is a good option if you are not

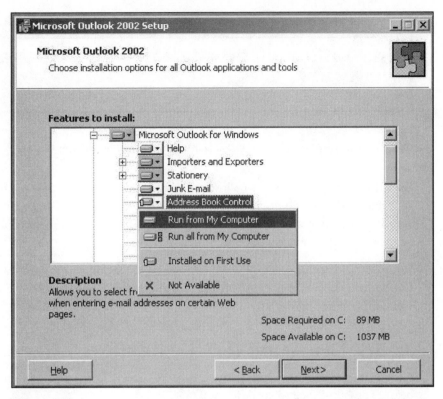

Figure 3-7
Choose exactly which options you'd like to install.

really sure, for instance, whether you are going to use Word as your HTML editor or use another application. By setting the install option to Install on First Use, you install only those features that you actually end up using.

The downside is that you have to know where your Office installation CD is at all times. Otherwise, you could someday be left in a lurch. Suppose you're just crazy about Links, the friendly orange tabby Office Assistant, and you want him to appear in your work window every time you open an Office document. Without the Custom installation CD on hand to install the Office Assistant personalities the first time you press the F1 key, you'll be stuck with that suspicious-looking paper clip.

Run Setup to Remove Useless Components

Check your installation by running the Office installation CD. If you are upgrading from a previous version of Office, Setup will display a list of all the Office applications currently installed on your hard disk. These are the applications that Setup will remove when it installs the newest version of Office. To

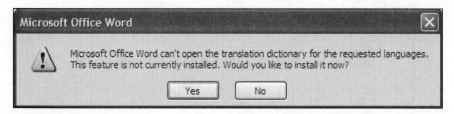

Figure 3-8
Office asks whether you'd like to install uninstalled features at first use.

keep things simple, it's best to allow Setup to remove old versions of Office applications so that you do not create a hodgepodge of application versions on your PC. Once Setup runs and the installation is complete, extraneous components will be permanently removed.

Regarding the new installation, click the Add/Remove button and then change features you do not want to Not Installed or Install on First Use. Office Setup will perform the appropriate actions to remove the unwanted features.

What to Do After the Installation

Now that installation is complete, you have just a few more tasks to complete before you put Office to work for you.

Activate and Register Your Applications

You must activate your application software on the Microsoft site. This required step ensures Microsoft that you have installed a genuine Microsoft product and that you accept the End User License Agreement for terms of use. During activation, no personal information is exchanged with Microsoft, and the activation is completely anonymous and for the purposes of validating the license for your installation. You must activate the software for it to work properly.

Registration, on the other hand, is completely optional. You want to register your installation with Microsoft to be eligible for product updates and to be able to report errors or bugs in the application. At the end of the activation process, if you choose to register your products, it will enable Microsoft to send you information and offers about future products. Registration also enables you to receive improved product support and product update information. The personal information that you supply for product registration is kept confidential by Microsoft and enables Microsoft to tailor messages about other products according to the answers you supplied.

The first time you start an Office program, you have the opportunity to fill in the electronic registration form and return it to Microsoft by using your Internet connection or e-mail. If you don't have an Internet connection or e-mail, you can print the form and then send it to Microsoft by postal mail or by fax. You can also register by telephone by following the instructions in the Office Registration Wizard. This is your only opportunity to fill in the registration form. If you choose not to register when you first start an Office program, the only method available for you to register later is through the Microsoft Office Update Web site.

Check for Product Updates

Periodically, Microsoft releases software updates and patches that you can download to keep your computer up-to-date. These downloads can include the latest security information to help protect your computer against new viruses and other security threats, software upgrades and drivers to help your computer run more smoothly, and the latest Help files.

Microsoft Office Update is a Web site that Microsoft updates regularly, and it acts as a portal to information and answers to your questions about all of the Office products. The Microsoft Office Update site provides Office updates for free. Because the Windows Installer program requires access to the original installation CDs to apply an update, you might as well check for updates right now, while you have the installation media handy. Go to **http:// office.microsoft.com/officeupdate/** and click Check for Updates to see whether any updates for your installation are available. Thereafter, make a habit of periodically checking the Microsoft Office Update Web site for security patches for your installed version of Office. Remember, you're required to have the installation discs handy to complete the updates successfully.

How to Get Help

If you have a question about a Microsoft Office program, first ask the Office Assistant (the embedded context-sensitive help system that comes with the program). If you don't find what you need, you can get information from the following technical resources:

√ Microsoft Knowledge Base (**http://support.microsoft.com**). A Web site that contains a wealth of information about all Microsoft products and technologies. The Microsoft Knowledge Base gives you tips to find the information and the technical answers you're looking for. It contains templates, macros, and clip art that you can download.

√   Microsoft TechNet (**www.microsoft.com/technet/default.mspx**) and
Microsoft Developer Network (**http://msdn.microsoft.com/**), Web sites
that contain comprehensive (Office developer) information for product
support and comprehensive programming information and toolkits. They are
usually searched from the Knowledge Base.

Summing Up

In this chapter you learned how to apply the important degunking process to
get Office installed or upgraded on your PC. We showed you how to get focused and assess your specific needs, and then examine the various versions of
Office that are available so that you can match your needs to the best version.
To install Office, we suggested you use the Custom installation feature to ensure that you get everything you need without gunking up your PC in the
process. Finally, you learned how to perform some important degunking tasks
after you installed Office.

In the next chapter, you'll learn how to start organizing your Office-related
files and folders so that you can work much more efficiently.

Organizing Office–Related Files and Folders

Degunking Checklist:

√ Remove the excess junk in the default folders: My Documents, My Pictures, My eBooks, My Music, and My Downloads.

√ Remove gunk from personal folders you've created.

√ Delete or move files that are inappropriately placed in other areas, such as the root directory (C:).

√ Delete unnecessary archive files, such as those with .zip, .sit, .tar, and .dmg extensions.

√ Remove temporary files stored on your system.

√ Remove excess files that might be shared by multiple users on your PC.

√ Set up a subfolder system that makes sense for the types of files you save.

√ Defragment your hard drive to make it work more efficiently.

n this chapter, we'll show you how to roll up your sleeves and get some real degunking done. Files that you create using Microsoft Office applications take up space on your PC's hard drive—a lot or a little, depending on how many kilobytes or megabytes of memory they consume. Even in this age of seemingly unlimited hard drive space, you do need to be concerned about conserving disk space. This is because when you open any Office file—an Excel workbook, for instance—the application has to search the entire hard disk (including any auxiliary disks or disk partitions, which we'll explain later in this chapter) to find the file you specified. The more stuff on your hard drive, the longer it takes for your PC to search for and open the file. Deleting unnecessary files that you no longer need can therefore optimize disk performance. You'll notice that Office responds more quickly to your Open and Save commands after you've degunked your file and folder system using the tips we provide in this chapter.

Clean Up the Default Folders

On the C: drive, also called the root directory, Windows provides default folders called My Documents, My Music, My eBooks, My Pictures, and My Downloads to which Office automatically attempts to save files you create. The first time you click Save to store a file, Office reads the file extension (the last few letters of the file name after the rightmost dot) and, based on whether it recognizes the file type, offers to save the file in the default save location for that type of file. For example, if you try to save a file with a .jpg extension, Office offers to save it for you in the My Pictures folder, which is the default save location for images. In a similar way, Office will offer to save files with .txt (text), .doc (document), .ppt (PowerPoint), .xls (Excel), and .pdf (PDF) extensions to your My Documents folder. Table 4-1 lists the types of files based on file extension that each default folder is associated with.

Table 4-1   File Extensions Associated with Default Folders

Default Folder	Associated File Extensions
My Documents	.doc, .dot, .eml, .pdf, .xls, .ppt, .txt
My eBooks	.pdf, .doc, .lit, .pdb
My Music	.midi, .wav, .mp3
My Pictures	.jpg, .jpeg, .bmp, .tif, .tiff, .gif, .emf
My Downloads	.htm, .html

If you're in the habit of saving Office files to the C: drive, or if you save everything—from Word files to PowerPoint presentations and Outlook e-mail attachments—to the default My Documents folder, you will be gunking up your system unnecessarily. You'll soon find (if you haven't already) that you've got a jumbled mess of Office-related files piled in one place and you can't find the data you need easily, or at all. Although you might find it convenient to accept the default file save location Office offers when you are saving a file, by doing so you are likely creating a clutter problem for yourself in the long run. Believe us when we say it's in your best interest to keep your default folders clean and organized as we explain here.

We're going to help you take inventory of the Office-related files stored on your PC. Then we'll share some guidelines on how you can get rid of the unnecessary files and folders. And finally, we'll help you organize what remains on your hard drive so that you can keep a shipshape Office-related file system going forward.

Take a Look at What's Gunking Up Your PC

Before you start cleaning, it's best to see what you've accumulated and begin to make decisions on what is worth keeping, what needs deleting, and how you might logically group what's left. Log on to your PC as the administrator so that you can have ultimate authority over degunking the files and folders. Then right-click the Start button and choose Explore All Users. This opens Windows Explorer, which enables you to view all the files and folders stored by all users on your PC. If a list of folders is not showing in the left pane of Explorer, click the Folders button in the menu bar.

GunkBuster's Notebook: Learn How Your Hard Drive Is Partitioned

In Windows Explorer, you can check whether your PC is using a single hard drive, multiple hard drives (such as the basic hard disk plus a peripheral data storage device), or a partitioned hard drive. A disk partition is a portion of a hard disk that behaves as if it were a separate disk. Sometimes large hard drives are broken into one or multiple partitions to allow programs and system files (files used by the operating system) to be kept separate from user files (files created by users that hold user data). For instance, if your drive is partitioned, you might see a C: and a D: drive in the Folders list, where C: is smaller and set up to hold system files and D: is larger and meant to store user data. If your drive is partitioned and you've been storing your files in the default folders, which are usually located on C:, that drive quickly becomes

> filled and cluttered, whereas D: remains a vast expanse of un-
> used storage space. Later we'll show you how to move the loca-
> tion of the default folders to the larger partition so that you can
> continue to store your data in them. Many PC users simply get in
> the habit of saving their files in one partition and then forgetting all
> about the other partition. As you continue on with your degunking
> tasks, make sure you take a moment to acquaint yourself with how
> your drive is partitioned.

Browse through the folders on your hard disk to see what's piled where. Explore under All Users, as well as the folders under your own logon name. Peek in the My Documents folder, glance at the Shared Documents folders, and skim through the other default folders. Right-click any file that you recognize as unneeded, and choose Delete to remove it. Be careful not to move or remove program file folders, downloaded installation files, or any file that you did not create; doing so could cause system instability and unexpected data loss.

Once you've got a good idea of what's stored on your system, you're ready to move on to the next step in degunking your files and folder system: separating the wheat from the chaff.

Delete Unnecessary Files and Folders

In this section, we offer guidelines on how to search out old and unneeded files from every nook and cranny of your file system so that you can eliminate them to optimize Office. After you've read this section, you will know how to bust gunk from the following locations:

√   Default folders, such as My Documents, My Music, My eBooks, and My Pictures

√   Shared folders, such as Shared Documents, Shared Music, and Shared Pictures

√   The root directory

We'll also help you accomplish the following degunking feats:

√   Remove unnecessary files according to file extension

√   Clean up archive files (.zip, .tar, .arc) that have already been extracted and saved elsewhere

√   Locate and delete duplicate files

√   Delete old temporary files

√   Delete unused user accounts and related files

√   Degunk your Outlook e-mail folders

Restore Order to the Default Folders

Here's your chance to make a clean sweep through each user folder, tossing the old and tired files you no longer need as you go along. Under each user logon name, make sure you scour the following folders to locate the gunk:

√   My Documents

√   My Music

√   My Pictures

If you worry that you might accidentally delete something that you'll need later, copy specific files or whole folders to removable media, such as a Zip disk or a CD. When you see something you don't need or want, complete the following steps to remove it:

1.   Right-click the item.

2.   Choose Delete from the context menu.

3.   Choose Yes in the Confirm File Delete dialog box.

Keep in mind that when you choose to delete a folder, the folder and all of its contents will be moved to the Recycle Bin, which is a holding place for unwanted items. Also, if you wish to select multiple files and remove them all at once, hold down the Shift key (to select a contiguous group) or the Ctrl key (to select nonadjacent files) as you highlight items, and then right-click one of the selected items to delete them all.

TIP: *When you delete files or whole folders using this method, they are removed from view and stored in the Recycle Bin. Only when you choose Empty Recycle Bin from the Recycle Bin File menu are items permanently removed from your PC. This provides you with a sort of safety net, allowing you to try out how the deletion of an item will work before erasing the item irretrievably.*

Do be careful about what you delete—don't remove anything that might be an executable file (with the .exe extension) or related to running an application. When you find you need encouragement to keep going, in Explorer navigate to the Recycle Bin and take a look at how many files and folders you have banished. The number in the lower right corner of the Explorer window tells you how many kilobytes (or megabytes!) of data this trash heap contains—and later, when you finally do empty the bin, you'll feel exhilarated that you just recycled the space consumed by these superfluous files and put all those kilobytes back into circulation.

Straighten Up Shared Folders

The default shared folders, called Shared Documents, Shared Pictures, and Shared Music, enable you to share files with the other users who share your PC or with others on your network. In Explorer, these folders are listed under All Users, and you must be logged on as Administrator to clean out the gunk from them. Shared folders sometimes act as gunk magnets because they are public space and no one in particular feels responsible for keeping the commons clean. If you share files often with coworkers or other logon accounts, you might find several items here that are no longer needed and that can be removed. Right-click each item to be removed and choose Delete from the context menu. On the other hand, if you do not share your PC with other users and do not share files on a network, you might find you have very little gunk buildup in the shared folders.

Cleanse the Root Directory

Next, move on to the root directory, or C: drive. Sometimes it can be so easy to save files directly to C:, but after even just a short while you'll experience all sorts of problems having your data files mixed in with system folders and application files. Plus, you'll find you're wasting time scrolling through screens and screens of file names just to find the file you need amidst the system folders. If you've cultivated the unfortunate habit of using the root directory as a catch-all, you must break free of this conditioning and clear out C: now. Remove only files—never folders!—from the root directory. Later, when we show you how and where to create relevant subfolders for your stuff, you'll have a place to move the remaining user files.

Clean Up Old ZIP Files

If you use WinZip or another compression program to compress (archive) files and folders, you might be harboring a whole lot of gunk that you can very easily remove. Think about it: a friend e-mails you a ZIP file containing the rough draft of his business and marketing plans. You save the ZIP file to your hard drive, and then, to open and modify the documents, you must extract them from the ZIP file and save them to a permanent location on your hard disk. So now you have an e-mail message in Outlook with a ZIP file attachment, a ZIP file on your hard disk containing the business files, as well as a copy of the individual files saved on the hard drive—that's three sets of the same information, two of which are pure gunk! Later in this chapter we'll show you how you can degunk your message list in Outlook, which will take care of the ZIP file attachment. Right now, you can find and remove ZIP files saved to your hard disk by browsing user folders for files ending with .zip. Delete all ZIP files that you have already extracted and see how much space you free up.

Search and Destroy by File Extension

Use the Search feature, located in the Start menu, to find specific files by file extension. Your hard drive might be so cluttered with superfluous files that even you can't remember where you've stored them all. To save yourself the trouble of clicking open each folder to search for gunk, you can ask Windows to find all the files that end with a specific file extension, for instance, .bmp. This approach lets you easily glance through the list and decide which ones to keep and which ones to lose, no matter where their actual location is in the file system. Here are the steps to follow:

1. Select Search in the Start menu (or use the Search button on the Windows Explorer menu bar).

2. In the left pane of the Search results dialog box, select "All files and folders" under "What do you want to search for?"

3. Type a file extension, or several, in the "All or part of the file name" box under "Search by any or all of the criteria below."

4. Choose your local hard drive from the Look In drop-down menu, and then click Search.

All files meeting the search criteria are displayed in the right pane of the Search Results dialog box as shown in Figure 4-1. From there, you can right-click specific items and decide whether to open them to view the contents or to delete them. Search for and remove extraneous files with the following file extensions:

.txt	.doc	.pdf	.ppt	.pps
.xls	.jpg	.jpeg	.psd	.gif
.tif	.bmp	.tiff	.midi	.mp3
.wav	.avi	.wma	.msg	.zip

Locate and Delete Duplicate Files

Just as in the ZIP file scenario discussed previously, you might have duplicate copies of the same files saved in different locations on your hard disk. Ultimately, a duplicate is just gunk waiting to be discovered and eliminated. You can search manually through all the user folders on your file system, hoping you'll be able to recognize doubles, but this can take inordinate amounts of time and mental concentration, especially if you have not been in the habit of using a consistent file-naming strategy and file properties (explained later in this chapter in the section entitled "Use Descriptive Names") to identify your files. You'll be better off using a third-party software tool to skim through your files, matching byte by byte and pointing out exact duplicates so that you can remove them. Some third-party tools can be downloaded for this task; simply use a search engine and search for "duplicate files."

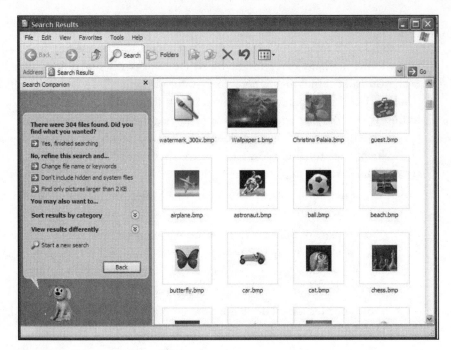

Figure 4-1
Use the Search Results dialog box to search for files by file extension.

Remove Temporary Files

In Chapter 1, "Why Is Office So Gunked Up?" we explained how Office uses temporary files and why these files might linger longer than they're welcome. Other types of temporary files are stored on your system as well, such as copies of recently viewed Web pages and temp copies of files recently accessed on your system. Temporary files, as their name suggests, are necessary only in the short term to enhance system or application performance. Later, after their usefulness has expired, they can be safely deleted. If you are not vigilant, temporary files can hog up thousands of kilobytes on your PC. You might not think to delete them because you did not overtly create them and they are not stored in any user data folders. The other problem is that some temp files are invisible! Windows provides a handy tool called Disk Cleanup that you can use to identify and then delete various temporary files stored on your system. To open Disk Cleanup, follow these steps:

1. Click Start, and then choose All Programs.
2. Point to Accessories, then select System Tools, and click Disk Cleanup.

First, Disk Cleanup will calculate how much space you can save by using the utility; this sometimes takes a few minutes. Then Disk Cleanup provides a Files

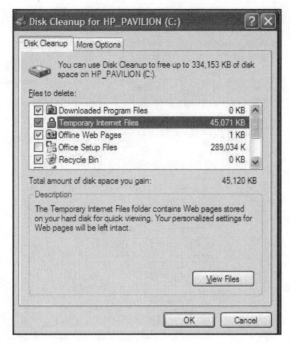

Figure 4-2

Disk Cleanup lists temporary files that you can safely
delete.

to Delete list (see Figure 4-2) containing files it found across your hard drive
that you can safely remove to free up space.

Select an item in the Files to Delete list to read a description. Be sure to place
a check mark beside each category of files that you would like Disk Cleanup to
delete, and remove the check mark beside file types that you would not like
removed. When you're ready, click OK to authorize the utility to start deleting;
click Yes to confirm the decision. It's a great degunking strategy to run Disk
Cleanup to remove temporary files once a week or so—you'll regain thousands
of kilobytes of usable space each time.

After running Disk Cleanup, you can also use the Windows Search feature to
find any stowaway temporary files. Enter the file extension .tmp in the "All or
part of the file name" box under "Search by any or all of the criteria below" in
the Search Results dialog box. If you haven't recently been on a mission like
this one, you'll likely see hundreds of temporary files listed in the Search Results dialog box. To delete the unnecessary temp files, follow these steps:

1. In the right pane, right-click the Name column heading and be sure that
    Date Modified is checked (see Figure 4-3).

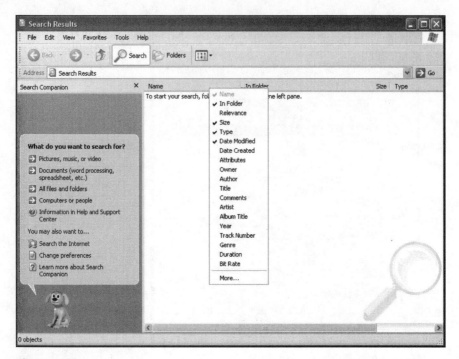

Figure 4-3
Make the Date Modified column visible in the Search Results window by right-clicking the Name header.

2. Left-click the Date Modified column heading to toggle the ascending/descending sort of the files by date. Sort in ascending order so older items are listed first and more recent items are near the bottom of the list as you scroll down.

3. Left-click to select the first file in the list that is more than one week old, scroll to the end of the list while holding down the Shift key, and left-click to select the oldest temp file (end of list). (Alternatively, press the Ctrl key while you simultaneously left-click files to individually select/deselect them from the list.) See Figure 4-4.

4. Right-click a highlighted file name and choose Delete.

5. Click Yes to confirm you want to delete the selected files. The files will be moved to the Recycle Bin. Note that the delete action will terminate if a file in the list is locked and in use by another program, so close down other applications and files while you complete this bit of degunking.

It might take a few minutes, and several files may not be deleted as requested, but you can be assured that you just did a very good thing. For instant gratification, open the Recycle Bin and view how many items and megabytes of

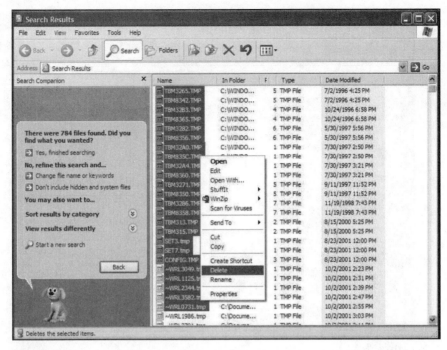

Figure 4-4
Select the files to delete, right-click them, and then choose Delete from the context menu.

to-be-removed data it contains. Soon, your system will be permanently purged of the unneeded files that have been bloating your folder system and slowing performance.

Eliminate Vacant User Accounts and Related Files

If you share your PC with others, you might have created personalized user accounts for those people. As good security practice, when such accounts are no longer needed, they should be removed, along with any unnecessary related files, by completing the following steps:

1. Log on as Administrator to manage user accounts.

2. Click Start, and then choose Control Panel.

3. In Control Panel, double-click User Accounts to open the User Accounts dialog box.

4. In the "Pick an account to change" section, click the user account you want to remove.

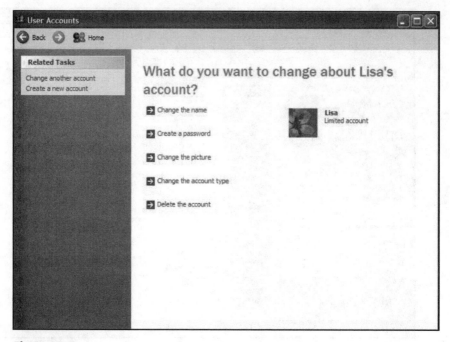

Figure 4-5

You can delete old or unused user accounts to help degunk your file system.

5. Select "Delete the account" (see Figure 4-5), and then on the next screen decide whether you'd like to keep the files stored in the account's My Documents folder.

6. On the last screen, click Delete Account to confirm that you'd like to remove the account.

Use this procedure to eradicate all extraneous user accounts.

Degunk Your Outlook Mail Folders

Most plain e-mail messages take up just a few kilobytes of space. But when Outlook is clogged with hundreds and thousands of messages—most of which, we have to remind you, you no longer need because they contain expired content—those few kilobytes here and there add up to monstrous file sizes that will eventually begin to slow down your PC. And e-mail attachments, oh-ho-ho! They significantly contribute to folder bloat—in fact attachments usually are the prime culprit. We dare you to examine the size of your folders by following these steps:

1. Open Outlook and right-click any folder name in the folders list.

2. Choose Properties from the context menu.

3. In the folder Properties dialog box, click the Folder Size button to see the verdict (Outlook 2003 users can use the Mailbox Cleanup utility on the Tools menu to see a list of all folders and their sizes).

In most cases—excluding folders for current projects you are involved in and current correspondence—there is no need to allow your Inbox and Sent Items mail folders to grow beyond one week's worth of messages in size. For some people this may be 150 messages, whereas others might receive twice that in a week. Then to degunk your e-mail folders is a minor task and the time expended is limited to just a few minutes. Archive folders with more than 1000 messages in them to a local Personal Folders file (which uses the .pst extension; we'll show you how to create these in just a moment), and limit archive files to no more than 2 megabytes (MB) to reduce the risk of corruption. Target your largest folder, and prepare to trim the fat.

As mentioned, beware of attachments cluttering up Outlook. Usually, for every attachment file that you send, the original file is safe and sound, tucked away in another location on your hard disk—this duplication is gunk! And every attachment that you receive, if it is safe and worthy, should immediately be saved to a more permanent location; *the Inbox and its subfolders are not the place to store attachment files.* If attachments in your mail folders and the Sent Items folder run into the thousands or hundreds of thousands of kilobytes, they are hogging space unnecessarily and it's time to clear them out.

TIP: Let us just remind you here: never open an attachment from an unknown or suspicious source because it could contain a virus or other malware.

In Outlook 2003, you can sort your messages by attachment size. This is a great help and should provide great motivation for deciding which attachments gotta go. On the View menu, select Arrange By, and then choose Size from the submenu. Suddenly, you are confronted with the evidence—you have been aiding and abetting gunk. In earlier versions of Outlook, sort messages in the message list by attachment by clicking the attachment icon (which looks like a paper clip) in the list header; you won't be able to see the attachment size, but at least you can focus your energy on clearing messages with attachments first.

As we mentioned earlier, important attachments that you receive should be saved immediately to a more permanent location, so there should be no need to keep them here in Outlook. To ease into it, pick 10 of the largest attachments or a bunch of attachments grouped at the top of your message list that you have already saved elsewhere on your hard disk. Then make the cut in one of two ways:

√ Delete the message, attachment and all, by right-clicking the message and choosing Delete from the context menu.

√ Delete only the attachment by opening the message, right-clicking the attachment, and choosing Remove from the context menu. (You cannot delete an attachment while viewing a message in the Reading Pane/preview pane.)

Don't you feel better after lightening the load? Perhaps a little later, try to degunk another 10 large attachments, and keep going until you've demolished them all. Don't forget to patrol the Sent Items folder, too; when it comes to hiding fugitive attachments, it's usually the biggest offender.

Compacting Your E-Mails

After you have made so many deletions, you can reduce the size of your data file, the Personal Folders (PST) file that holds all your Outlook items, by compacting it. Compacting a PST file is analogous to defragmenting your hard drive. Compaction permanently removes (never to be retrieved) deleted items and moves all items into heel-to-toe order. To compact a PST file, complete the following steps:

1. In the Outlook Mail pane, on the File menu, choose Data File Management.
2. In the Outlook Data Files dialog box, click the data file that you want to compact, and then click Settings.
3. In the Personal Folders dialog box, shown in Figure 4-6, click the Compact Now button and then click OK.
4. Click Close in the Outlook Data Files dialog box.

Another sure way to decrease folder size and allow yourself to keep Outlook items you just cannot bear to get rid of is to archive items over a certain age, say, all mail messages older than three months. We provide detailed information on how to customize archiving settings in Chapter 9, "Degunking Microsoft Outlook." What you must do now is right-click the names of each of your mail folders in the folder list and choose Properties from the context menu. In each folder's Properties dialog box, select the AutoArchive tab. Ensure at a minimum that the "Archive items in this folder using the default settings" option is selected as shown in Figure 4-7. Click Apply, and then click OK. If you wish, you can review or configure the default AutoArchive settings or create per-folder archiving settings now using the steps given in Chapter 9, but the main thing is to be sure that the AutoArchive feature is enabled on a folder-by-folder basis, especially for overly large mail folders. Once AutoArchive runs, folders will be trimmed down in size.

Figure 4-6

Compact your Personal Folders file after making many deletions.

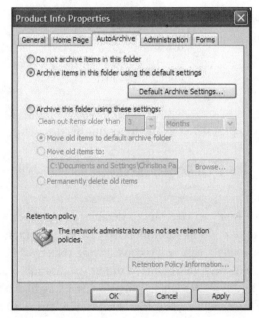

Figure 4-7

In folder Properties dialog boxes, ensure that archiving is turned on.

It's best to make the folder size reduction procedure a two-step process as we've outlined here. First, go through your mail folders—do this persistently in small bits if you're strapped for time—and delete all messages and attachments that you no longer need to keep (remember to empty your Deleted Items folder afterward). Then archive the remaining items that are over the specified age; there's no sense archiving first because you'll simply end up shifting deletable gunk from a current folder to an archive folder, never to be seen again.

Organize What Remains

After all that deleting, you might be exhausted, but you should be happy. It's like cleaning out your closets at home. Think of all the wasted space you've reclaimed! Now it is time to arrange the Office-related files that you've decided to keep into logical subfolders. If you have a single hard disk and only one partition on your drive, you can create a personalized subfolder system right inside the My Documents folder. If you have more than one hard drive or multiple disk partitions, you can keep yourself organized by creating personalized subfolders on the larger partition and saving your user data there. We'll show you how.

Putting your Office files in order involves a four-step process:

1. Organize default folders by creating subfolders.
2. Move data into subfolders.
3. Empty the Recycle Bin.
4. Run Disk Defragmenter.

We'll walk you through each step in detail in the following sections.

Create Subfolders to Personalize the Default Folders

Office applications are set up initially to save files to default file-save locations, namely, the My Documents folder and its subfolders: My Music, My Pictures, and My eBooks. You, however, likely create and receive a wide variety of Office files and you won't be able to get them all organized unless you use subfolders. To streamline how you open and save files with Office, the best way to arrange your subfolders is within the My Documents folder. That way, when an Office app politely offers to save a file in the default My Documents folder containing all your own subfolders, you have very little navigation to do to deposit the file exactly where you want it and where you'll easily find it again later. Use the following techniques to help you create meaningful and useful subfolders:

√ Identify file categories (such as work-related files, home-related files).

√ Define an organizational scheme (such as subfolders arranged according to project name).

√ Use descriptive names for files and folders (such as Revisions, Chapter 1, Images, as shown in Figure 4-8).

√ Use file properties to add descriptive details about files (such as author name, title, or subject).

√ Adjust Explorer so you can view the file properties (such as date created, author, or title)

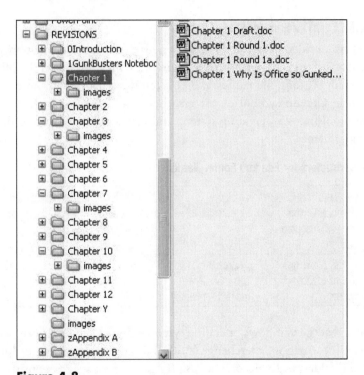

Figure 4-8

This is a folder hierarchy organized by project.

Scan your Office-related files and try to determine themes by which you can group them into subfolders. Here are some tips to help you come up with an organizational scheme:

√ Look for a clear way to divide work-related files from home-related files.

√ See if you can further categorize your work files by project name or by client.

√ Consider organizing your documents by user, creator, file type, date received, or some other similar identifying trait.

√ Create a folder to store files that you might need to review or take action on. These might be files that you receive as e-mail attachments and that you are not sure where to store just yet.

√ For your home-related files, try to organize them into categories that reflect your hobbies or activities.

√ For documents you are currently working on, create shortcuts and place them in a "work in progress" folder.

Use Descriptive Names

When you have decided how you'd like to organize your subfolder system, use descriptive names for subfolders to make them more meaningful. Most Office applications support long file names, and you can use a name with up to 255 characters in it. Certain symbol characters, shown in Table 4-2, hold special meaning to the Windows operating system, and you should avoid using them in file or folder names.

Table 4-2   Illegal Characters for File and Folder Names

\ (backslash, used in file path name)	/ (forward slash, universal naming convention source location)	: (colon, indicates drive)	* (asterisk, multicharacter wild card)	? (question mark, single-character wild card)
" (quotation mark, programmer's literal designator)	< (less than sign, command-line redirect symbol)	> (greater than sign, command-line redirect symbol)	| (pipe symbol)	. (period, designates file extension)

Also consider that the Windows operating system employs the American Standard Code for Information Interchange (ASCII) file-ordering system to alphabetize files and folders in Explorer. The ASCII character set assigns a numerical value to letters of the alphabet and can then sort words in alphabetical order. ASCII is case sensitive, so uppercase letters are assigned a higher value than lowercase letters and will fall earlier in a sort. ASCII sorts according to this order: 0–9, ABC–XYZ, abc–xyz. How this relates to your file- and folder-naming system is that file or folder names that begin with a numeral will be sorted before ones beginning with letters; if, for instance, you would like the chapter files of your book project to be sorted in book order, meaning that the Preface and Introduction fall first in the folder list, followed by individual chapters, and finally by the appendixes, as shown in Figure 4-8, you can start folder names with numbers or letters to force a nonalphabetic sort order.

GunkBuster's Notebook: Use File Properties to Better Label Your Files

To make it even easier to find files in Explorer, you can add to a document file properties that can be displayed in the Explorer window. File properties are small details about documents that can help you identify them, such as a descriptive title, author name, subject, comments, or specific keywords. To add file properties to a Word, Excel, or PowerPoint file, in the open document, complete the following steps:

1. On the File menu, click Properties.

2. Select the Summary tab, and then fill in the information you'd like to display later in the appropriate text boxes as shown in Figure 4-9.

3. Click OK.

Figure 4-9

Add file properties to an open document that will help you identify it later.

To get the full benefit of using file properties, you must next adjust your view in Explorer so that you can see file details. To view file properties in Explorer, complete the following steps:

1. Open Explorer, and on the View menu, select Details.

2. If the particular file properties that you would like displayed are not listed in the right pane as column headings, on the View menu, select Choose Details.

3. In the Choose Details dialog box, place a check mark next to each type of detail you'd like displayed in the file listing. Keep in mind that the more details you choose, the more narrow the columns in the Explorer window will be and the more scrolling you'll have to do to see the data. Therefore, pick between five and six detail categories for display, such as Name, Size, Type, Date Modified, Author, and Title, as shown in Figure 4-10.

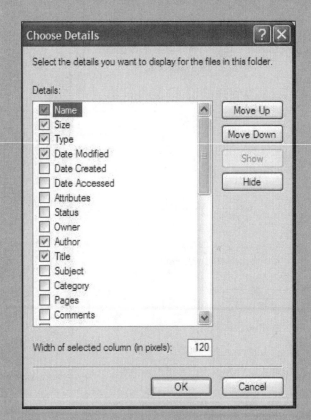

Figure 4-10

Choose which file properties you'd like displayed in Explorer by using the Choose Details dialog box.

Figure 4-11 shows the resulting Explorer window that displays the chosen details.

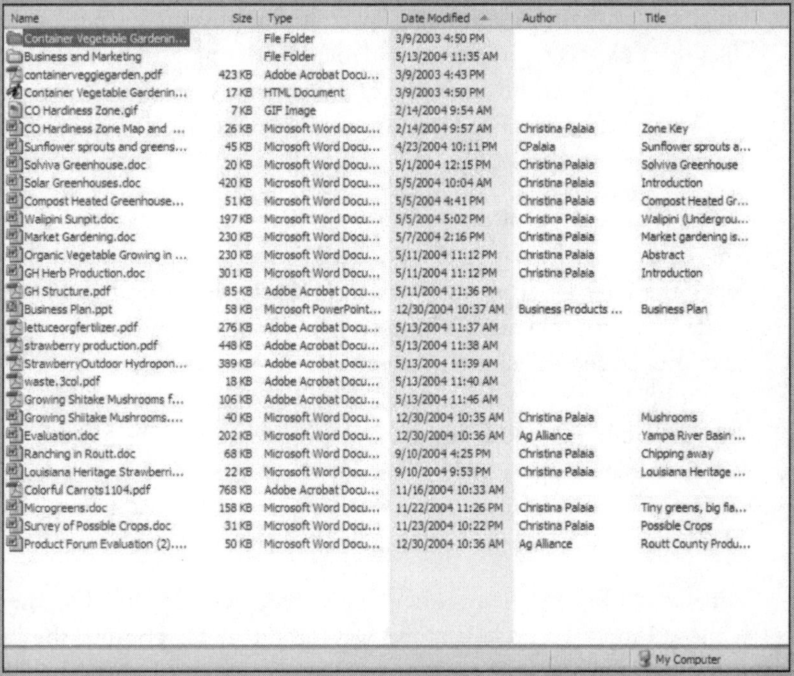

Name	Size	Type	Date Modified ▲	Author	Title
Container Vegetable Gardenin...		File Folder	3/9/2003 4:50 PM		
Business and Marketing		File Folder	5/13/2004 11:35 AM		
containerveggiegarden.pdf	423 KB	Adobe Acrobat Docu...	3/9/2003 4:43 PM		
Container Vegetable Gardenin...	17 KB	HTML Document	3/9/2003 4:50 PM		
CO Hardiness Zone.gif	7 KB	GIF Image	2/14/2004 9:54 AM		
CO Hardiness Zone Map and ...	26 KB	Microsoft Word Docu...	2/14/2004 9:57 AM	Christina Palaia	Zone Key
Sunflower sprouts and greens...	45 KB	Microsoft Word Docu...	4/23/2004 10:11 PM	CPalaia	Sunflower sprouts a...
Solviva Greenhouse.doc	20 KB	Microsoft Word Docu...	5/1/2004 12:15 PM	Christina Palaia	Solviva Greenhouse
Solar Greenhouses.doc	420 KB	Microsoft Word Docu...	5/5/2004 10:04 AM	Christina Palaia	Introduction
Compost Heated Greenhouse...	51 KB	Microsoft Word Docu...	5/5/2004 4:41 PM	Christina Palaia	Compost Heated Gr...
Walipini Sunpit.doc	197 KB	Microsoft Word Docu...	5/5/2004 5:02 PM	Christina Palaia	Walipini (Undergrou...
Market Gardening.doc	230 KB	Microsoft Word Docu...	5/7/2004 2:16 PM	Christina Palaia	Market gardening is...
Organic Vegetable Growing in ...	230 KB	Microsoft Word Docu...	5/11/2004 11:12 PM	Christina Palaia	Abstract
GH Herb Production.doc	301 KB	Microsoft Word Docu...	5/11/2004 11:12 PM	Christina Palaia	Introduction
GH Structure.pdf	85 KB	Adobe Acrobat Docu...	5/11/2004 11:36 PM		
Business Plan.ppt	58 KB	Microsoft PowerPoint...	12/30/2004 10:37 AM	Business Products ...	Business Plan
lettuceorgfertilzer.pdf	276 KB	Adobe Acrobat Docu...	5/13/2004 11:37 AM		
strawberry production.pdf	448 KB	Adobe Acrobat Docu...	5/13/2004 11:38 AM		
StrawberryOutdoor Hydropon...	389 KB	Adobe Acrobat Docu...	5/13/2004 11:39 AM		
waste,3col.pdf	18 KB	Adobe Acrobat Docu...	5/13/2004 11:40 AM		
Growing Shitake Mushrooms f...	106 KB	Adobe Acrobat Docu...	5/13/2004 11:46 AM		
Growing Shitake Mushrooms...	40 KB	Microsoft Word Docu...	12/30/2004 10:35 AM	Christina Palaia	Mushrooms
Evaluation.doc	202 KB	Microsoft Word Docu...	12/30/2004 10:36 AM	Ag Alliance	Yampa River Basin ...
Ranching in Routt.doc	68 KB	Microsoft Word Docu...	9/10/2004 4:25 PM	Christina Palaia	Chipping away
Louisiana Heritage Strawberri...	22 KB	Microsoft Word Docu...	9/10/2004 9:53 PM	Christina Palaia	Louisiana Heritage ...
Colorful Carrots1104.pdf	768 KB	Adobe Acrobat Docu...	11/16/2004 10:33 AM		
Microgreens.doc	158 KB	Microsoft Word Docu...	11/22/2004 11:26 PM	Christina Palaia	Tiny greens, big fla...
Survey of Possible Crops.doc	31 KB	Microsoft Word Docu...	11/23/2004 10:22 PM	Christina Palaia	Possible Crops
Product Forum Evaluation (2)...	50 KB	Microsoft Word Docu...	12/30/2004 10:36 AM	Ag Alliance	Routt County Produ...

My Computer

Figure 4-11
The right pane of Explorer shows the file details selected in the Choose Details dialog box.

Populate Your Subfolders

Now that you have a bunch of appropriate subfolders set up, you can begin moving data files into them. This is the fun part, as you watch the number of individual files lingering in the My Documents folder dwindle as you place them securely in their new homes. In Explorer, click an item you'd like to move and drag it to a subfolder listed in the left pane. To grab groups of files all at once, hold down the Shift or Ctrl key as you select files, and then simply drag the group to the relevant subfolder.

Prepare to Empty the Recycle Bin

With all the cleaning and rearranging you've done, we can imagine you have virtual piles of garbage heaping over the top of the Recycle Bin. But before you go and recycle the contents, you need to make sure that you have not accidentally deleted something important, such as a system file that Windows needs to start up or an application file that Office uses. The easiest way to make sure that the files and folders that are in the Recycle Bin are actually garbage that you don't need any more is to shut down and then restart your PC. You might think that this step is not necessary, but if you have been deleting a lot of files, it could save you from accidentally deleting a file you need. If the boot process goes smoothly and you can successfully open each one of the Office applications and other applications you use on your PC, you can be assured you haven't removed a necessary file.

Next, make one final pass through your file system and delete anything you missed previously. When you are certain you've degunked to the *n*th degree, open the Recycle Bin and check through the contents. Double-click the Recycle Bin icon on your desktop to open it, or navigate to the Recycle Bin in Explorer to see the contents. Run a careful eye over the files and folders you plan to delete to assure that they are all simply gunk cluttering up your system. At this point, it's a good idea to run Disk Cleanup (in the System Tools folder in the Start menu) again before deleting the contents of the Recycle Bin, just to be sure you haven't missed even the latest temp files that have accumulated over the last several hours.

Finally, the big moment is here: clear the Recycle Bin! On the File menu, choose Empty Recycle Bin and wave goodbye for good to the junk that was clogging your file system.

Defragment Your Hard Drive

In Chapter 3, we introduced the topic of defragmenting your hard drive after you install Office. Recall that this is necessary because of the way files are stored on a hard drive. When Windows permanently deletes files, the space each of those files consumed on the hard disk is freed to be written over by new data. Often little slots of space open here and there, scattered over the hard drive platter (the spinning magnetic medium in your hard disk on which data is stored electronically). The next time you ask Office to save a file, to use this free space it must skip around and find a spot big enough to put the file. This skipping around inhibits performance—it's like when you have a huge pile of bills, but each cubby hole in your desk is mostly filled up and you must therefore split the pile into little chunks to shove into the bits of free space. It'd really be better, and you'd more easily and quickly find the bills when it's time to pay them, if you could rearrange the cubbies and designate one whole space to bills; similarly, it's much better if Office knows it has a large swath of contiguous free space all in one area of the hard disk to which it could write data.

The Disk Defragmenter utility (as discussed in Chapter 3) can help the Windows operating system consolidate fragmented files (files saved in bits and pieces all over the disk) and gain more efficient access to your folder system. Start Disk Defragmenter by clicking Start; selecting Programs, Accessories, System Tools; and then clicking Disk Defragmenter. The defragmenting process might take a few minutes to complete, so it's a good time to go celebrate your successful file and folder system degunking over a hot cup of joe.

Summing Up

Congratulations! You did a great thing by degunking your folder system in this chapter. From now on, when you save an Office file to your hard drive, be sure you place it in an appropriate subfolder. As time goes on, you'll find you need to create many different subfolders, and even new sub-subfolders inside of them. But as long as you use descriptive folder and file names and stick to your organizational scheme, whether that's grouping files by project, by date, by user, or by file type, you'll be able to quickly and easily find what you need when you need it.

Degunking Office's Common Features

Degunking Checklist:

√ Get rid of the annoying Office Assistant.

√ Change the default file save locations so you can open and save files much faster.

√ Use default file views to make new file creation more efficient.

√ Simplify and customize menus so that you can use them more efficiently.

√ Take control of toolbars so that the tools you need are within easy reach.

√ Use keyboard and navigation shortcuts to suit your work style and increase productivity.

√ Take full advantage of the printing settings in each Office application.

This chapter is the first of five chapters that will show you how to really degunk and configure the main Office applications—Word, Excel, PowerPoint, and Outlook. We'll be showing you how to dig in and degunk each application in detail, but before we start, we'll show you how to configure Office so that all of your applications will benefit. We call this "shared" degunking because you'll be able to apply your degunking efforts to more than one application in some cases. We'll focus on showing you how to fine-tune Office so that you can save time (and reduce clutter) in performing tasks such as saving and opening files, setting up views, using menus and toolbars to perform operations, and using shortcut keys. With the degunking techniques we show you here, you'll be able to make your Office apps work more efficiently and consistently.

Microsoft designed Office so that the various applications work together seamlessly to help you perform all of your virtual office work, from creating letters and worksheets to creating presentations. One goal Microsoft had was to help you use the skills you learn in one application, such as Word, to get work done in another application, such as Excel. All Office apps contain some common features. The good news is that you can use similar methods with only minor differences to customize the apps. The bad news is that there are some differences, here and there, so you have to be careful. In this chapter, we'll use Word as the example app to show you how to set up common productivity features, but we'll also describe any nuances Excel, PowerPoint, and Outlook may have.

Hide the Annoying Office Assistant

If you're stuck with that whacky paper clip as an Office Assistant, you'll want it to go away and never come back—the thing is just creepy looking, with its sly smirks and springy eyes. (You can now choose between nine incarnations, from cheerful Dot to Mother Nature herself.) If you think the animations prove distracting (as we do) and you'd rather use the Help menu when you've got a question, you can easily hide the assistant. Just right-click it and choose Hide from the context menu. If you get lonely and want your pal back, on the Help menu, choose Show the Office Assistant.

Change the Default Open and Save As Folders

When you're developing several files related to a single project, it's handy to change the default folder path that the application displays in the Open and Save As dialog boxes. You can specify that a particular folder be automatically displayed to avoid wasting mouse clicks navigating to a specific document location. Say for the next week you will be preparing a set of important documents and you are on a tight deadline. You can have Word, Excel, and PowerPoint open automatically into a folder you specify instead of the My Documents folder (the default file location) whenever you need to open or save a related file. This might not seem like a big deal, but if you are opening and saving numerous files for a project, you can actually save a lot of time by not having to navigate the folder hierarchy. After all, degunking is often about making subtle changes that pay back big over time.

Word, Excel, and PowerPoint each offer a Default File Location option that you can customize; however, each is stored in a slightly different place in the Options dialog box. To change the default file location, follow these steps for Word, Excel, or PowerPoint:

1. Choose Options from the Tools menu.

2. In the Options dialog box, do one of the following:

   a. In Word, select the File Locations tab. In the File Types list, select Documents as shown in Figure 5-1, and then click Modify. In the Modify Location dialog box, navigate to the folder you'd like Word to use and click OK.

   b. In Excel, select the General tab. Type the path name of the location you'd like to use as a default in the Default File Location text box.

   c. In PowerPoint, select the Save tab. Type the path name of the location you'd like to use as a default in the Default File Location text box.

3. Click OK in the Options dialog box to apply the changes.

TIP: *If you switch projects and find it'd be more useful to have Word, Excel, or PowerPoint automatically open a different folder when you select Open, Save, or Save As from the File menu, repeat the preceding steps and designate a new folder as the default file location.*

Set Up Default Views to Better View Your Documents

Remember that one of the goals for degunking Office is to get the applications set up so that you feel like you are slipping on a well-worn glove whenever you use them. One smart way to do this is to set up a default view for each application, so that your documents are displayed exactly as you want to see them. That way, each application will open a document window arranged exactly as you like it right from the start.

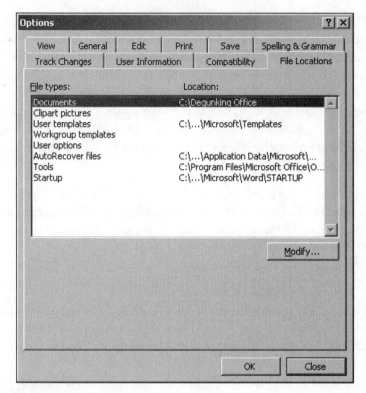

Figure 5-1
Change the default folder in the File Locations tab of the Options
dialog box in Word.

---

*TIP: Remember, the way an existing document opens depends on how it was saved the
last time it was open. Saving and closing a document using a particular screen setup
overrides any preferences you set for new documents using the methods we discuss
next.*

Customizing a view in a newly created Excel and PowerPoint document is a
matter of applying your preferences in the Options dialog box. It's a little trickier
to create a default view in Word because it entails modifying either the global
template or another one. And because Outlook contains numerous features, we'll
need to devote several pages to explaining the different ways you can organize
and arrange Outlook items to maximize your efficiency and organization.

Customize the Look of the Word Window

Unlike the other applications, Word saves each document's view as a setting in
the document's properties. You can save any document with the view settings
you want by saving the file with a particular view displayed. To select a view for

a document you are working in, choose an option from the View menu and then save and close the document. Likewise, documents you receive from others, which have been saved with the document creator's view settings applied, will open displaying those pre-existing properties.

You can, however, create a default view for all Word documents you *create in the future*. You do this by modifying the Normal.dot (global) template, which is the template of styles and configuration settings that is applied automatically (unless otherwise specified) to any new Word document you open.

GunkBuster's Notebook: Backing Up the Normal.dot Template

It's a good idea to make a backup copy of the original Normal.dot template just in case you decide you don't like the global changes you've made and want to revert back to Word's original default settings. To make a backup copy of the original Normal.dot template, follow these steps:

1. Close all Word documents and exit Word.
2. Right-click Start, and then select Explore.
3. Navigate to C:\Documents and Settings*username*\Application Data\Microsoft\Templates, where *username* is your logon name. If you are working on a PC to which multiple users have access, it's polite to change *only* the global settings that apply to you specifically (unless you have the other users' permission to change their settings, too).
4. In the Templates folder, right-click the Normal.dot file, and then select Copy from the context menu.
5. Right-click any open space in the Templates folder, and select Paste from the context menu.
6. The new file you just pasted is named Copy of Normal.dot by default; you can rename it if you like, or leave it as is, but just know that this is a copy of the original Normal.dot template.

To make changes to Normal.dot that will affect each subsequent new Word document that you open (existing Word files will not be affected by the changes you make to the Normal.dot template), follow these steps:

1. Close all Word documents and exit Word.
2. Right-click Start, and then select Explore.

3. Navigate to C:\Documents and Settings*username*\Application Data\Microsoft\Templates, where *username* is your logon name.

4. Right-click the Normal.dot file and select Open from the context menu. Don't double-click the Normal.dot file because that would simply open a single new Word document; you want to open the template itself.

5. On the View menu, choose which view you prefer: Normal, Web Layout, Print Layout, or Outline (in Word 2003, Reading Layout is available, too).

6. On the View menu, choose Toolbars, and then select a toolbar that you would like to have displayed. Repeat this process until you've selected all the toolbars you want available upon opening a new document. If you select a toolbar that already has a check mark in front of it, the selection acts as a toggle and deselects that toolbar.

7. On the Format menu, choose Font, and then configure the settings for the default font in the Font dialog box. Click OK to apply the changes.

8. On the Format menu, choose Paragraph, and use the Paragraph dialog box to set up the default page formatting. Click OK to apply the changes.

9. On the Tools menu, choose Options, and use each tab in the Options dialog box to configure default settings. Click OK to apply the changes.

10. On the File menu, click Save to save the changes to the template.

11. Close the Normal.dot file.

Refer to the section entitled "Create, Customize, and Organize Templates" in Chapter 6, "Degunking Microsoft Word," for a closer look at how to create individual customized templates. But if you simply want things to look a certain way as soon as you open Word, modifying the Normal.dot template as described in the preceding steps is an easy way to save yourself from having to reorganize the Word window each time you open a new doc.

Customize Views in Excel

In Excel, you can assign a set of display and print settings to individual workbooks by customizing the workbook's view using the Custom Views command on the View menu. You can save multiple views of a workbook and name each view to make it easy to distinguish between them. This makes great degunking sense because it enables you to quickly arrange spreadsheet data in multiple meaningful ways—without saving multiple copies of a file! To save customized views for an Excel document, follow these steps:

1. Set up the worksheet exactly as you'd like it to be represented by the named view, including setting print options (see the section "Degunk Application Printing" later in this chapter for more info on how to customize print options), view options, toolbars shown, and anything else that organizes your data just so.

2. Choose Custom Views from the View menu.

3. In the Custom Views dialog box, click Add, and then type in a name for the view and decide whether you want to include the print settings and any hidden data.

4. Whenever you want to see your data arranged according to a particular view, choose Custom Views from the View menu and then select a view.

In Excel, you can also personalize how newly created Excel workbooks look and behave by using the Options dialog box, shown in Figure 5-2. You can customize how many worksheets are automatically displayed in new workbooks by using the Sheets in New Workbook option. Use the two drop-down menus to select the font and font size of text in new workbooks.

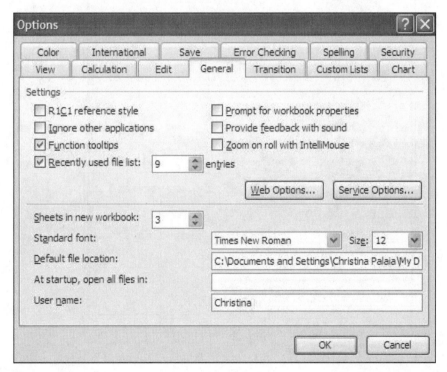

Figure 5-2
Use the General tab of the Excel Options dialog box to set the defaults for how workbooks appear upon opening.

Also, check out the View tab in the Options dialog box. In the View tab, you can decide which toolbars will be displayed on startup, as well as customize how the window appears for new Excel workbooks.

Customize Views in PowerPoint

In PowerPoint, you can select a default view into which PowerPoint will always open. The original PowerPoint default is to open in Normal view with the Outline tab open, the Slides tab available, the notes pane showing, and the slide pane displayed. You can use the View tab in the Options dialog box (Tools menu) shown in Figure 5-3 to enable the view settings you'd like to make the default view for all new PowerPoint files. In the View tab, you can decide which toolbars you'd like displayed upon startup, as well as create a default view

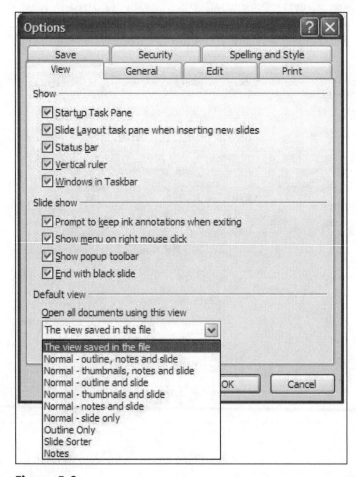

Figure 5-3

Use the View tab in the PowerPoint Options dialog box to customize the PowerPoint window.

for all PPT files you create thereafter. If you choose "The view saved in the file" from the drop-down list as shown in the figure, PowerPoint will use the view you saved for a file to open it; other PowerPoint files will open in the original default Normal view. When you choose any other option from the "Open all documents using this view" menu, PowerPoint will open all PPT files with the selected view options displayed. Also in the View tab, you can decide whether you'd like the Status bar and ruler to appear on startup, and you can tell PowerPoint exactly how to display slide shows by default.

Personalize Outlook Views

In Outlook, it is also quite useful to be able to see at a glance what you need to do next to stay on schedule and in the loop. When you first start using Outlook, your screen setup displays the Microsoft defaults. You can make the following quick changes to these defaults to become better organized and reduce clutter:

√ Configure Outlook to open in Outlook Today.

√ Show the Navigation Pane.

√ Show the Reading Pane.

√ Change fields that are displayed.

Open in Outlook Today View

Wouldn't it be nice if for a brief instant during every hectic day you got a clear vision of what you need to do next? Fortunately, Outlook offers the Outlook Today screen to help you stay focused. You can configure Outlook to open showing Outlook Today, which provides you with a preview of the day ahead, including a list of upcoming appointments, unfinished tasks on your to-do list, the number of unread messages in your Inbox or other folders, and the number of unsent messages in your Outbox or Drafts folder.

To set Outlook to open in the Outlook Today screen, follow these steps:

1. In the Mail utility, click Personal Folders to open the Outlook Today screen. Personal Folders is usually located at the top of your mail folder hierarchy in the Navigation Pane.

2. In Outlook Today, click the Customize Outlook Today button.

3. In the Customize Outlook Today screen, be sure the "When starting, go directly to Outlook Today" option in the Startup section is checked, as shown in Figure 5-4.

4. While you're there, configure the other information you'd like Outlook Today to display. In the Messages section, click the Choose Folders button and select which mail folders you want displayed on the Outlook Today

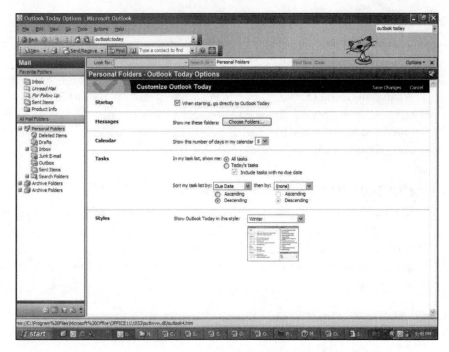

Figure 5-4
Configure Outlook Today to give you a snapshot of the day and the coming week.

screen. (After we show you how to use rules and filters to sort your incoming mail into custom folders in Chapter 9, "Degunking Microsoft Outlook," you might add the custom folders to the Outlook Today list to get a quick view of how much unread mail has accumulated in various places.)

5. In the Calendar section, use the drop-down list to select the number of days of your calendar you'd like displayed. Outlook Today will show a list of all appointments scheduled on the days you choose to display.

6. Use the Tasks section to set up the display of tasks, including which tasks should be displayed and how tasks should be sorted.

7. Finally, use the Styles section to pick the screen style for Outlook Today—experiment to see which one you like best. Figure 5-5 shows Outlook Today in Winter style.

8. Click Save Changes when you are finished.

Show Navigation Options

Outlook 2003 includes a feature called the Navigation Pane, which is the area on the left side of the Outlook window that includes the folder list and shortcuts to other panes. In earlier versions, this feature is called the *Outlook bar*.

Figure 5-5
This is Outlook Today in Winter style.

Whatever you call it, it provides an excellent way to zoom around the different features Outlook offers. Click a folder name in the Favorite Folders list, for example, to see the contents of that folder. Switch quickly to the calendar using the Calendar shortcut or by clicking the Calendar button. One more click can fire up your whole contacts collection.

This is such an expeditious way to navigate the features of Outlook, we wonder why Microsoft makes its display optional. It streamlines and increases the application's ease of use, which falls well within degunking philosophy. To be sure that your Navigation Pane or Outlook Bar is showing when you open Outlook, on the View menu, check to see whether the Navigation Pane option or the Outlook Bar option, depending on your Office version, is selected (see Figure 5-6). If not, select the option and enjoy easy navigation.

Show the Reading Pane

Another time-saver is the Reading Pane (called the *preview pane* in versions earlier than Outlook 2003). This screen area shows the contents of a selected e-mail message without you having to double-click to open the message (see Figure 5-7). If you can save the double-click necessary to open message after message and still view the contents of your mail, why not do so?

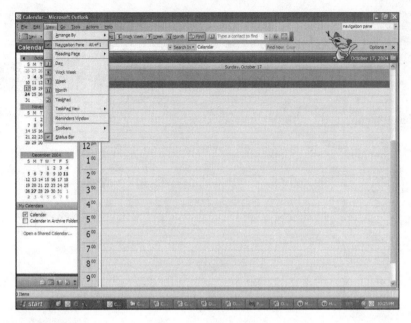

Figure 5-6

On the View menu, make sure the Navigation Pane (as shown here) or the Outlook Bar is selected.

The Reading Pane also offers some security benefits: you can view the text of messages without automatically activating attachments or potentially malicious scripts (see Chapter 11, "Securing Office," for more on Office security), thus decreasing your chances of allowing your computer to be infected by a virus or commandeered by a rogue program. Turn on the Reading Pane or preview pane by selecting Reading Pane or Preview Pane on the View menu, and then use the submenu to decide whether you want the pane displayed across the bottom of the Outlook window as shown in Figure 5-7 or along the right side.

You can customize how the Reading Pane handles messages, too. To do so, complete the following steps:

1. Choose Options from the Tools menu.

2. Select the Other tab in the Options dialog box.

3. Click the Reading Pane button in the Reading Pane section.

4. In the Reading Pane dialog box, check the "Mark items as read when viewed in the Reading Pane" option as shown in Figure 5-8.

5. In the text box, type in the number of seconds you'd like Outlook to wait before marking an item as read. A lower number allows you to quickly dispatch messages to other folders or the trash, for instance, without having to linger on them to get the unread designation to disappear.

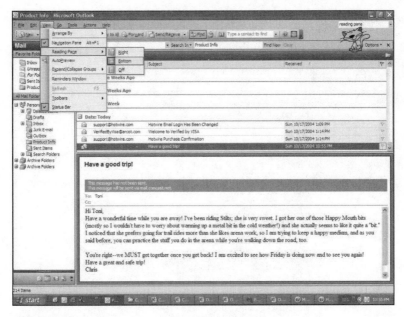

Figure 5-7

On the View menu, turn on the Reading Pane or preview pane and select whether you'd like it displayed to the right or on the bottom of the screen.

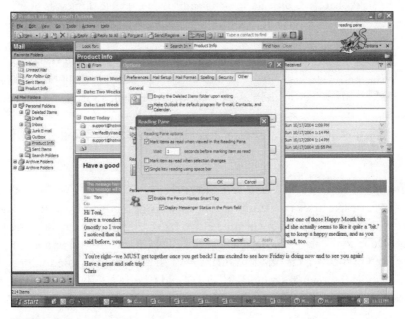

Figure 5-8

Configure how the Reading Pane handles mail.

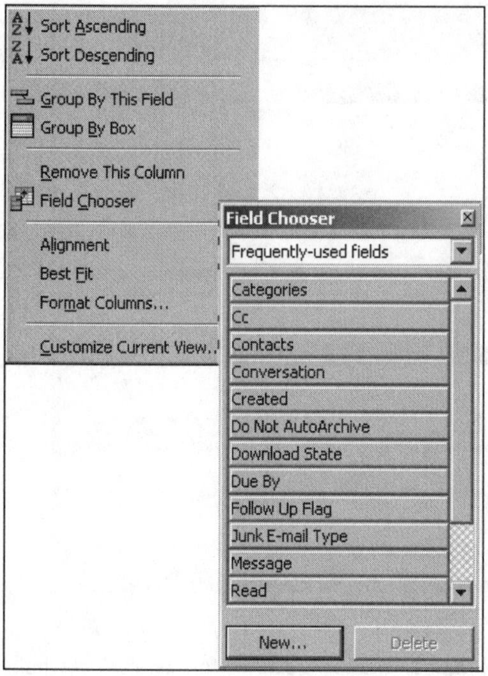

Figure 5-9
Use the Field Chooser to pick the column headings you want to display in the message window.

6. Alternately, you can use the "Mark item as read when selection changes" option to remove the unread status as soon as you switch to another message.

7. Select "Single key reading using space bar" to be able to navigate through each e-mail message simply by tapping the spacebar.

8. Click OK in the Reading Pane dialog box, and then click OK in the Options dialog box.

Change Fields That Are Displayed

Typically, we like to see the size of each message in our Inbox and Sent Items folders to get an idea of the attachment size (and to make later degunking easier), but the size field is not displayed by default. Use the Field Chooser to add or remove fields displayed in the message window. Right-click the column heading to display the context menu shown in Figure 5-9. Select Field Chooser, and then drag and drop the field where you want to insert it in the column headings for the message list.

Each of your folders can display different fields as well as display messages sorted in different list order. List messages in your Inbox by date in descending order so that you can quickly find the newest messages at the bottom of the list. Toggle the sort order by clicking the column heading.

Simplify and Customize Your Menus

We're sure you've noticed by now that a consistent style is used for the menus and toolbars in all of the Office apps. Office was purposely designed this way to help you easily move from one application to another. This is degunking nirvana: if you are aware of an option or command available in one app (such as the AutoRecover time interval setting in Word), when you see a need to employ a similar feature in another Office app (AutoRecover in Excel), you'll have a good idea of where to look for it and how to activate it (Save tab in the Options dialog box). In the following sections, we'll show you how to really take control of menus and toolbars, from personalizing how menus are displayed to adding and removing commands and buttons.

Change Personalized Menus Settings

Whenever you click a menu name such as File or Edit in an Office app, you'll only see some of the menu choices. To see the full set of choices, you must either click the down arrows or wait about five seconds. Five seconds is too long to wait when you're trying to get something done, and why should you have to waste an extra mouse click just to see all your menu options?

The Office apps track how you use menu options and toolbar buttons and then displays only those commands you've used recently. This often becomes frustrating because the menu options and toolbar buttons that are displayed change constantly based on your use, and the commands you need are usually hidden. (Murphy's Law dictates what you need will rarely be shown!)

This feature, called *personalized menus,* is enabled by default in new installations, but you can easily turn it off if it bothers you. To enable full menus to be displayed automatically when you click them, complete these steps:

1. In any of the Office applications, select Customize from the Tools menu.
2. In the Options tab of the Customize dialog box, do one of the following:
   a. In Office 2003, select the "Always show full menus" option.
   b. In earlier versions of Office, clear the check mark in front of the "Menus show recently used commands first" option as shown in Figure 5-10.

   You'll notice that the "Show full menus after a short delay" option simultaneously becomes unavailable, in effect turning off that feature.
3. Click Close to apply the changes.

TIP: *Alternately, if you're a minimalist and you find you like the way Office condenses your menus into the options you use most regularly but you hate the way a tiny, clutter-free menu unexpectedly balloons into a huge one while you're in the middle of reading it, you can disable the expansion feature separately. In the Customize dialog*

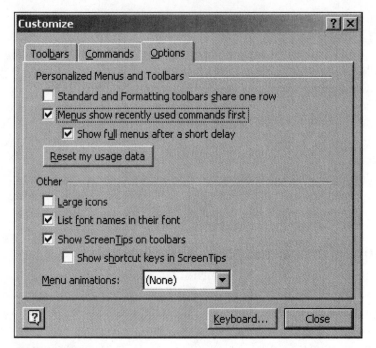

Figure 5-10
Change personalized menu settings in the Options tab of the
Customize dialog box.

*box, uncheck the "Show full menus after a short delay" option, but either uncheck the
"Always show full menus" option in Office 2003 or leave the "Menus show recently
used commands first" option checked in earlier versions.*

Remember the good ole days when you'd click a menu name and be presented
with a smorgasbord of choices? You felt plush with options! Well, now the good
ole days are back.

Clean Up Your Menus

Let's face it: if you don't intend to write a fairy tale using medieval-style text in
Copperplate Gothic Bold font, you probably won't need Word's Format menu
Drop Cap command. If you use your Excel workbooks simply to track your
household budget, it's unlikely you'll need the XML command on the Data
menu or Hyperlink option on the Insert menu. We guess there are numerous
other menu commands you ignore in each Office app as well. So why let
unused commands such as these sit there taking up space? They're just blobs of
gunk. To streamline your menus by removing unused items, follow these steps:

1. Choose Customize from the Tools menu, and then select the Commands tab in the Customize dialog box.

2. Once the Customize dialog box is open, you can click a menu name in the application window and then select and drag off any item you want to get rid of. Repeat this step for each item you'd like to remove.

3. Choose the template you'd like to apply this change to in the Save In box of the Customize dialog box, then click Close.

Adding a Command to a Menu

After using Office for a while, you might come across a few great commands that are not displayed on any menu. Adding a command to a menu is simple:

1. Choose Customize from the Tools menu, and then select the Commands tab.

2. Select a command category in the Categories list, and then drag the command you select from the Commands list onto any of the menus in the application window. An I-beam will appear to help you place the item precisely. Note that you can drag a command from any category onto any menu; you are not limited to taking items from the File category and placing them on the File menu only, for instance.

3. Repeat the preceding step to insert any other commands you wish, and then click Close.

If you make a mistake or want to restore the default selections to any menu, open the Commands tab in the Customize dialog box, right-click the menu name that you want to restore in the application window, and then select Restore from the context menu. Voila! Good as new.

Streamline Your Toolbars

The Office apps provide handy toolbars to help you get your work done quickly. But they often are often gunked up with commands and options you never use. Toolbars should reflect your work habits. To keep your work area as clutter-free as possible, you'll want to display only the buttons you use frequently and ensure that the toolbars display only the options you need. So now it's time to remove those options you don't need.

Add and Remove Buttons from Toolbars

You can easily customize your toolbars by adding and removing buttons and telling applications like Word and Excel which toolbars you want to appear automatically when you open a new document (we showed you how to do this in the sections "Customize the Look of the Word Window," "Customize Views in Excel," and "Customize Views in PowerPoint" earlier in this chapter).

For example, if you find yourself often editing documents and changing font sizes, in Word you can add the Grow Font by 1 Pt and Shrink Font by 1 Pt buttons to the Format toolbar (Excel and PowerPoint have similar commands called Increase Font Size and Decrease Font Size). Also, as you are writing, creating, moving text, and rearranging sentence parts, you are frequently required to change the case of words to set section headings as title case and paragraph text as sentence case. Add the Change Case button to the Format toolbar in Word and PowerPoint to reduce the number of mouse clicks required to change words from uppercase to lowercase, and vice versa.

To add a button to a toolbar, follow these steps:

1. Click Toolbars on the View menu, and then select a toolbar that you'd like to customize. If the toolbar name has a check mark next to it, that toolbar is already displayed on-screen. If the toolbar you want to customize does not have a check mark, select it to display it.

2. Select Customize from the Tools menu.

3. In the Commands tab in the Customize dialog box, select an item in the Categories list (which lists the available toolbars by name).

4. Scroll through the list of commands presented in the Commands list and select a command. In versions of Office earlier than 2003, you can click the Description button to see a description of what a command does, as shown in Figure 5-11.

5. Drag the command out of the Customize dialog box and drop it into a toolbar (be sure that the toolbar you want to customize is open and already in view as described in step 1). An I-beam cursor appears to help you place the new command button precisely where you want it. In earlier versions of Office, by default the new button has only a text label. In Office 2003, the button appears as an icon or a text label; you can skip over the renaming instructions given in steps 6 and 7.

6. With the Customize dialog box open, right-click the new toolbar button and select Default Style to convert the button into a plain square.

7. Right-click the new button again, choose Change Button Image, then select a button image. Alternately, you can allow your new button to keep its original text label, and you can add an image to the text label as well.

8. In the Customize dialog box, in the Save In box, choose the template in which you'd like to save this customization.

9. Click Close.

To remove a button from a toolbar, complete the following steps:

1. Select Customize from the Tools menu.

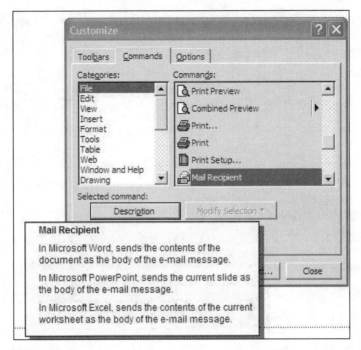

Figure 5-11
Learn what a particular command does in the Commands tab of the
Customize dialog box.

2.   Select the button you want to remove and drag it off of the toolbar. When
     you release it, it disappears.

3.   Click OK.

Create Your Own Toolbars

You can even create your very own toolbars and populate them with whichever commands you'd like. To do so, complete these steps:

1.   Select Customize from the Tools menu.

2.   Select the Toolbars tab in the Customize dialog box then click New.

3.   In the New Toolbar dialog box, type in a name for the toolbar in the
     Toolbar Name box as shown in Figure 5-12.

4.   Use the drop-down list to choose which template you'd like to make this
     new toolbar available in.

5.   Click OK.

6.   Click Close in the Customize dialog box.

7.   A tiny blank toolbar will appear on your screen. Follow the steps discussed
     in the previous section to add buttons to your new toolbar.

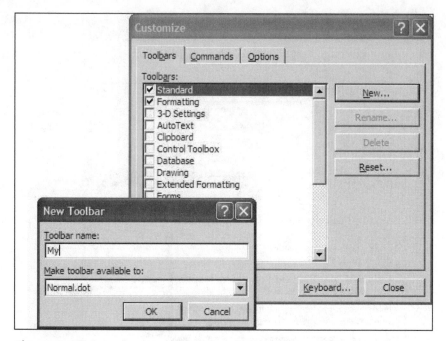

Figure 5-12
Create a new toolbar in the Toolbars tab of the Customize dialog box.

Take a Shortcut Using Keyboard Shortcuts

Shortcut keys can help you bypass menus and carry out commands directly. You can use shortcut keys in many ways, including accessing commands and toolbar buttons, opening new e-mail messages, and mailing workbooks to specific recipients. Shortcut keys are sometimes listed next to the command name on menus. For example, in Outlook if you look at the Edit menu, you'll notice that the Delete command lists the keyboard shortcut Ctrl+D.

Useful Shortcut Keys

For a comprehensive list of keyboard shortcuts for whichever Office application you find yourself in, ask the Office Assistant for help. Press F1 to display the Office Assistant, and then type **shortcut keys** in the search query box. There are several shortcuts that will work across applications; these are listed in Table 5-1. Table 5-2 lists useful Word shortcuts, and Table 5-3 lists useful Excel shortcuts. Useful PowerPoint shortcuts are listed in Table 5-4, and you'll find useful Outlook shortcuts in Table 5-5.

Table 5-1   Shortcut Key Combinations Common to Word, Excel, PowerPoint, and Outlook

Action	Shortcut Key Combination
Open a new object (file, workbook, presentation, message, contact, etc.)	Ctrl+N
Open an existing object	Ctrl+O
Close an object	Ctrl+W
Save an object	Ctrl+S
Print an object	Ctrl+P
Open Help files	F1
Toggle between Help files and document	F6
Undo	Ctrl+Z
Redo last action	Ctrl+Y
Cut	Ctrl+X
Copy	Ctrl+C
Paste	Ctrl+V
Apply bold formatting to selection	Ctrl+B
Apply italic formatting to selection	Ctrl+I
Apply underline formatting to selection	Ctrl+U
Change case of selection	Shift+F3
Find	Ctrl+F
Replace	Ctrl+H
Go To	Ctrl+G
Open a specific menu and select a menu item	Alt+right or left arrow+*underlined letter in menu name*+ *underlined letter in command name*
Delete a word	Ctrl+Backspace
Select all	Ctrl+A

Table 5-2   Word Shortcut Key Combinations

Action	Shortcut Key Combination
Display shortcut menu for selected item	Shift+F10
Decrease font size	Ctrl+Shift+<
Increase font size	Ctrl+Shift+>
Copy text formatting	Ctrl+Shift+C
Paste text formatting	Ctrl+Shift+V
Remove paragraph or character formatting	Ctrl+spacebar
Select text	Shift+right or left arrow
Turn on/off Track Changes	Ctrl+Shift+E
Open the Spelling and Grammar dialog box	F7

(continued)

Table 5-2   Word Shortcut Key Combinations *(continued)*

Action	Shortcut Key Combination
Insert a nonbreaking space	Ctrl+Shift+spacebar
Insert the copyright symbol (©)	Alt+Ctrl+C
Insert the registration symbol (®)	Alt+Ctrl+R
Insert the trademark symbol (™)	Alt+Ctrl+T
Insert an ellipsis (...)	Alt+Ctrl+.

Table 5-3   Excel Shortcut Key Combinations

Action	Shortcut Key Combination
Select the entire worksheet. If the worksheet contains data, Ctrl+A selects the current region, and then pressing Ctrl+A a second time selects the entire worksheet.	Ctrl+A
Apply the General number format.	Ctrl+~
Apply the Currency format with two decimal places (negative numbers in parentheses).	Ctrl+$
Apply the Percentage format with no decimal places.	Ctrl+%
Apply the Exponential number format with two decimal places.	Ctrl+^
Apply the Date format with the day, month, and year.	Ctrl+#
Alternate between displaying cell values and displaying formulas in the worksheet.	Ctrl+'
Copy a formula from the cell above the active cell into the cell or the formula bar.	Ctrl+'
Copy the value from the cell above the active cell into the cell or the formula bar.	Ctrl+"
Use the Fill Down command to copy the contents and format of the topmost cell of a selected range into the cells below.	Ctrl+D
Display the Find dialog box. Shift+F5 also displays this dialog box, whereas Shift+F4 repeats the last Find action.	Ctrl+F

Table 5-4   PowerPoint Shortcut Key Combinations

Action	Shortcut Key Combination
Move clockwise among panes of Normal view	F6
Move counterclockwise among panes of Normal view	Shift+F6
Switch between Slides and Outline tabs of the Outline and Slides pane in Normal view	Ctrl+Shift+Tab
Perform the next animation or advance to the next slide	N, Enter, Page Down, right arrow, down arrow, or spacebar
Perform the previous animation or return to the previous slide	P, Page Up, left arrow, up arrow, or Backspace
Go to slide *number*	*Number*+Enter
Stop or restart an automatic slide show	S or plus sign
End a slide show	Esc, Ctrl+Break, or hyphen
Return to the first slide	1+Enter

Table 5-5   Outlook Shortcut Key Combinations

Activity	Shortcut Key Combinations
Open an e-mail message	Ctrl+Shift+M
Open the Address Book	Ctrl+Shift+B
Open an appointment	Ctrl+Shift+A
Open a contact	Ctrl+Shift+C
Open a meeting request	Ctrl+Shift+Q
Open a task	Ctrl+Shift+K
Make the Find a Contact box active	F11
Switch to Inbox	Ctrl+Shift+I
Switch to Outbox	Ctrl+Shift+O
Check for new mail	F5 or Ctrl+M
Open the Advanced Find dialog box	Ctrl+Shift+F
Mark an e-mail message as read	Ctrl+Q
Delete an e-mail message, contact, calendar item, or task	Ctrl+D

GunkBuster's Notebook: Customize Keyboard Shortcuts for Symbols and Characters in Word

Certain people are exclusively mouse clickers and others find they can work faster using keyboard shortcuts. If you're the latter sort, you can certainly increase your speed by customizing the keyboard shortcuts you use for common symbols and characters in Word. Some of the default Word shortcuts are nearly impossible to get your fingers around: the keyboard shortcut for Ø is Ctrl+/+Shift+O. That painful contortion is one good reason to change the shortcuts for characters and symbols you use often into something easy to type and easy to remember. To do so, complete these steps:

1. Choose Symbol from the Insert menu.

2. Select a symbol in the Symbols tab of the Symbol dialog box, and then click Shortcut Key.

3. In the Customize Keyboard dialog box, type the new key sequence you'd like to use. The new keyboard shortcut will appear in the "Press new shortcut key" box, as shown in Figure 5-13.

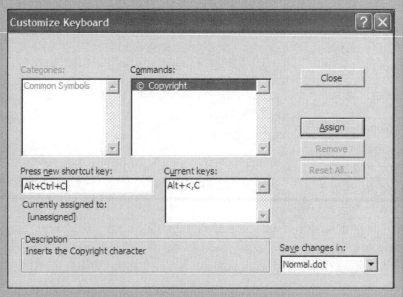

Figure 5-13

Assign keyboard shortcuts to symbols and characters in the Customize Keyboard dialog box.

4. Word will inform you whether that key combination is already assigned to another symbol or character. If it is, you can decide whether you'd like to commandeer the key combination and apply it to this symbol or make up a new combination. Click Assign.

5. Select which template you'd like to save the changes to in the Save Changes In box, and then click Close.

6. Pick another symbol character to reassign or select a character in the Special Characters tab and follow the same procedure.

TIP: You can print out a list of all the Word keyboard shortcuts very easily, including ones you have reassigned—there's a macro designed to do this. On the Tools menu, select Macro, and then click Macros. In the Macros dialog box, in the Macros In section, select Word Commands. In the Macro Name list, select ListCommands, and then click Run. In the List Commands dialog box, make sure the Current Menu and Keyboard Settings option is selected, and then click OK. In a new document, Word will print a 10-page table listing all the keyboard shortcuts.

Being in the word business over the years, we've found that creating handy shortcuts for the em dash (Ctrl+Alt+M), the en dash used in number ranges (Ctrl+Alt+N), a lowercase é (Ctrl+Alt+E), and the styles we apply often, as well as knowing the shortcuts for turning on and off Track Changes (Ctrl+Shift+E), undoing an edit (Ctrl+Z), saving (Ctrl+S), and opening the Find and Replace dialog box (Ctrl+H), has been invaluable and has saved our mouse hands from early decrepitude. As you use Word, notice which actions, symbols, and characters you do and type most, and then configure keyboard shortcuts for them.

Navigation Shortcuts

Suppose you're working on the ultimate document—the longest document you've ever written—and navigating through all those pages is a huge back-and-forth between the keyboard and the mouse. Plus, it's making you dizzy scrolling around like a nut.

Keyboard Navigation Shortcuts

The keyboard shortcuts listed in Table 5-6 can ease the pain of navigating your document (they apply with varying results in each of the Office applications)—so hopefully you won't need aspirin anymore.

Table 5-6   Keyboard Navigation Shortcuts

Keyboard Shortcut	Description
Arrow keys	Move one space or line in the arrow direction
Ctrl+left or right arrow	Moves the cursor one word left or right
Home	Moves the cursor to the beginning of the current line
Ctrl+Home	Moves the cursor to the top of the document
End	Moves the cursor to the end of the current line
Ctrl+End	Moves the cursor to the bottom of the document
Page Up	Moves the cursor up the length of one screen
Page Down	Moves the cursor down the length of one screen
Ctrl+Page Up	Moves the cursor to the previous page in your document
Ctrl+Page Down	Moves the cursor to the next page down in your document

Word and PowerPoint have some application-specific navigation features, too. When you click and hold the mouse pointer on the vertical scrollbar scroll box, a text box appears telling you which page or slide you're scrolling past and the section title that begins on that page or the slide title. (In Word, having the section title appear is really only helpful in very long documents when you have applied the default heading styles, Heading 1 through Heading 9; otherwise, only the page number is displayed in the ScreenTips box as you scroll.)

GunkBuster's Notebook: Browse Object Navigation in Word

The three buttons below the vertical scrollbar in the lower-right corner of a Word document window can be enormously helpful for navigating. The top and bottom buttons (double up and double down arrows) are for moving up or down by one object. The middle button (the dot) is called the Select Browse Object button. It enables you to select which item or object the double up and double down arrows jump to. For example, if you set the Select Browse Object button to Graphic, the up and down arrows jump you from graphic to graphic regardless of how many pages are in between each graphic.

Click the Select Browse Object button to see your browsing choices displayed in a small palette as shown in Figure 5-14. You can choose to browse by page, section, comment, footnote, endnote, field, table, graphic, heading, edits, find text, or Go To choice.

Figure 5-14
The browsing choices available in the Word Select Browse Object button.

Based on your document structure, select a browse object from the palette that will help with your editing. The icon name will appear in the gray box at the bottom of the palette as you move the mouse pointer over each icon. We guess you'll use either Browse by Page or Browse by Section most times, but definitely choose whichever browse object will be the most useful, and you can always change this setting as appropriate.

Degunk Application Printing

When you choose to print an Office file, each application will present you with the Print dialog box. Though each Print dialog box at first appears deceptively similar to every other, examine it closely and you will find a wealth of options to help you print your files according to very exacting specifications. In this section, we present each application's Print dialog box and call out specific features. But don't stop there. Explore the choices available in all the nooks and crannies in each application. You're bound to find something new and useful that can help you streamline and customize your printing.

Tweaking Printing in Word

Microsoft built several features into the print option to improve the way you work. Check out all the options available in Figure 5-15. And we're just scratching the surface here—many more choices hide behind the Properties and Options buttons. In addition, you can customize the printer tray assignment and reverse the print order, as described in the following sections.

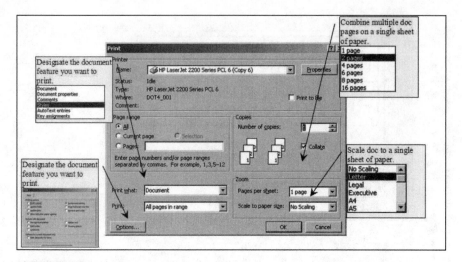

Figure 5-15

The Word Print dialog box presents you with a plethora of choices.

Customize the Default Printer Tray Assignments

With most printers located out of arm's reach, under the desk or down the hall, printing is an opportune task to customize in Word so you can make sure it's hassle-free. Some printers have separate trays that can hold different types of paper, and you can designate the paper source from which Word should pull paper to print documents. To change the default printer tray assignments, complete these steps:

1. Select Page Setup from the File menu.

2. In the Paper Source tab, select the appropriate printer tray choices. You can have Word pull paper from one tray for the first page of the document and from a different tray for the other pages in the document.

3. Click Default. (If you do not click Default and instead click OK, the changes will apply only to this document and will revert to the defaults after the current print job is finished.)

4. A message appears, as shown in Figure 5-16, to inquire whether you want this change to the page setup defaults to apply to all new documents based on the Normal template (or whichever template you are currently using). Click Yes.

Reverse the Print Order

Another step to take toward printing efficiency is to reverse the print order so that the last page prints first, and is therefore on the bottom of the stack, and the first page prints last, ending up on top. This saves you from having to manually reorder the pages to put them in the proper page sequence. To have the document pages print in reverse order so that page 1 is on top hot off the presses, complete the following steps:

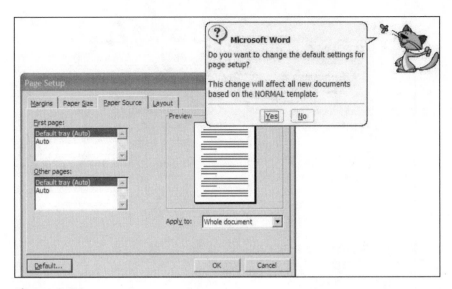

Figure 5-16
Reassign the default printer tray assignment in the Page Setup dialog box.

1. Select Options from the Tools menu.
2. Select the Print tab in the Options dialog box.
3. Click to place a check mark in front of the Reverse Print Order option as shown in Figure 5-17.
4. Click OK.

Practice No-Fuss Printing in Excel

The Print dialog box in Excel (see Figure 5-18) is the perfect example of short and to the point: print what, and print how many, print selection from where to where. If you are unsure how a monstrous worksheet that takes up the entire screen will translate into hard copy, click the Preview button and make adjustments as necessary.

You can also reverse the print order in Excel in the Layout tab of the printer Properties dialog box. On the File menu, choose Print, click the Properties button, and in the Layout tab, enable the Start Printing from Last Page option.

Specify Print Settings in PowerPoint

The PowerPoint Print dialog box (see Figure 5-19) enables you to choose specifically which parts of your show will be printed and how they will look on paper.

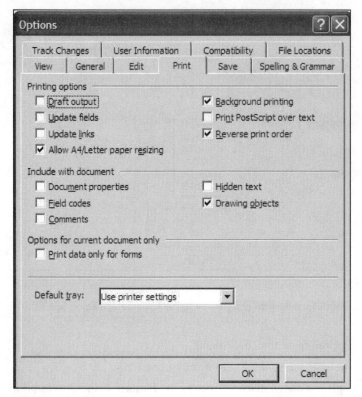

Figure 5-17
Reverse the print order in the Print tab of the Options dialog box.

Again, choose whether you'd like to reverse the print order of your presentation (in the Layout tab of the printer Properties dialog box), whether to print slides in color or black and white, whether to place a border around slide edges, and whether to print the whole show to a file on disk, among other things.

Get to Know Outlook Printing Options

As usual, Outlook seems to be the winner in offering the most printing choices. Select multiple messages in your Inbox by holding the Ctrl key and clicking items with the left mouse button, then choose to print the selected messages without even opening each one using the Print dialog box. You can also choose a style in which to print the messages: Table style or Memo style. Explore the choices this Print dialog box (see Figure 5-20) makes available, and experiment with the results.

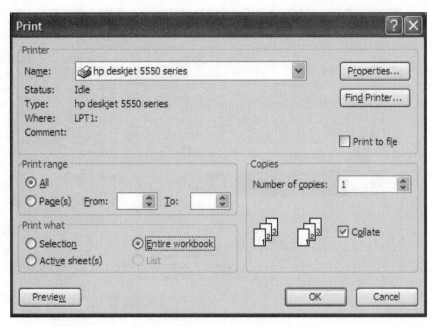

Figure 5-18

The Excel Print dialog box is a bit tamer, but still full of options.

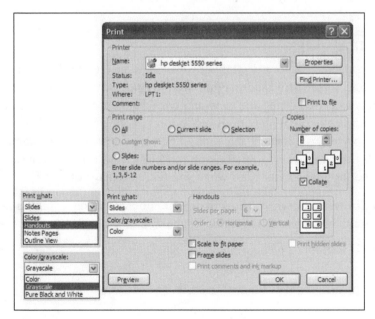

Figure 5-19

The PowerPoint Print dialog box enables you to specify exactly how printed slides or shows will appear.

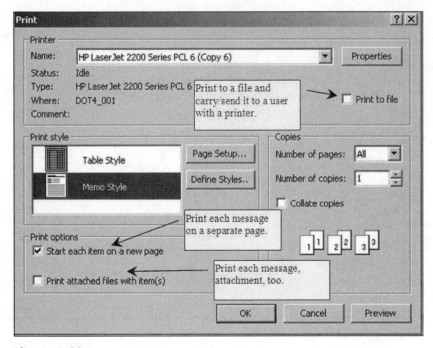

Figure 5-20
The Outlook Print dialog box contains many useful features.

Summing Up

This chapter is all about degunking your experience using the features common to all Office applications. From decluttering and customizing menus and toolbars to personalizing the view and tweaking printing settings, you'll find that your familiarity with options and features in one program will easily translate into greater efficiency across all Office applications. Office components were written to have a consistent look and feel across the board. You can realize tremendous productivity gains when you take advantage of that fact.

Now that we've shown you how to degunk some of the key common features, we'll start our application-specific degunking work with Word in the next chapter.

Degunking Microsoft Word

Degunking Checklist:

√ Understand Word's linear nature and how this affects your editing experience.

√ Use our 10 important degunking techniques to tweak Word settings to increase your efficiency and productivity.

√ Discover how you can pry open documents locked for editing.

√ Use styles to reduce your formatting time dramatically.

√ Create and modify templates to simplify document creation and layout.

This is the first of four chapters in which we explain, application-by-application, an easy system for degunking Microsoft Office and keeping it gunk free. We'll start with Microsoft Word because you likely use Word more than any other application. Word is so amazingly useful, but it can get really gunked up if you are not careful.

Everybody does word processing with Microsoft Word these days. If you work in an office, probably all your reports, letters, memos, faxes, and corporate forms are in Word. If you're in a business such as advertising, marketing, or communications, or involved in any creative endeavor, you probably use Word to create brochures, flyers, self-mailers, postcards, sell-sheets, and press releases. If you're an attorney, all your firm's documents are done in Word. If you're a student, you probably use it to write all your papers and reports. In short, it's probably the most widely used application in the world.

Understand the Uses of Word

Microsoft Word is amazingly useful. Contrary to its name, Word enables you to do so much more than, well, fidget with words! Slick image-heavy promotional materials, your 462-page text-only doctorate dissertation, a whimsical hand-drawn bookmark to be placed in your child's first hardbound book—if you need to get practically anything down on paper, Word's your thing.

Word is more than an electronic typewriter. It transcends simple word processing and is a multifunctional program that you can use to not only develop traditional word-processing-type documents such as letters and reports, but also to accomplish a host of other tasks such as the following:

√ Create desktop publishing documents, such as flyers and brochures

√ Build hypertext documents such as Web pages

√ Twist text into funky shapes using the WordArt feature

√ Use the Drawing toolbar to insert objects or wrap words around graphics

√ Build elaborate multicolumn, multirow tables to display data

√ Use the Equation Editor to insert and manipulate numerical data

√ Add bits and pieces of Excel documents or other Office files into your Word docs

√ Write a book on degunking Microsoft Office, replete with colorful screen captures and lots of cheery witticisms

Word is so versatile you might not need a single other piece of software to accomplish your work.

Unfortunately, Word can also be one of the worst gunk offenders in Office. The good news is that this gunk is not hard to fix. To degunk Word, you just have to understand exactly what Word is and how it goes about its business.

How Word Works

Word documents are linear in nature; that is, each element, text or graphic, follows another on the two-dimensional plane of a page, as shown in Figure 6-1. The advantage to Word's linear documents is that everything stays in order, even after you add or delete elements. As you add objects to your document—pictures, paragraphs, or tables—the rest of the text adjusts from the insertion point down.

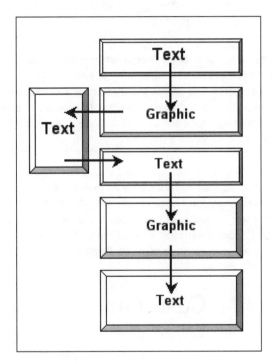

Figure 6-1
Word documents are linear: one element follows another sequentially.

Word stores everything—pictures, tables, and text—in a single file. Even when you have a 100-page document that contains 56 graphics, Word stores all those graphics with the text in the document file. The size of the file can become humongous, which affects application performance. We'll show you later how to optimize Word when you work with extra-large and complex documents. You can take several degunking steps to improve document-handling efficiency.

This will keep you from drumming your fingertips on the desktop waiting for Word to catch up to you!

When you first start Word, several events occur that affect the application's behavior and performance. The Word Data Registry key, which contains many of the customized options used in the application, is loaded first. The Normal.dot global template, which contains formatting, AutoText, and macros, is loaded next. Any templates or add-ins that are stored in the Startup folder are loaded. Any Component Object Model (COM) add-ins installed by programs that interact with Word are loaded. And finally, the Options Registry key, which contains default settings (established by Setup.exe and configurable in the Options dialog box) and optional settings (configured by changing the actual Options key settings in the Registry), is loaded.

TIP: The Registry is the database Windows uses to store and retrieve important configuration data. During operation, Windows and any running applications refer to this database so they know how to act—it's sort of like the director of a theatrical production who tells you when to smile, when to frown, and when to drop down dead on the stage. The Registry contains settings for each user on a system, as well as information about hardware and software property settings.

CAUTION: To customize the way Word works, you will ultimately be making changes (indirectly) to the Registry. However, you should not need to edit the Registry keys directly—doing so could damage your system and cause data loss if you make a mistake. Instead, we'll be using the application property settings, such as the Options dialog box discussed later, and we'll let the application make the necessary Registry edits.

Important Settings to Customize After Installation

Soon after you install Office and open Word, you should tailor the application to enhance your productivity. Even if you've been using the same version of Word for years, you can tweak it now to help you work more efficiently.

Your installation of Word came set up to work a certain way; that was Microsoft's best guess at how you might use the application. But no two Word users are alike, and the default settings simply may not suit your situation. Fortunately, we can apply a little degunking magic to help you get things set up.

We suggest the following customizations be made in Word:

1. Enable AutoRecover.
2. Enable background saves.
3. Enable backup copies.
4. Show more recently used documents on the File menu.
5. Change the default margins.
6. Make text boundaries visible.
7. Make the style area visible.
8. Customize AutoCorrect features.
9. Configure Word to use picture placeholders in large documents.
10. Customize the spelling checker dictionary.

You can also make other customizations, and we'll be showing you how to perform them in Chapter 10, "Improving How Office Applications Work Together." For now, we want to focus on giving you an immediate productivity boost.

You can turn features on and off and change the way Word works mostly by using the dialog boxes available in Word—including the Options, Customize, and Page Layout dialog boxes—and various other menu commands.

TIP: *In Word, the dialog boxes we just mentioned are not available unless a document is open. To make the Options, Customize, and Page Layout dialog boxes available, for instance, open Word, then open a document—any document will do.*

GunkBuster's Notebook: Using the Touch-It-Once Approach

Adopt a "touch it once" mentality. Think through how you expect to get stuff accomplished with Word and decide which features you use most often, and then customize to your heart's content. The configuration changes we suggest are on an application-level scale, meaning that you tweak a feature once and the changes apply to *every Word document* you create thereafter. Doing it this way prevents you from having to tinker around each time you open a document. Think how much time you'll save!

TIP: *Wasted time is just another form of gunk. As a GunkBuster, you need to find ways to increase efficiency in how you use Office applications. By saving time here and there, you'll find your gunkbusting load magically lightened as you go forward.*

Enable AutoRecover

When you can least afford a crash and lost data, that's when it happens. Fortunately, the built-in feature called AutoRecover provides a first line of defense against data loss.

At an interval specified by you, the AutoRecover feature saves the changes you make in a document to a separate, temporary recover file. Then, even when Word terminates abnormally before you've had a chance to save your work, you can usually recover most of your work, depending on the setting of the AutoRecover interval.

Recover files are assigned a temporary name by Word in the form of "AutoRecover save of *filename*.asd," where *filename* is the name of the original file. Word by default saves AutoRecover files in the C:\Documents and Settings*username*\Application Data\Microsoft\Word folder, where *username* is your Windows logon name.

To enable the AutoRecover option, follow these steps:

1. Choose Options from the Tools menu.
2. Select the Save tab in the Options dialog box.
3. Make sure the "Save AutoRecover info every" option is checked, and then use the up and down arrows to set the number of minutes (as shown in Figure 6-2), which tells Word how often you want the AutoRecover feature to save the data. A good setting to use is 10 minutes, although you might want to make this interval smaller if you are especially concerned about losing data. (Here's the trade-off: the shorter the interval, the less efficient Word will be.)
4. Click OK to apply the changes.

After a crash, the next time you open Word, it searches for and automatically opens any AutoRecover files (there may be one for each document open with unsaved changes at the time of the crash). You will know you are working with a recover file because the title bar will display the document name as "*FileName* (Recovered)," where *FileName* is the original file's name. In the recovered document, choose Save from the File menu to save it using the original document name. This in effect replaces the original document with the one containing the latest changes. Or choose Save As from the File menu to save the recover file using another name. If you choose to ignore the recover file and do not save it at all, it is deleted when it is closed and any unsaved changes are lost.

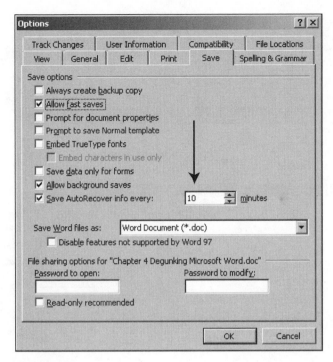

Figure 6-2

Set the AutoRecover interval in the Save tab of the Options dialog box.

TIP: The AutoRecover feature is for preventative use and is not a replacement for regularly saving your documents. You'll notice that some of the very last changes you made to a document just before it crashed are not captured in the recover file. For instance, if AutoRecover is set to save every 10 minutes and your document crashes 9 minutes after the last automatic save, AutoRecover won't have a chance to save those last few edits and you'll have to redo them. That's why you need to regularly save your work using the Save command—initiate the save function often to minimize lost data.

GunkBuster's Notebook: Specifying Where Recover Files Are Stored

You can specify another location (other than the default) for Word to save AutoRecover files by completing these steps:

1. Select Options from the Tools menu.

2. Select the File Locations tab in the Options dialog box.

3. In the File Locations tab, select the AutoRecover Files option as shown in Figure 6-3, and then click the Modify button.

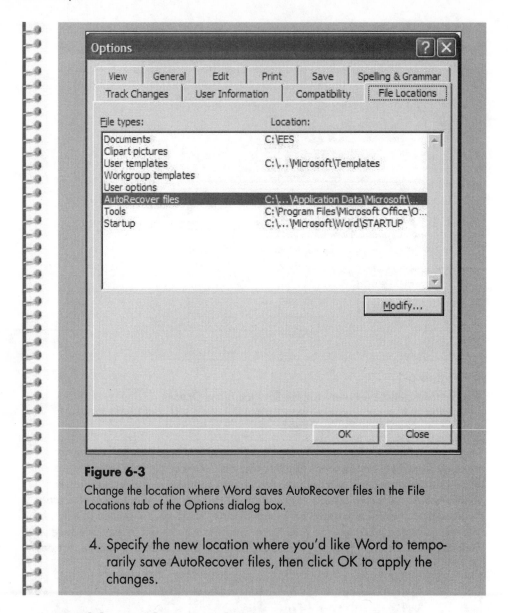

Figure 6-3
Change the location where Word saves AutoRecover files in the File
Locations tab of the Options dialog box.

4. Specify the new location where you'd like Word to temporarily save AutoRecover files, then click OK to apply the
changes.

Enable Background Saves

Word has the ability to perform background saves, making it possible for you to
continue working in a document without having to wait until the save operation (when Word writes the information to disk) is complete. You'll notice that
a disk icon appears in the status bar at the bottom of the Word editing window
when Word is performing a save operation in the background. When you see
this, you can blithely go on typing. Word will make sure it's all captured on disk
without interrupting your train of thought.

To enable background saving, complete these steps:

1. Select Options from the Tools menu.

2. Select the Save tab in the Options dialog box.

3. Click to insert a check mark in front of the Allow Background Saves option as shown in Figure 6-4.

4. Click OK to apply the changes.

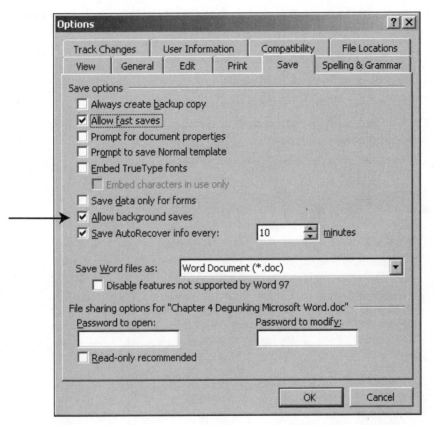

Figure 6-4
Enable background saves in the Save tab of the Options dialog box.

Enable Backup Copies

Sometimes, after you've opened a document and made all sorts of changes to it, you decide you'd rather revert back to the original and somehow wish you could erase everything you've just done. Word has a feature, which is by default disabled, that makes a backup copy of your document before your current edits are saved. When you enable this feature, you can have a backup copy of every document you edit.

Word creates the backup copy of your file only after you open the document and save it at least twice. The first time you select Save or Save As, Word creates the original document and writes it to disk. After you add text or make some editing changes and save it again, Word writes the changes into the original file and also creates the backup copy without the latest editing changes; the backup copy is a copy of the original file before you made any edits. The backup copy is stored in the same folder as the original document.

To enable the backup copy feature, complete these steps:

1. Choose Options from the Tools menu.
2. Select the Save tab in the Options dialog box.
3. Click to place a check mark in front of the Always Create Backup Copy option as shown in Figure 6-5.
4. Click OK to apply the changes.

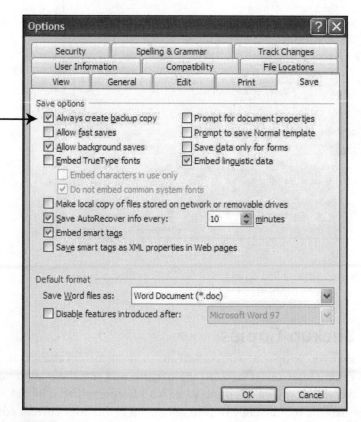

Figure 6-5
Enable backup copies in the Save tab of the Options dialog box.

Take care not to allow backup copies of your documents to gunk up your system. Delete backup copies when you complete your document.

Backup copies are automatically named "Backup of *filename*.doc," where *filename* is the name of the original document. To open a backup copy, choose Open on the File menu. At the bottom of the Open dialog box, in the File of Type box, select All Files. Navigate to the folder containing the original document, select "Backup of *filename*," and then click Open to open the backup copy.

TIP: In the Details view of the Open dialog box, backup files are listed as "Microsoft Word Backup Document" in the Type column.

TIP: When you enable the Always Create Backup Copy option, the Allow Fast Saves option is automatically turned off because Word cannot create a backup copy when it fast-saves the changes to a document. Conversely, if you enable the fast saves option, such as when you're working with extremely large files, the Always Create Backup Copy option will automatically be disabled.

Show More Recently Used Documents on the File Menu

In a typical work session, don't you usually find yourself opening and closing the same handful of documents? It's a pain to continuously have to navigate the folder hierarchy in the Open dialog box or Windows Explorer just to get to the Word doc you need. At the bottom of the File menu, you'll notice a list of document names. This is called the File menu Most Recently Used (MRU) list. The File menu has the capability of displaying the last nine Word documents you've had open; the most recently used file is listed first. This is a handy shortcut enabling you to open a document quickly without having to navigate any folder hierarchies.

Word usually comes with only four documents showing in the File menu Most Recently Used list. To set the number of document names shown in the File menu Most Recently Used list, follow these steps:

1. Select Options from the Tools menu.
2. Select the General tab in the Options dialog box.
3. Make sure that the Recently Used File List option is checked as shown in Figure 6-6.
4. Use the up and down arrows to select the number of files you'd like displayed in the File menu Most Recently Used list, and then click OK to apply the changes.

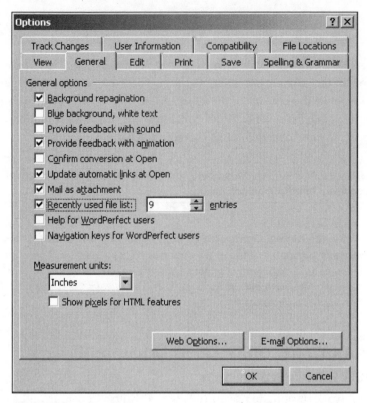

Figure 6-6
Reset the File menu Most Recently Used list in the General tab of the Options dialog box.

Change the Default Margins

Whether you're writing a formal business letter, a report, or a term paper, standard document margins are typically 1 inch all around the page. A 1-inch margin provides a visually symmetric and pleasingly even white border around all the edges of a document. Why Word comes with default left and right margins of 1.25 inches, we don't know.

Instead of manually modifying the margin settings for each individual document you work in, you can change the margins globally for all the Word documents you'll create thereafter. This entails making a change to the global template, Normal.dot, so if you have not made a backup copy of the original Normal.dot template (or your preferred document template), you should do so now. (Details about making a backup of Normal.dot are given in the section "Customize the Look of the Word Window" of Chapter 5, "Degunking Office's Common Features.")

To change the default settings for page margins for all your Word documents, follow these steps:

1. Close all Word documents and exit Word.

2. Right-click Start, and then select Explore.

3. Navigate to C:\Documents and Settings*username*\Application Data\Microsoft\Templates, where *username* is your Windows logon name.

4. Right-click the Normal.dot file and select Open from the context menu. Don't double-click the Normal.dot file because that would simply open a single new Word document; rather, you want to open the template itself.

5. Select Page Setup from the File menu.

6. In the Margins tab of the Page Setup dialog box, shown in Figure 6-7, use the down arrows to decrease the Left and Right margin settings to 1".

7. Click OK to apply the changes.

8. On the File menu, click Save to save the changes to the template.

9. Close the Normal.dot file.

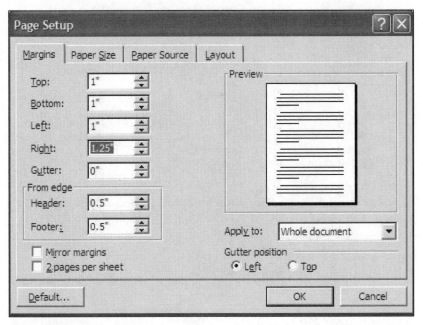

Figure 6-7
Change the default left and right margins in the Margins tab of the Page Setup dialog box of the Normal.dot template.

Make Text Boundaries Visible

We know it's a bit intimidating to be in Page Layout view staring at that big, blank open page. How will you possibly fill up all that white space? For one, you can make the text boundaries visible, which might make you feel better psychologically, as well as make it easier to know where the margins are when you are placing objects on a page, especially while you create flyers and brochures.

To make the text boundaries visible, follow these steps:

1. Select Options from the Tools menu.
2. Select the View tab in the Options dialog box.
3. In the Print and Web Layout Options section, click to place a check mark in front of the Text Boundaries option as shown in Figure 6-8.
4. Click OK to apply the changes.

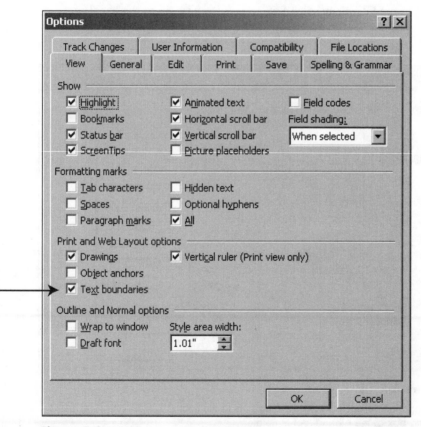

Figure 6-8

Make the text boundaries visible in the View tab of the Options dialog box.

Make the Style Area Visible

If you apply styles to your text elements to give documents an organized look and feel, it's helpful to be able to see how paragraphs are styled without having to click them and read the style name in the Styles drop-down box on the Formatting toolbar. In Normal view and Outline view, you can allocate the far left margin of your monitor screen as the Style Area in which applied paragraph styles are visible, as shown in Figure 6-9.

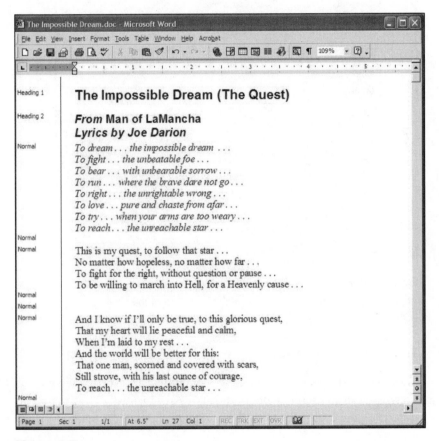

Figure 6-9
The Style Area appears in the left margin of the screen in Normal or Outline view.

Here's how to make the Style Area appear:

1. Select Options from the Tools menu.

2. Select the View tab in the Options dialog box.

3. In the Outline and Normal Options section, use the up and down arrows to adjust the Style Area Width setting to a comfortable size, as shown in Figure 6-10. A setting of .75" to 1.00" is usually adequate.

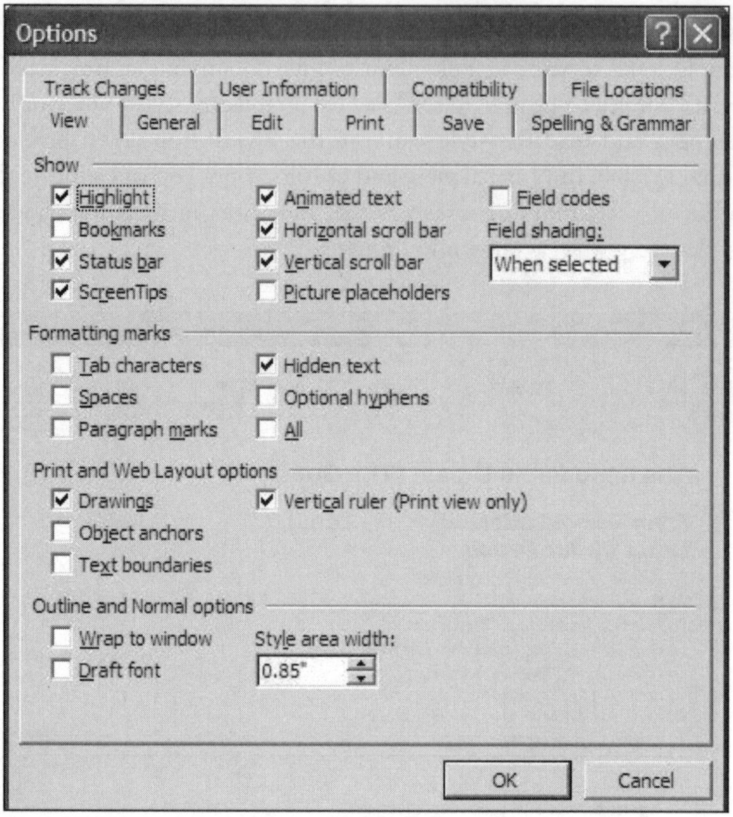

Figure 6-10
Adjust the Style Area Width setting in the View tab of the Options dialog box.

4. Click OK to apply the changes.

Keep in mind that when you view a document in Normal view or Outline view, you can adjust the width of the Style Area manually. Drag the vertical line separating the Style Area from the document text area to where you want it.

You'll notice that only *paragraph* styles are listed in the Style Area. You still must click directly on a text element and observe the style name in the Styles drop-down box to see which *character* style has been applied to it. The section entitled "Understand Types of Formatting" later in this chapter explains more about paragraph and character styles.

Customize AutoCorrect Features

Have you ever been around one of those people who likes to finish your sentences before you're halfway through them? Sometimes Word can be like this too; with certain AutoCorrect features enabled, Word tries to complete your words after you've typed only a few letters, automatically replaces straight quotes with curly ones, and corrects the words you commonly misspell, among other things. You can find this helpful, or it can drive you up the wall.

Word offers many options for you to customize the way it tries to help you work. For instance, suppose you're writing a short article for the garden club newsletter explaining to local green thumbs how they can keep *Melittia satyriniformis* out of their *Cucumis sativus* vines using *Bacillus thuringiensis*. Now how many times are you going to feel like typing that Latin? Instead, by adding those words to the AutoText list you can have Word automatically insert the multiletter monsters as if it's reading your mind.

To customize the myriad AutoCorrect options, complete these steps:

1. Select AutoCorrect from the Tools menu.
2. Click each of the tabs and choose which features you'd like to enable.
3. Click OK to apply the changes.

Table 6-1 lists the AutoCorrect features available in each tab. Once you know what's available, you can decide which ones will help improve your efficiency.

Table 6-1   Useful AutoCorrect Features

Tab	Options
AutoCorrect tab	Correct two initial capitals Capitalize first letter of sentences Capitalize names of days Correct accidental usage of Caps Lock key Replace text as you type Automatically use suggestions from the spelling checker
AutoFormat As You Type tab	*Apply as you type:* √ Headings √ Borders √ Tables √ Automatic bulleted lists √ Automatic numbered lists

(continued)

Table 6-1 Useful AutoCorrect Features (continued)

Tab	Options
AutoFormat As You Type tab	*Replace as you type:* √ Straight quotes with smart quotes √ Ordinals (1st) with superscript √ Fractions (1/2) with fraction characters ($^1/_2$) √ Symbol characters (--) with symbols (—) √ *Bold* and _italic_ with real formatting √ Internet and network paths with hyperlinks *Automatically as you type:* √ Format beginning of list item like the one before it √ Define styles based on your formatting
AutoText tab	Show AutoComplete tip for AutoText and dates Enter AutoText entries here
AutoFormat tab	*Apply:* √ Headings √ Lists √ Automatic bulleted lists √ Other paragraphs *Replace:* √ Straight quotes with smart quotes √ Ordinals (1st) with superscript √ Fractions (1/2) with fraction characters ($^1/_2$) √ Symbol characters (--) with symbols (—) √ *Bold* and _italic_ with real formatting √ Internet and network paths with hyperlinks *Preserve:* √ Styles *Always AutoFormat:* √ Plain text WordMail documents

Configure Word to Use Picture Placeholders in Large Documents

At some point you will be working in a document that contains numerous graphics. You'll notice that Word slows down in the process of displaying those graphics as you scroll through your document. An easy way to speed up the display is to have Word display an empty box as a placeholder for the more resource-hungry graphics.

To enable the Picture Placeholders feature, complete the following steps:

1. Choose Options from the Tools menu.

2. Select the View tab in the Options dialog box, and click to insert a check mark in front of Picture Placeholders in the Show section as shown in Figure 6-11.

3. Click OK to apply the changes.

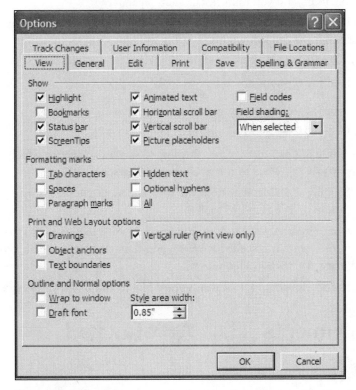

Figure 6-11

Enable picture placeholders to speed up display in the View tab of the Options dialog box.

Customize the Spelling Checker Dictionary

Besides being able to customize exactly how you want the spelling checker to work (use the Spelling & Grammar tab in the Options dialog box), you can tell Word which dictionary you'd like to use to check the spelling in a document and you can add specific words to the dictionary. To specify which dictionary to use, complete these steps:

1. Choose Options from the Tools menu.

2. In the Spelling & Grammar tab, use the drop-down list to choose which dictionary you'd like Word to use to check the spelling.

3. If you'd like to add a new dictionary file, click the Dictionaries button or Custom Dictionaries button (depending on the Office version you're using).

4. In the Custom Dictionaries dialog box, click New or Add, and then navigate to the folder in which a dictionary list is contained. Dictionary files have the .dic file extension and you must install them separately.

5. If you'd like to associate the dictionary with a language, choose the language from the Language drop-down list.

6. Click OK.

7. Click OK in the Options dialog box to apply the changes.

To add new words to a dictionary, complete these steps:

1. Choose Options from the Tools menu.

2. In the Spelling & Grammar tab, use the drop-down list to choose which dictionary you'd like Word to use to check spelling. Click OK.

3. Choose Spelling and Grammar from the Tools menu, or click the spelling checker button on the Standard toolbar.

4. When Word presents a word it doesn't know that you'd like to add to the dictionary, make sure it is spelled correctly, and then click Add to add it to the dictionary as shown in Figure 6-12.

5. Repeat the previous step for all words you'd like to add to the dictionary.

Open Documents That Are Locked for Editing

Here's a situation you are likely to experience: you attempt to add a few last-minute updates to a letter on your PC before you send it, but Word tells you the document is locked for editing by another user. Typically, Word invents this imaginary "user" when you try to open a document that was open when Word crashed or when your PC experienced a system failure that affected Word. When a document becomes locked for editing by another user and you know there can't possibly be someone else using the file, it's an indication that some of the document's temporary files were not released correctly.

When Word shuts down abnormally because of an application failure or act of nature, frequently the operating system is unable to terminate (computer geeks say "kill") the Word (Winword.exe) process. If you like, you can view the process

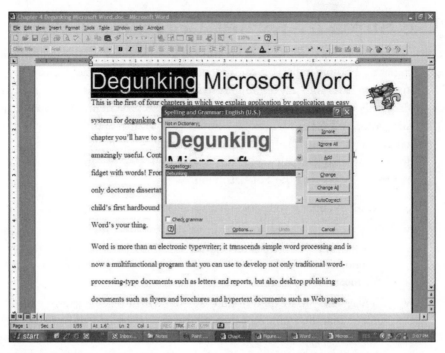

Figure 6-12
Click Add in the Spelling and Grammar dialog box to customize the dictionary.

in the Processes tab of the Task Manager: press Ctrl+Alt+Del or right-click the Taskbar and select Task Manager from the context menu. The Windows operating system perceives that orphaned Word process as another user editing the document and maintains links to the temporary files automatically created when a Word document is open. The temporary files that you cannot delete are usually Clipboard files (they might be named something like ~df*xxxx*.tmp, where *xxxx* is a string of numerals) left over from copy and paste operations you performed while editing the original document.

There are two ways to solve this dilemma:

√   In the Processes tab of the Task Manager, you can highlight the Winword.exe process and click End Process to delete the Clipboard temporary files and release the document for read and write operations.

√   You can simply reboot the computer and let the Windows operating system end the process during shutdown.

Either way, you'll finally be allowed to access your document the next time you open it.

Use Styles to Format Content

Word provides a plethora of formatting options for your text—you can make it a giant 72 points high; you can indent it with 14 tab characters; you can even turn each letter into a Wingding. A *style* is a *set* of formatting characteristics you can apply to a single word or whole paragraph. A style delineates the font, point size, color, and other formatting options you wish to apply on a character-by-character or paragraph basis. Styles make it easy to apply a predefined set of formatting characteristics with just a single click of the mouse as opposed to repetitive forays into the Format menu.

Styles work to degunk your documents and your work sessions in two main ways:

√   They enable you to organize your work into a document that has a standardized look and feel. Like elements are formatted identically and readers can understand the document layout and organization intuitively, which adds meaning beyond your words.

√   They enable you to apply a multitude of formatting characteristics all at once so that the amount of time it takes to format a document and the number of clicks you have to make are drastically reduced. Best of all, if you later decide to change the formatting, you can simply modify a style or styles and all the corresponding text elements will automatically be updated with the new formatting.

Before you start slinging styles every which way, you should understand a little about Word formatting. Once you know how Word applies formatting, you'll be able to use it (and styles) to the fullest extent with a minimum of frustration. And remember how we mentioned that Word documents are linear by nature? Formatting is one of the areas where this most comes into play.

Understand Types of Formatting

In Word, there are *paragraph* formats and *character* formats. Paragraph formats apply formatting to an entire paragraph, whether that is the font, point size, indentation, line spacing, or bulleted list characteristics. It's all about how you want a paragraph to look. Character formats apply formatting to a single letter or contiguous group of letters and can designate whether italics, bold, underline, or superscript is applied, as well as which font and point size to use, among other things.

Even though character formatting (font, point size, and small caps, for instance) might be included in a defined paragraph formatting style, you cannot apply paragraph formatting to a single word. Conversely, you cannot apply character formatting to an entire paragraph (unless you manually select each word in the whole paragraph and apply the character format to it).

Character formatting transforms selected text, storing the character formatting configuration in invisible codes "after" the selected text. Word is linear, so character formatting elements stack up around characters. When you move a word that has been styled a particular way, sometimes the formatting travels with the word and arrives intact at the final destination, and other times the formatting seems to get lost in transit. This is because you might have inadvertently left behind the character formatting coding. We can't fault you for that: it's invisible. The easiest way to ensure that character formatting travels with the target word is to double-click the word to select it rather than dragging over each character manually; the double-click selects the invisible codes automatically.

Work Efficiently with Paragraphs

To start a new paragraph, you press the Enter key. Word then inserts a line break designated by a paragraph mark, which is a funny-looking backward *P* as shown at the end of the text lines in Figure 6-13. When a hard return is inserted in this manner, the current paragraph formatting is applied to the new paragraph. When you want to combine two paragraphs into one, you can delete the paragraph mark and the text merges into one block with the paragraph formatting of what was the second paragraph applied. In other words, the paragraph formatting is stored in that little paragraph mark. Wherever that paragraph mark goes, so goes the formatting. To retain the paragraph formatting when you move or copy text, include the paragraph mark in the selection.

TIP: *We use the term* **hard return** *when we mean press Enter and insert a paragraph mark. On the other hand, a* **soft return** *is a line break that is inserted automatically by the word processor and allows words to "wrap" from one line to the next when no more characters will fit between the margins of one line. Although no special character represents them, in Figure 6-13 you can see that Word inserted soft returns on the lines where the words just wrap back and start anew at the left margin.*

To display paragraph marks, tab characters, spaces, and other nonprinting characters, toggle the Show/Hide button ¶ on the Standard toolbar or place a check mark in front of the All option in the Formatting Marks section of the View tab in the Options dialog box, as shown in Figure 6-14.

As you can see in the figure, you can designate individually which formatting marks you'd like displayed by using the check boxes adjacent to specific choices.

Standardize with Styles

Styles are easy to work with. You can view all the styles available in a particular template as well as modify them quickly and painlessly. On the Format menu,

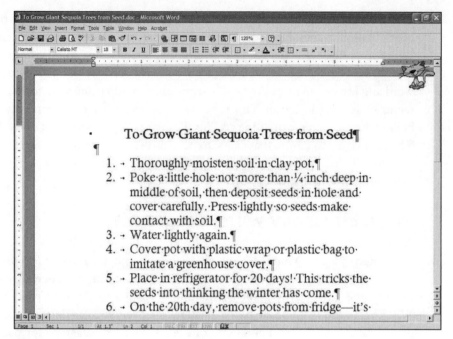

Figure 6-13

The paragraph marks indicate a line break inserted by the user and contain the paragraph formatting.

choose Style. In the Style dialog box, click any style name in the Styles list to see a paragraph preview, a character preview, and a description of the formatting that style comprises. Paragraph styles are denoted by the paragraph mark preceding the style name, and character styles are preceded by an underlined lowercased *a*.

TIP: *To apply styles quickly, forget about double-clicking to select a word or triple-clicking to select a whole paragraph and then choosing a style to apply—instead, simply place the insertion point anywhere in a word to apply a character style to it and anywhere in a paragraph to apply a paragraph style.*

Use the New button in the Style dialog box to create a new style. When you define a new style, Word lets you base your new style on an existing one so that you don't have to reinvent the wheel. You can also choose which style you'd like to apply to following paragraphs. This comes in handy when, for example, you want every H1 heading to be followed by a No Indent paragraph: when you define the H1 style, use the "Style for following paragraph" drop-down list in the New Style dialog box to select the No Indent style. The next time you type an H1 heading in your document, when you press Enter you will automatically be in No Indent style.

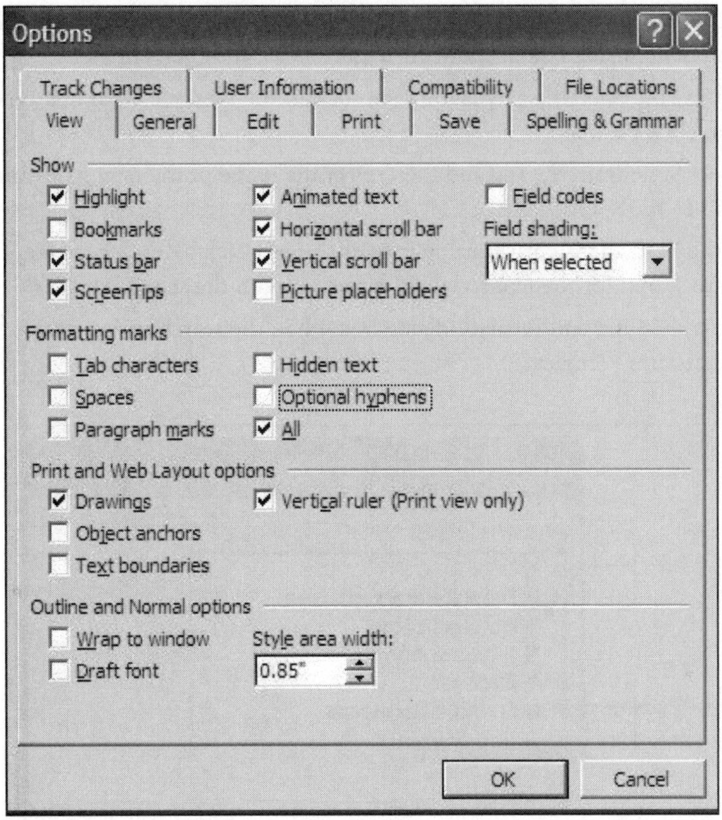

Figure 6-14

To see paragraph marks and other nonprinting characters, check All in the View tab of the Options dialog box.

Use the Modify button in the Style dialog box to tweak an existing style. The Modify Style dialog box and the New Style dialog box contain nearly identical configuration options. You can choose whether you'd like this style change to be saved in the current template. You can create a shortcut key to use to apply the style. You can even choose whether you want the formatting of text elements using this new or modified style to be automatically updated.

An alternative way to change text formatting and update styles is to use Search and Replace. To do so, follow these steps:

1. Choose Replace from the Edit menu.

2. In the Find and Replace dialog box, click More; then click Format in the fully expanded Find and Replace dialog box.

3. Select Style from the list.

4. Choose the style you want to replace from the Find What Style list in the Find Style dialog box as shown in Figure 6-15, and then click OK.

5. In the Find and Replace dialog box, click in the Replace With text box, and then click Format.

6. Select Style from the list, and then select the name of the new style you want to apply. Click OK.

7. In the Find and Replace dialog box, click Find Next, Replace, or Replace All to search for the first style and replace it with the second style.

8. Close the Find and Replace dialog box when the search and replace operation is complete.

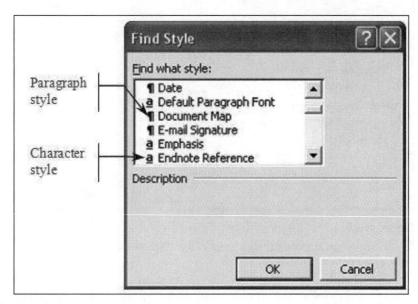

Figure 6-15
Select a style to find in the Find Style dialog box.

A Few More Formatting Tips

In many fonts, Word uses proportional spacing, where each letter character varies in width. For example, the letters *w* and *m* are wider than most other letters, whereas the space character and the letter *i* are less wide. This is important to consider when you are formatting a document because when you are using a proportional font you will then not be tempted to indent lines or align text columns by inserting spaces or tab characters, respectively. Instead, use tab characters to indent text uniformly (on the Format menu, choose Paragraph, and then click the Tabs button to set up tab stops), and use tables (on the Table menu, choose Insert) or actual column formatting (on the Format menu, choose Columns) to align text vertically. Tab stops and tables automatically adjust as you edit content, which saves you from trying to keep track of misaligned spaces.

Remember not to apply more than two or three different fonts throughout the document; any more than that and the final product begins to look amateurish and disorganized. Arial and Times New Roman are two widely used, easy-to-read fonts in the business world. Save the unusual fonts for your creative work.

Point size is another consideration. Depending on the font you use, the point size will have dramatic effects on readability. Word will allow you to make the point size as small as you like; however, the smaller the type, the less likely your prose is to be read—people will see your tiny text as "the fine print" and will avoid reading it even for their own good.

Create, Customize, and Organize Templates

A Word template is like a cookie cutter you can use to churn out files with similar characteristics and formatting. Word comes with a number of built-in templates that you can use as is, or modify to suit your needs (select New on the File menu to see the available templates). For example, use the Elegant Letter "shape" to stamp out a routine business letter, and in so doing, take advantage of the preconfigured formatting and layout it contains. Use the Contemporary Resume shape to cut a smart-looking résumé. Or create your own cookie cutter that includes personal settings and layout preferences.

A template is a central storage location that holds such items as special formatting, macros, AutoText entries, shortcut key assignments, toolbars, font choices, styles, and layout structure so that you can access these characteristics as a group and apply them all at once to new documents. For example, you can insert boilerplate text such as a signature block or company logo into a template and have it appear on every subsequent file you create using that template.

There are two types of templates: global templates and document templates. *Global templates*, such as Normal.dot, make settings available to all documents. A *document template*, on the other hand, makes its settings available only to documents based specifically on that template. If you use a specific document template, you can also apply settings from any global template or from any other document template that you have loaded.

We've mentioned the Normal.dot template already in this chapter. By default, Word applies the Normal.dot template to all new Word docs you create unless you tell it otherwise. In the following sections, we'll explain why Normal.dot is special and how Word uses it. We also talk about how you can create, load, and organize your own templates.

Using Normal.dot

The global Normal template is also considered a user template because you can customize it and change its storage location. A Word document cannot be opened without an associated template, and unless you have specified another template to use, Word applies Normal by default whenever a new Word doc is opened.

Normal.dot defines the default paragraph styles, heading styles, margins, page sizes, headers, and footers of a new Word document. The following components are stored in the Normal.dot global template:

√   Boilerplate text and graphics

√   Styles (text formatting)

√   Default settings (font, margins, page size, and so on)

√   AutoText entries

√   Macros

√   Custom menu and toolbar settings

The Normal template contains the Word defaults. Unless (and until) you alter them, the defaults include the following settings (or something similar):

√   8.5-by-11-inch letter-sized paper

√   Portrait page orientation

√   Arial font style

√   10-point font size

√   1-inch top and bottom margins

√   1.25-inch left and right margins

√   Single line spacing

√   Left alignment

√   English language

√   The Standard toolbar, menus, and key commands

How Word Finds Normal.dot

It's important to understand how Word goes about locating the Normal.dot template, especially if you have multiple versions of the template on your computer—the search order determines which version will be opened for new docs. Also, where Normal.dot is stored obviously affects how you go about locating it whenever you want to use it or modify it.

Word looks first in the installed templates location at C:\Program Files\Microsoft Office\Templates\1033. If Normal is not there, Word looks in the user templates file location at C:\Documents and Settings*username*\Application

Data\Microsoft\Templates, where *username* is your logon name. If it still doesn't find Normal, then Word looks in the workgroup templates file location, which has no default location set.

TIP: *At initial installation if you chose the Run from My Computer or the Run All from My Computer install option, the search order that Word uses is slightly different: first it looks in the user templates file location at C:\Documents and Settings**username**\Application Data\Microsoft\Templates, then in the program folder (where Winword.exe is stored) at C:\Program Files\Microsoft Office\Office11, and finally in the workgroup templates area, which has no set default location.*

*If you chose the install option Run from Network or Run All from Network, Word searches for Normal.dot first in the program folder at C:\Program Files\Microsoft Office\Office11, then in the user templates location at C:\Documents and Settings**username**\Application Data\Microsoft\Templates, and then in the workgroup templates area. Table 6-2 shows the Word search order based on installation type. If Word cannot find Normal.dot in any of these places, it will create a new one!*

Table 6-2 Search Order for Normal.dot

Install Option	Search Path 1	Search Path 2	Search Path 3
Typical	Installed templates path[a]	User templates path[b]	Workgroup templates path
Run from My Computer or **Run All from My Computer**[c]	User templates path	Word program folder	Workgroup templates path
Run from Network or **Run All from Network**[d]	Word program folder	User templates path	Workgroup templates path

[a] Installed templates path = C:\Program Files\Microsoft Office\Templates\1033

[b] User Templates path (default folder) = C:\Documents and Settings*username*\Application Data\Microsoft\Templates

[c] Run from My Computer or Run All from My Computer install option Word program folder (Winword.exe location) = C:\Program Files\Microsoft Office\Office

[d] Run from Network or Run All from Network install option Word program folder (Winword.exe location) = *Drive*:*Server_Folder*\PFiles\MSOffice\Office, where *Drive* is the hard drive and *Server_Folder* is the name of the server on which the Word program is stored

Specifying a New Location for Normal.dot

If you want to change the default User Templates location for Normal.dot, you can specify a new location using the Options dialog box. Complete these steps:

1. On the Tools menu, choose Options.

2. In the File Locations tab of the Options dialog box, select User Templates in the File Types list, and then click Modify.

3. Specify a new location in the Modify Location dialog box.

User and Workgroup Templates

You should store templates that you share with others in the Workgroup Templates file location. You can specify exactly where this location is by using the File Locations tab in the Options dialog box. No default location is preconfigured for workgroup templates, so you must set one up if you intend to enable others to access specific templates on a network location.

Save your custom user templates in the Templates folder. The location of the Templates folder varies based on the version of the Windows operating system you have installed:

√ In Windows 95 and Windows 98, the Templates folder is located at C:*Windows_folder*\Application Data in the Microsoft folder or at C:*Windows_folder*\Profiles*username*\Application Data in the Microsoft folder.

√ In Windows 2000, Windows XP, and Windows 2003, the Templates folder is located by default at C:\Documents and Settings*username*\Application Data in the Microsoft folder.

Template files that you save in the Templates folder appear in the General tab of the New dialog box (on the File menu, choose New) as shown in Figure 6-16. Template files have a .dot file extension. However, any document (.doc) file that you save in the Templates folder also acts as a template.

If you want to create a custom tab in the New dialog box in which to save frequently used or newly created templates, you can create a new subfolder in the Templates folder and save your templates there. In Windows Explorer, navigate to your Templates folder location. Then, using the File menu, choose New, select Folder from the submenu, and name the new folder. The name you give that subfolder appears as the label of the new tab as shown in Figure 6-17.

Create, Modify, and Load Templates

It's easy to create a new template—the hardest part is deciding which way to do it. If you'd like to base the new template on an existing template, follow these steps:

1. Choose New from the File menu.

2. In the Create New section of the New dialog box, choose the Template option.

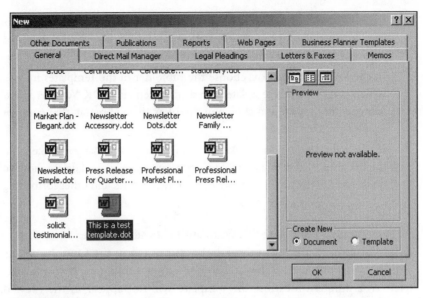

Figure 6-16

Available templates appear in the General tab of the New dialog box.

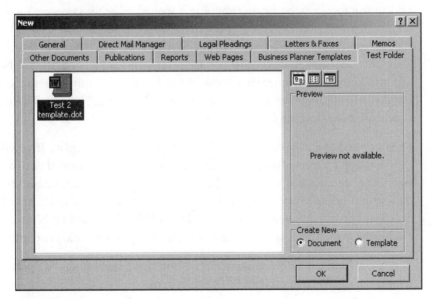

Figure 6-17

A subfolder added to the Templates folder results in a new tab in the New dialog box.

3. In one of the tabs of the New dialog box, select a template similar to the one you'd like to create, and then click OK. Word will open the document window, ready to accept your modifications.

4. Choose Save As from the File menu. In the Save as Type box, be sure that the Document Template (*.dot) option is selected, then type a name for your template into the File Name text box.

5. In the Save As dialog box, choose the subfolder of the Templates folder in which you'd like this template stored, and then click OK. Your template will subsequently appear as a choice in the New dialog box tab that corresponds to the subfolder name.

6. In the document window, make the changes to the file that you'd like to save in the template. Add text and graphics you want to appear and delete those you don't. Modify the page layout, styles, AutoText entries, and other formatting.

7. Save and close the template.

When you save a template file, Word automatically switches to the User Templates location that is set in the File Locations tab in the Options dialog box, which by default is the Templates folder and its subfolders. If you save a template in a different location, the template will not appear in the New dialog box. When you want to use that template, you'll have to navigate to it manually.

Another method to use to create a new template based on an existing one is to open a document to which the existing template is applied, make the necessary modifications (delete text, add formatting and styles, change the layout, and so forth), then choose Save As on the File menu. In the Save as Type box, select the Document Template (*.dot) option, and then type a name for your template into the File Name text box. Again, as in the preceding method, the default folder offered in the Save In box is the Templates folder. Choose the subfolder (New dialog box tab location) in which you'd like this template to be stored, then click Save.

Keep in mind that all Word docs are based on at least one template. If you don't choose to apply a specific one, the document will be based on Normal.dot. You can determine whether you want to make changes to the Normal.dot template (see the section entitled "Customize the Look of the Word Window" in Chapter 5 for directions) or whether you would rather open a blank doc based on Normal.dot, modify the settings, and save it as a new template using the preceding two methods.

When you have a document open and wish to make the settings of a particular template available, complete the following steps:

1. Choose Templates and Add-Ins from the Tools menu.

2. In the Templates and Add-Ins dialog box, click Attach.

3. In the Attach Template dialog box, navigate to where the target template is stored, then click Open.

4. In the Templates and Add-Ins dialog box, be sure the Automatically Update Document Styles option is selected if you wish Word to apply the template's styles to the document's existing text elements.

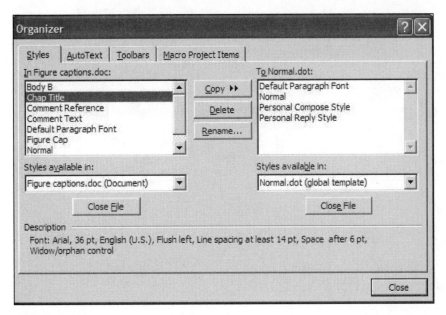

Figure 6-18
View a description of a style in the Styles tab of the Organizer dialog box.

5. In the Global Templates and Add-Ins section, be sure that there is a check mark in front of the other templates you wish to use.

6. Click OK.

What's that Organizer button in the Templates and Add-Ins dialog box? It's actually another way Word enables you to modify existing templates. The four tabs of the Organizer dialog box enable you to copy AutoText entries, toolbars, and macro project items back and forth between the document you are working in and the templates that are available. The Organizer is also a handy place to get a description of a particular style or item, as shown in Figure 6-18.

Summing Up

Word is a feature-intensive application that goes almost above and beyond the call of duty when it comes to providing functionality—but watch out for the junk that accumulates along the way! There are at least 10 ways you can tweak how Word is configured to make your Word environment more efficient and convenient. Now you also know how to open documents that are locked for editing. And you've learned how to use and customize the built-in capabilities of styles and templates to get your work done faster and with much higher quality.

Degunking Microsoft Excel

Degunking Checklist:

√   Perform some simple but important changes to make Excel run more efficiently.

√   Use the built-in automatic save features to protect your workbooks.

√   Use workspace files to save you lots of time and energy.

√   Incorporate templates to simplify new workbook and sheet creation.

√   Discover several fundamental principles of worksheet design.

√   Use Excel to create simple databases to organize your information.

Microsoft Excel is an excellent tool for manipulating large amounts of data. With Excel, you can organize discrete bits of information into columns and rows and then do all sorts of things to it that would take forever to do by hand. You can sort and filter the data, run calculations on it, generate reports on it, work interactively with it, chart it, and display it as a Web page, among other things. The good news is that even with all this functionality, Excel manages to stay on task and doesn't accumulate too much gunk. Even so, you can use the few easy degunking techniques we show you in this chapter to get Excel working even more efficiently for you.

Excel documents are called workbooks, and they use the .xls file extension. A *workbook* is a collection of worksheets, chart sheets, and Microsoft Visual Basic for Applications modules. A *worksheet* is the primary location in which you store data in a workbook. When you open a blank worksheet, you see a grid containing what seems to be an almost endless number of columns and rows— by default there are 256 columns and 65,536 rows. That's a lot of space! Each individual grid block, called a *cell,* can store data and formulas and has associated formatting, such as fonts, colors, and layout options. Figure 7-1 shows the different features of an Excel workbook.

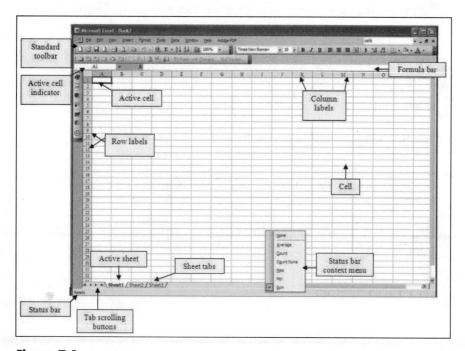

Figure 7-1
Some specialized terminology is used to describe Excel workbook and worksheet items.

In this chapter, we'll start with the top 10 changes you should make to degunk Excel. We'll also show you how to employ the AutoSave and AutoRecover features to keep your data safe, how to work with workspace files, and how to use templates to save time. Along the way we'll offer a few file-layout best practices, and finally we'll discuss how Excel can be used as a database tool to help you better organize the data clutter you may be encountering.

Top-10 Changes to Make

Many of the tips and techniques we show you here follow the touch-it-once approach: make a few easy configuration changes one time so that by default Excel works the way that's most convenient for you thereafter. You'll notice that most of the degunking strategies in this chapter focus on saving you time rather than de-cluttering the application. As mentioned, Excel manages to keep from getting too gunked up, so we want to capitalize on that and optimize it in other ways. The next time you open Excel, make these changes:

1. Group and ungroup sheets.
2. Change the default number of sheets in a new workbook.
3. View two sheets simultaneously.
4. View multiple formulas simultaneously.
5. Copy formatting from cell to cell.
6. Create styles based on cell contents.
7. Enable word wrapping in cells.
8. Pick from a list to enter data.
9. Calculate values quickly using the status bar shortcut.
10. Change cell selection behavior.

Group and Ungroup Sheets

In Excel, you perform actions in the active sheet. Normally, when you must enter the same data or formatting in multiple sheets, you have to copy cell contents manually by cutting and pasting. However, you can group the sheets so that they are active simultaneously. Grouping sheets has several time-saving advantages and enables you to accomplish the following tasks:

√   Set the print options for a number of sheets at once.

√   Change a setting that applies to all the sheets in the View tab of the Options dialog box (Tools menu). (We discuss how to customize views in Excel in Chapter 5, "Degunking Office's Common Features.")

√ Apply formatting to selected cells in the sheets.

√ Unhide rows and/or columns simultaneously.

√ Type and/or insert data or formulas at the same cell address in all grouped sheets.

To group all sheets in a workbook, select the first sheet tab, hold down the Shift key, and click the last sheet tab. Alternately, you can right-click a sheet tab and choose Select All Sheets from the context menu. You know sheets are grouped when the sheet tabs appear selected as shown in Figure 7-2a. Sheets stay grouped until you click an individual sheet tab. If you'd like to ungroup the sheets but do not want to switch your view to another sheet, hold down the Shift key and click the active sheet tab.

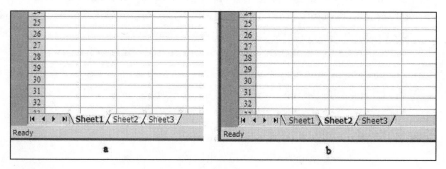

Figure 7-2

(a)The three sheets are grouped, and (b) Sheet2 is the active sheet.

TIP: To group sheets that are next to each other, hold down the Shift key and click the desired sheet tabs. To group nonadjacent sheets, hold down the Ctrl key and click each sheet tab to add it to the group.

With the sheets grouped, you can enter data or formatting into one sheet and it will automatically appear at the exact same cell address in the other selected sheets.

Change the Default Number of Sheets in a New Workbook

The number of sheets that an Excel workbook can hold is limited only by the memory available on your PC. If you work in Excel a lot, you might find that your typical projects require more sheets in a workbook than the default three provided. To change the default number of sheets in a new workbook, follow these steps:

1. Select Options on the Tools menu.

2. In the General tab of the Options dialog box, use the up and down arrows to select a number for the Sheets in New Workbook option, shown in Figure 7-3.

3. Click OK.

New Excel workbooks that you create from now on by default will contain the number of sheets you entered.

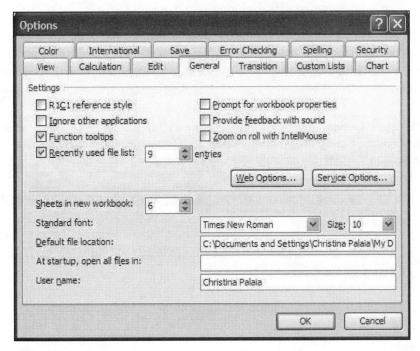

Figure 7-3

Set the default number of sheets in new workbooks in the General tab of the Options dialog box.

TIP: As you can see from Figure 7-3, you can set several other default behaviors in the General tab of the Options dialog box, including the default font and size for text, how many file names appear in the File menu Most Recently Used list, and whether you want to enable zoom on roll if you have a roller ball on your mouse.

View Two Sheets Simultaneously

There are times when you want to be able to view two sheets in the same workbook side by side so you can compare data. Follow these steps to be able to see two sheets at the same time:

1. Close all workbooks except the one that contains the sheets you want to see.

2. Select New Window on the Window menu; this opens a second instance of the active workbook. You'll see an icon representing the second instance appear on the Windows Taskbar. The instances are numbered to help you keep track.

3. In the first workbook instance, select the first sheet you want to see. In the second workbook instance, select the second sheet you want to see.

4. Select Arrange on the Window menu and choose how you'd like the windows arranged: Tiled, Horizontal, Vertical, or Cascade. Click OK.

Figure 7-4 shows the sheets arranged horizontally. Note that any change you make to the data in one instance is automatically made in all instances of the workbook. To restore normal view, click the Maximize button in the upper-right corner of the active worksheet and then close either instance of the workbook.

TIP: You can view more than two worksheets at once. Simply open the desired sheets and arrange them using the preceding steps. To view multiple workbooks simultaneously, open the target workbooks and choose Arrange on the Window menu.

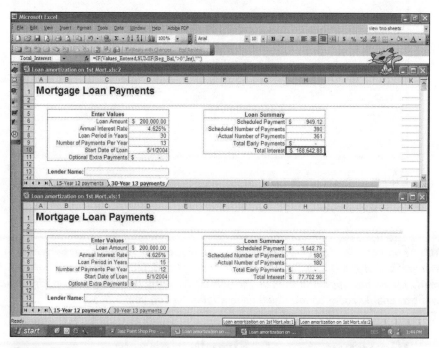

Figure 7-4

You can view two sheets simultaneously. Notice that the workbook instance names are numbered in the Windows Taskbar ScreenTips.

View Multiple Formulas Simultaneously

As you know, you enter a formula into a worksheet cell, and when data is available, the formula calculates and the results are displayed in the cell. To see the underlying formula, you must click the cell so that the formula is displayed in the formula bar. Sometimes, however, you might need to see more than one formula displayed simultaneously and the formula bar cannot accommodate you. To see the underlying formulas in all cells at once, follow these steps:

1. Select Options on the Tools menu.

2. In the View tab of the Options dialog box, enable the Formulas option in the Window Options section as shown in Figure 7-5. Click OK.

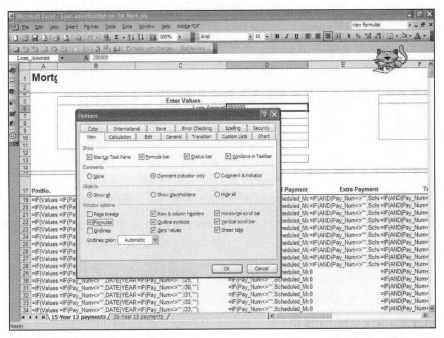

Figure 7-5

In the View tab of the Options dialog box, you can choose to display all the underlying formulas.

A handy way of switching views instead of using the View tab is to toggle back and forth between the formulas view and the results view by pressing Ctrl+' (accent key located above the Tab key).

TIP: We discuss other handy keyboard shortcuts in Chapter 5, "Degunking Office's Common Features."

Copy Formatting from Cell to Cell

Each cell in a worksheet contains formatting. If you have not applied formatting, such as a number style, alignment, or font attributes, the default formatting is applied. You can copy formatting between cells by using the Format Painter tool, which is represented by the paint brush button on the Standard toolbar. Follow these steps:

1. Select the cell with the formatting you want to copy; then double-click the Format Painter button.

2. Click cells to which you want to apply the formatting.

3. Click the Format Painter button to turn it off.

TIP: If the Format Painter button does not appear on the Standard toolbar, you can make it show by clicking Toolbar Options on the Standard toolbar and selecting it from the list of extra buttons shown.

Create Styles Based on Cell Contents

Styles in Excel are collections of formatting options, such as font style, alignment, and number style, bundled into one handy setting. Styles enable you to apply standard formatting to like data with just the click of a button. It's easy to create styles, too, by basing them on the contents of a cell that already displays the desired formatting. Using styles will save you gobs of formatting time!

To save yourself from having to use a series of menu items and dialog boxes when working with styles, add the Style drop-down list to the Formatting toolbar by following these steps:

1. Click the Toolbar Options button on the Formatting toolbar, and then select Add or Remove Buttons, Customize from the submenus.

2. In the Commands tab of the Customize dialog box, choose Format from the Categories list.

3. Click the Style text box icon and drag it to the Formatting toolbar. An I-beam cursor will appear to help you place the new button precisely where you want it.

4. Click Close.

To create a style based on the contents of a cell, format the cell as you wish, enter a name for the style in the Style box on the Formatting toolbar, and then press Enter. In Figure 7-6, you can see that the style name is Loan Rate. Any data styled thereafter as Loan Rate will match the formatting of the active cell and will include three decimal places and the percent sign. To apply a style to another cell or range of cells, select the cells and then choose the style from the Style list.

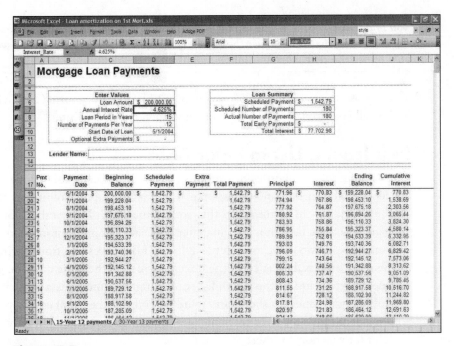

Figure 7-6
Create a style based on the formatting applied to a specific cell.

TIP: *You can use AutoFormat to apply a formatting effect to a range of cells. Select the range of cells, and then choose AutoFormat on the Format menu. Choose one of the preconfigured formats for the range. If you want to apply only part of a format, click the Options button and uncheck the options you do not want applied.*

Enable Word Wrapping in Cells

Although Excel is not meant to contain large strings of text, sometimes it is necessary to add cell labels or other textual material. Unless you adjust column width to accommodate the length of the text string, Excel default settings make longer lines of text difficult to read because they are not completely displayed, especially when adjacent cells contain data. One useful solution is to enable word wrapping in cells so that the text adjusts itself to the column width. As you change column width, the text wrapping adjusts automatically, as does the row height. To wrap text in cells, follow these steps:

1. Select the cells for which you want to enable word wrapping.

2. Choose Cells on the Format menu.

3. In the Alignment tab of the Format Cells dialog box, enable the Wrap Text option in the Text Controls section. Then click OK.

TIP: If you find that all of the wrapped text is not visible, it might be because a specific row height is set for that cell. Adjust the row height setting or adjust the column width to be able to see the text.

You can also insert a line break in a cell by entering a hard return. Click where in the cell you want to start a new line and then press Alt+Enter.

Pick from a List to Enter Data

Many workbooks contain large amounts of data, and usually this information has to be typed in by hand—row upon row, column upon column. Is there anything that can help automate this wearisome task? Why, yes! If you are entering repetitive data in a column, after you have entered unique information into at least two cells, you can use a shortcut that saves you from having to retype those entries thereafter. In the next blank cell in the same column, press Alt+down arrow and a drop-down list containing the unique data elements in the column will appear, as shown in Figure 7-7. Notice the list of entry options is even alphabetized for your convenience! You can choose from this list which piece of information to insert.

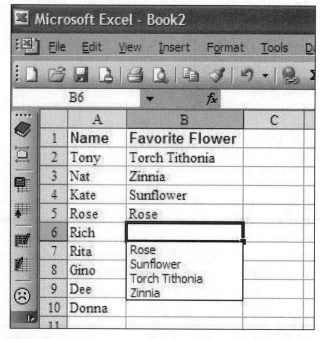

Figure 7-7

Excel saves you key strokes during data entry by providing a drop-down list of entry options.

TIP: The Excel AutoComplete feature also helps you save keystrokes. If the data you begin typing into a cell closely matches the contents of another cell in that column, Excel offers to fill in the rest of the word for you. To accept, press Enter or select another cell. To reject the default offering, just keep typing. The trick to getting the AutoComplete feature to work is to select the next blank cell in a column of entries. If you attempt to enter data into a cell separated from the previous data by one or more blank cells, AutoComplete will not activate.

Calculate Values Quickly Using the Status Bar Shortcut

Frequently, when you just need the sum or the average of a couple of cells, your first inclination might be to break out the calculator and do the calculation by hand. But hold on; you don't need a calculator when you work with Excel. You can get the answer quickly by using a feature of the status bar, and the best part is you don't have to enter a specific formula or function to do so. Select two or more cells containing numerical data and right-click the status bar at the bottom of the screen. Choose which operation to perform from the context menu. The result appears in the status bar as shown in Figure 7-8.

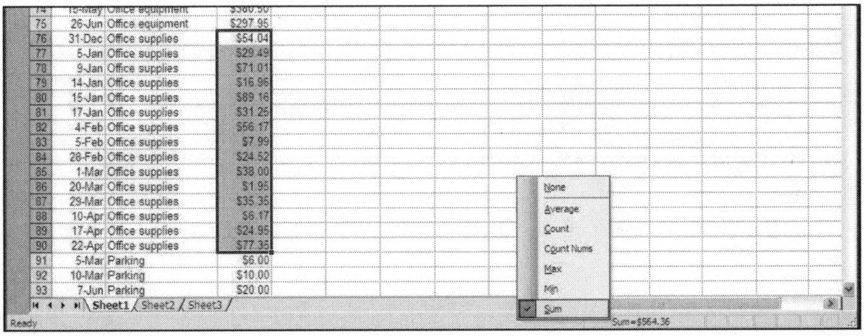

Figure 7-8
Perform a quick calculation using the status bar context menu.

Change Cell Selection Behavior

Oftentimes, when you finish working in a cell and press Enter to finalize the data, you remain in the active cell. You must use the Tab key to move to an adjacent cell or the up and down arrows to move within a column. You can, however, choose whether pressing the Enter key automatically moves you one cell to the right, to the left, up, or down by following these steps:

1. Choose Options from the Tools menu.

2. In the Edit tab of the Options dialog box, enable the Move Selection after Enter option, and then use the drop-down menu to choose Down, Right, Up, or Left, as shown in Figure 7-9.

3. Click OK.

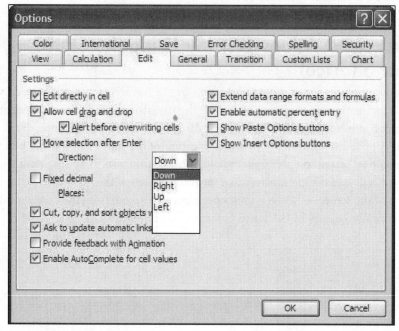

Figure 7-9
Set the behavior for the Enter key in the Edit tab of the Options dialog box.

Customizing this feature can save you a lot of time. For instance, it can save you time if you typically enter columns of data at one time and you enable the Move Selection after Enter Down option.

Use AutoSave and AutoRecover

Each Office application comes with built-in features to help protect your data from loss after an application failure or other disaster. In versions earlier than Excel 2002, this feature is called AutoSave; in later versions, the AutoRecover feature replaces the AutoSave add-in. Both tools periodically save changes you make as you work in an Excel workbook by writing them directly to the open workbook file. In earlier versions, AutoSave is not enabled upon installation, so you must manually turn it on by following these steps:

1. On the Tools menu, select Add-Ins.
2. In the Add-Ins dialog box, select the check box for AutoSave Add-in and then click OK.

You can modify the way AutoSave works, including how often it saves, which workbooks it saves, and whether it prompts you first before performing an automatic save. To customize AutoSave, follow these steps:

1. After enabling AutoSave, select AutoSave on the Tools menu.
2. In the AutoSave dialog box, select the AutoSave options you would like to enable, and then click OK.

AutoSave automatically saves every 10 minutes to the default location C:\ Documents and Settings*username*\Local Settings\Temp. You can distinguish Excel temp files from other temp files saved there by other applications because Excel files are saved as *xx*.tmp, where *xx* is a number, as in 28.tmp.

In Excel 2002 and Excel 2003, AutoRecover is similar to Word's AutoRecover feature. It automatically saves changes made to a workbook at an interval set by you (the default is 10 minutes). You can modify the way AutoRecover works, including how often it saves and where it saves the recover files, by following these steps:

1. Select Options on the Tools menu.
2. In the Save tab of the Options dialog box, enable the Save AutoRecover Info Every option, and then use the up and down arrows to set an AutoRecover save interval as shown in Figure 7-10. A setting of 10 minutes is usually adequate.
3. Review the AutoRecover Save Location information to be sure it suits you, and then click OK.

TIP: Remember, enabling AutoRecover is no substitute for saving your work often using Save on the Standard toolbar.

The next time Excel starts after an application crash or whatever caused it to shut down unexpectedly before you had a chance to save your work, it will open the most recent recover file. Excel recover files have wacky names such as ~ar*xxxx*.xar, where *xxxx* is a string of random letters and numbers that Excel calculates using an internal algorithm. You can choose to save the recover file using the same name as the original workbook, which replaces the original workbook, or you can choose a new name. If you close the recover file without saving it, it is deleted. Excel avoids clogging up the designated recover file save location by deleting recover files when they are no longer needed, for instance,

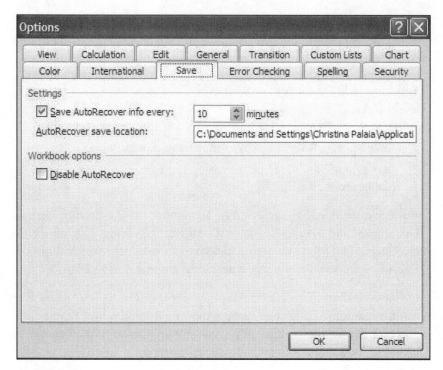

Figure 7-10
Enable AutoRecover and set the save interval and location in the Save tab of the Options dialog box.

when you manually save a workbook, close the workbook, or close Excel.

TIP: *We discuss other ways to protect your Excel data, including applying protection and removing metadata, in Chapter 11, "Securing Office."*

Use Functions to Degunk Your Formulas

If you didn't use formulas and functions in your Excel worksheets, they'd be nothing more than glorified Word tables. The awesome power of Excel shines through when you write formulas and use built-in functions to manipulate your data. A formula, as you know, instructs Excel to perform a mathematical calculation. All formulas begin with the equal sign, as in =2+6. (Notice that there are no spaces placed around the math operators.) The real bonus is that instead of using plain numbers in a formula, as you would on a regular ol' calculator, you can use cell references to perform the calculation on the contents of a cell or cells. When cell contents change, so will the results of the formula calculation.

One limitation with formulas is that you must use references to individual cells, not cell ranges, to specify the cells on which to perform operations. If you want to calculate the sum of the numbers in cells A2, A3, A4, and A5, you write the formula as =A2+A3+A4+A5. For long lists of numbers or complicated calculations, writing formulas in longhand can get gunked up and frustrating. This is where functions come in to save the day by degunking your formulas.

Functions are special words, such as SUM or AVERAGE, to which Excel has assigned a particular math operation. They are shorthand substitutes for performing longhand math operations. Again, all functions begin with an equal sign followed by the name of the function and then a set of parentheses containing the function's arguments or the instructions on how to perform the function and/or on which cells. Functions can have multiple arguments and can refer to ranges of cells, as in =MIN(A2:A5), which calculates the minimum value in cells A2, A3, A4, and A5. Even functions that do not need arguments must be followed by a set of empty parentheses; it's a syntax convention.

Don't shy away from using functions because you think they are too complicated. They can save you enormous amounts of time as well as simplify formula writing. Using functions means you don't have to reinvent the wheel every time you want to perform a complex math calculation. Excel provides plenty of help for finding just the right function to perform the calculation you want— and there's bound to be a built-in function that'll do exactly what you need done. On the Insert menu, choose Function. In the Insert Function dialog box, you can simply type a brief description of what you want to do and Excel will offer suggestions on which functions might work. Or click the Help on This Function link to read the Help file on the function's functionality. The Insert Function dialog box can even help you prepare arguments for the function in the correct format.

There are several ways you can enter functions. Pick the one that is most efficient for you:

√   Type the function and arguments into the formula bar.

√   Type the function and arguments into a cell.

√   Use the Insert Function dialog box.

√   Use voice command mode.

√   Type an equal sign (=) into a cell and then use the drop-down menu in the Name box (also known as the active cell indicator, see Figure 7-1) to choose a function (as shown in Figure 7-11).

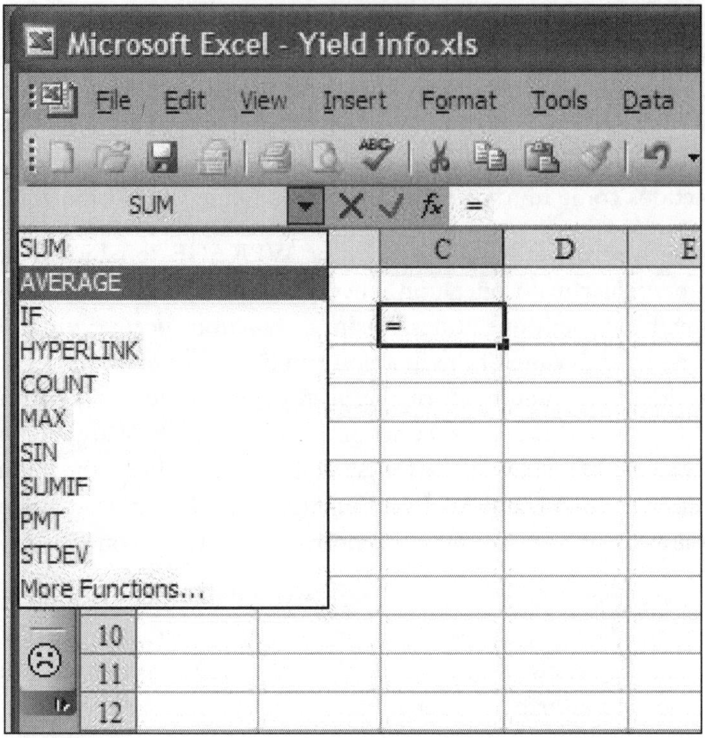

Figure 7-11
Use the Name drop-down list to quickly choose a function.

Use Named Ranges in Functions

Functions allow you to refer to ranges of cells in the function arguments. To make the purpose of a function even more clear, you can use descriptive names that you have assigned to ranges of cells. It's easier to understand what =AVERAGE(QuarterlySales) means as opposed to =AVERAGE(B2:B20). A *name* in Excel is a descriptive string of characters that you can use to refer to the contents of a cell, a range of cells, a constant, or even a formula. There are two ways you can create a named range of cells:

√   Select the range you want to name and type a name in the Name box.

√   Convert row and column labels to names.

To create a name for a range of cells, follow these steps:

1.   Select a cell or group of cells (hold down the Ctrl key to select nonadjacent cells).

2.   Click the Name box at the left end of the formula bar, and type a name in the box.

3.   Press Enter.

To convert existing row or column labels to names, follow these steps:

1. Select the range of cells you want to name, including the row or column labels.

2. Choose Name on the Insert menu, and then click Create on the submenu.

3. In the Create Names box, select the location that contains the label you want to use, and then click OK.

Now you can use these names in functions to simplify formula construction and ease readability of your worksheet. You can also edit or delete named ranges by selecting Name on the Insert menu and choosing Define on the submenu. But beware: if you remove a name, you'll have to correct the functions that use the name because they will display an error.

TIP: Tell Excel to read the label. By default, Excel doesn't recognize labels in formulas. Select Options on the Tools menu, and in the Calculation tab, enable the Accept Labels in Formulas option. Now Excel will recognize labels used in a formula to keep you from having to enter explicit cell references. When you use a relative reference like this, the reference updates itself when the formula is copied to another cell.

Create 3D Ranges

Named ranges can even become three-dimensional, which means they refer to cells contained in other worksheets. This is an easy way to allow your data to remain modularized in separate sheets but to perform calculations on the data and present a consolidated summary in one sheet. It's easy to create a 3D range reference:

1. Select Name from the Insert menu, and then click Define.

2. In the Names in Workbook box in the Define Name dialog box, type a name.

3. Clear the Refers To box by selecting the text there and pressing Backspace.

4. In the Refers To box, click the tab of the first worksheet to be referenced and hold down the Shift key as you click the last worksheet to be referenced.

5. Hold down the Ctrl key as you click the cells in each sheet that you want to be included in the range. Click OK.

---

*TIP: To refer to a cell in a different worksheet in a function or formula, simply precede the cell reference with the name of the sheet and an exclamation point, as in **SheetName!A2**, where **SheetName** stands for the name of the sheet containing the target cell.*

Use Workspace Files

When you're in the middle of a project, it's great to be able to leave everything out on your desk while you rush to lunch and come back later to find all as you left it. Excel offers a feature that enables you to save the screen arrangement when you work with a specific set of workbooks so you can later jump back into work without a lot of setup hassle. To open a group of workbooks in one step and find them exactly as you left them last time, you can create a workspace file. A *workspace file* contains information about which workbooks to open, where they are located, and the size and position of their windows on the screen. The workspace file does not contain the workbooks themselves, however.

To create a workspace file, follow these steps:

1. Open all the workbooks you want to include in the workspace. (If you work in a networked environment and plan to distribute the workspace file to other users, make sure all the workbook files are available on a shared network drive.)

2. Arrange each workbook as you want it to appear when you open the workspace, including which worksheets are displayed and whether they are tiled on-screen.

3. Select Save Workspace on the File menu, choose a save location for the workspace file, and then click Save. The default name Excel gives the workspace file is Resume.xlw (as in *begin again,* not *résumé!*). See Figure 7-12. You can certainly rename the file if you like.

TIP: The workbook names and folder locations are saved in the workspace file. If you move the underlying files to another location, Excel will not be able to find them to open the workspace. The best strategy is to save the workspace file and the workbook files it references in the same folder if possible.

Next time you want to open that group of workbooks, select Open on the File menu and choose the XLW file from its saved location.

GunkBuster's Notebook: Worksheet Design Best Practices

You'll have greater success working in Excel—and help it run more efficiently—if you follow a few practical layout and design principles. Thinking about sheet design ahead of time instead of actually jumping right in can save you much time and frustration and can increase the effectiveness and readability of your Excel files. Before you format the first cell or import a single piece of

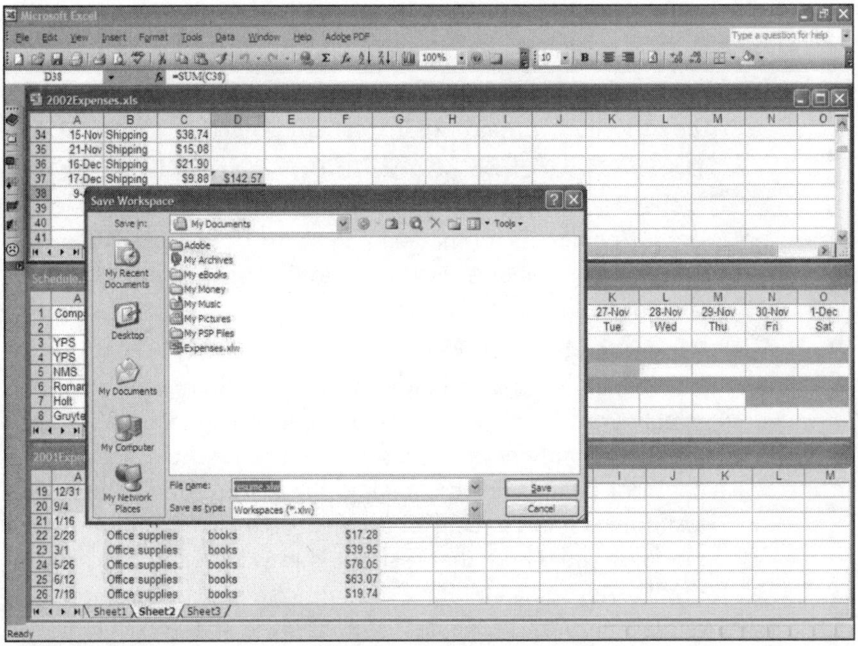

Figure 7-12

Save a bunch of open workbooks as a workspace file.

data, plan how you will make your workbooks and sheets ultimately useful by considering the following design best practices:

√ **Plan the sheet design thoroughly.** The number one rule when creating a spreadsheet is to start with the end in mind and never assume you won't need to add more data or formulas later. Chances are you will. To make a good and functional spreadsheet, you'll spend about 80 percent of your time planning and 20 percent implementing the design.

√ **Consider your audience.** Will you be sharing the sheet with others, either in print form or electronically? If so, you might make an extra effort to format the data to ease readability, to label rows and columns sufficiently, and to add comments where further explanation is needed. You can create various summary views and reports to make the data more meaningful for the target audience. On the other hand, if the sheet is strictly for your own reference, you might not need to spend as much time on making the presentation pretty, but do be sure that everything is clearly labeled and documented so that you don't get confused later. Is it necessary to present all of the data, or can a summary view or particular report convey the idea to the audience? You can use the outlining feature to collapse views to help emphasize the salient points.

√ **Decide how data should be arranged in a sheet.** Generally, it's best to put the more plentiful data in rows and use columns for the less-numerous data type. Place headings in columns and arrange the appropriate data beneath in rows.

√ **Modularize your data.** Break down data into discrete bits, which helps Excel features function more efficiently and effectively. For instance, instead of inserting people's names into a column where each cell contains a whole name, consider putting first names into the cells of one column and last names into the cells of another column. The more modular your data, the easier it is to work with. Similarly, don't try to squish all the data into one sheet. Break out related data and formulas into separate sheets, which allows you to reuse chunks of data more easily.

√ **Format data to ease readability.** Place column headings in row 1 and begin inserting data in row 2. Apply formatting to row and column labels (such as bold) to help Excel distinguish them from data during sorts and report generation. Place the sheet heading or report title in the header, not in one of the data rows. Format decimal points to align. Place subtotals in separate columns. Color-code various elements, such as sheet background, sheet tab, specific cells, and text, to distinguish them. Avoid repeating elements throughout a column or row to reduce visual clutter; for instance, place the dollar sign or the percent sign in only the top cell in a column of monetary values or percentages. Sort data as often as possible, which not only improves readability but enables built-in functions to operate more efficiently.

√ **Make important data stand out.** Consider using conditional formatting (choose Conditional Formatting on the Format menu) to format a cell depending on its contents. Use charts and graphs to help summarize data so reviewers can easily understand your data results. Consider WordArt or AutoShapes to emphasize specific cell contents. But remember, avoid letting the formatting distract from the content. Use special features and formatting only if they enhance your presentation of data, not detract from it.

√ **Avoid blanks.** Don't include leading or trailing spaces in a cell because they affect sorting and searching functions. Try to keep blank cells from interrupting columns or rows of data in the data area of a worksheet. Often, when Excel encounters a blank, it thinks it's reached the end of the data range and will calculate mistakenly using the abbreviated data set. If you insert a blank row or column to indicate a separation or the end of a range, consider instead placing the new range in a new sheet to modularize the data.

√ **Consider what the data will look like in print.** Decide whether you'll print using landscape or portrait orientation, and insert data into the sheet accordingly. For large sheets that print on many separate pages, repeating row and column labels are necessities.

Check whether you can improve your worksheets beyond the recommendations given here by looking at them with a fresh eye. Can you reorganize columns into a more logical order? Are totals and results sufficiently labeled? Have you included enough documentation to aid new users or readers?

Use Templates to Create Blueprints for Your New Files

Templates are like sewing patterns. You can use them to fashion new workbooks and worksheets based on a standardized set of previously configured options. Excel templates use the .xlt file extension. There are two types of templates in Excel: workbook templates and worksheet templates. A *workbook template* contains the formulas, styles, macros, default text, sheets, and other formatting you want to appear in new workbooks based on that template. A *worksheet template* contains the styles, formatting, default text, and other items you want to appear in new sheets added to a workbook. In Excel, it's optional whether you base a new workbook or sheet on a template, not mandatory, as it is in Word.

In Excel, you can create your own templates or download preconfigured ones from the Microsoft Office Online Templates Web site at **http://office.microsoft.com/ en-us/templates/default.aspx**. If you choose to create your own templates, you can make one the default workbook template by naming it Book.xlt and storing it in the XLStart folder. Then every new workbook you create will be based on the settings included in the Book.xlt template. Similarly, you can create a default worksheet template by naming it Sheet.xlt and storing it in the XLStart folder. When you choose to insert a new sheet in a workbook by choosing Worksheet on the Insert menu, the sheet will be based on the Sheet.xlt template. You can save other custom templates in the Templates folder or the alternate startup folder to make them available when you run Excel.

Where Have All the Templates Gone?

Excel stores templates in three places: the XLStart folder, the Templates folder, and any alternate startup folder you specify. The main XLStart folder is usually located at C:\Program Files\Microsoft Office\Office11\XLStart; the path might be slightly different depending on the version of Excel you are using. When you want to store a template or add an item to the XLStart folder, however, use the version of the folder contained in your user profile at C:\Documents and Settings*username*\Application Data\Microsoft\Excel\XLStart. Any workbook, workspace file, or template that you place in this XLStart folder is automatically opened when you are logged on and start Excel.

TIP: *If you access the XLStart folder through the Save As dialog box, the path is C:\Documents and Settings\username\Application Data\Microsoft\Excel\XLStart.*

The Templates folder is usually located at C:\Documents and Settings*username*\Application Data\Microsoft\Templates. Excel template files that you store in this folder are available when you run Excel. The Templates folder is the default location where Office applications store, well, templates. Rather than specify a different save location, use the Templates folder to keep all your custom templates, Excel and otherwise, organized and easily accessible.

You can also specify an alternate startup folder where you can store Excel files and templates that you want Excel to open upon startup. After it checks the XLStart folder, Excel will check the alternate startup folder, if you have named one. Beware, though. Excel attempts to open all files stored in XLStart and the alternate startup folder, so be sure you store only Excel-compatible files in these locations or you might generate an error message and Excel will fail to open.

To set an alternate startup folder, follow these steps:

1. Select Options on the Tools menu.
2. In the General tab in the Options dialog box, type the path pointing to the desired folder in the "At startup, open all files in" text box as shown in Figure 7-13.
3. Click OK.

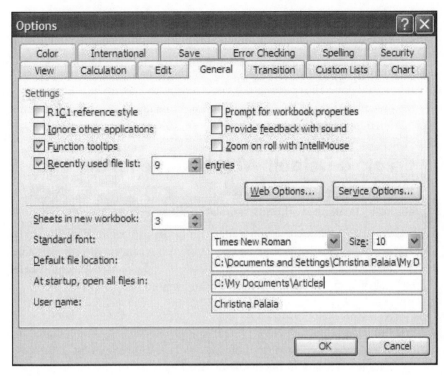

Figure 7-13
Specify the path name of the alternate startup folder in the General tab of the Options dialog box.

Templates Hold a Lot of Stuff

To save yourself the hassle of customizing new workbooks to fit your specs, try to take full advantage of saving settings and formatting in templates. You can save so many different things in Excel templates, including the following:

√ Cell and sheet formats that you set by using the commands on the Format menu.

√ Page formats and print area settings for each sheet.

√ Cell styles.

√ The number and type of sheets in a workbook.

√ Protected and hidden areas of the workbook. For example, you can hide sheets, rows, and columns and prevent changes to worksheet cells.

√ Text, data, graphics, and formulas, including the following:

   √ Text you want to repeat in each new workbook or worksheet, such as page headers and row and column labels

   √ Data, graphics, links, formulas, charts, and other information you want each new workbook or worksheet to contain

√   Toolbars.

√   Macros.

√   Calculation and view settings configured by using the Options dialog box.

If you find yourself repeating the same actions to customize a file just so, check the preceding list to see whether you might be able to include that configuration change in a template file.

Create a Default Workbook Template and Worksheet Template

To create a default workbook template, follow these steps:

1.   Open a workbook that you want to use as the pattern for all new workbooks, or create a new workbook and configure it as a pattern. Include data, formulas, formatting, styles, images, and default text (see the section "Templates Hold a Lot of Stuff" for a list of items that can be saved in a template).

2.   Choose Save As on the File menu.

3.   In the File Name box, type **book**.

4.   Select Template (*.xlt) from the Save as Type drop-down list. This adds the .xlt file extension to the file name. See Figure 7-14.

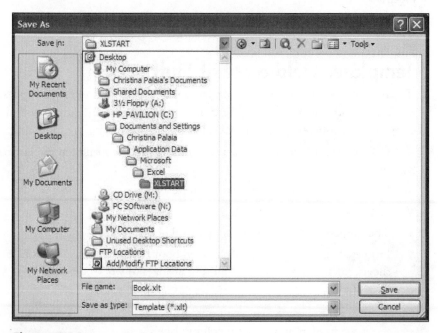

Figure 7-14

Name the default workbook template Book.xlt.

5. By default, Excel will offer to save this template in the Templates folder. Instead, navigate to the XLStart folder at C:\Documents and Settings*username*\Application Data\Microsoft\Excel\XLStart. Click Save.

From now on, whenever you create a new workbook by choosing New on the File menu or clicking the New button on the Standard toolbar, that new file will be based on the Book.xlt template.

TIP: *Be aware that you cannot create an Excel template just by adding the .xlt file extension to a valid file name. You must choose Template (*.xlt) from the Save as Type drop-down list to apply the extension and save the file as a valid template.*

To create a default sheet template, configure a worksheet exactly as you want new worksheets based on this template to appear. Include styles, formatting, default text and images, and anything else necessary. Then follow the Save As procedure in the preceding steps, except name this template Sheet.xlt and store it in the XLStart folder. New sheets you insert into workbooks are thereafter based on this sheet template.

GunkBuster's Notebook: How Are Excel Templates Different from Word Templates?

In Word, when you create a document, it must have at least one template attached to it (Normal.dot, by default), and multiple templates could potentially also be attached. In Excel, no default template exists (until you create one), and Excel workbooks and sheets need not have a template attached to run.

In Word, changing a template (redefining a style, for example) affects all documents to which the template is attached. In Excel, once a workbook is created from a template, no persistent link is maintained between the two, and changing one does not affect the other.

Use Excel for Simple Databases

Mention the word *database* and most people start to squirm as thoughts of tables filled with endless amounts of data, convoluted formulas, and a whole bunch of techy jargon fill their heads. A database is simply an information storage framework that contains data separated into discrete sets and organized for easy access and manipulation. Perhaps the preceding stereotypes fit other more complicated database systems, but Excel is one of the least expensive, easy-to-use, and user-friendly database systems around.

As a database system, Excel has only two limitations—which might turn out to not even be factors for you. First, only one user at a time can enter data into the database as opposed to multiple-user data entry available in larger, networked database systems. And second, Excel worksheets contain a limited amount of space—16,777,216 cells—so if you have more data elements than that, you might run out of room. Otherwise, Excel is a wonderful tool for small databases.

TIP: With Excel, you can create flat-file databases, which contain a single table and are two-dimensional. If you need to link multiple database tables or have huge amounts of data to organize, consider using a product like Microsoft Access.

First, you must enable Excel to recognize a particular data set or range of cells as a database. You do this by surrounding the target cells by an empty row and empty column. Check to see whether Excel recognizes your data as a database by choosing Go To on the Edit menu, clicking the Special button, and then selecting Current Region in the Go To Special dialog box. Click OK. The highlighted region is the database. When Excel recognizes a region as a database, you can then perform many of the functions contained on the Data menu.

TIP: In a database, it is essential that headings and labels be contained in a single row and that they be formatted differently from the rest of the data. If not, Excel will attempt to perform calculations on them.

Separate your data as much as possible into separate fields so that you can sort and filter it easily later. Also, remember to use single words, with no spaces, for field names. If you need to use more than one word to make a field name more meaningful, use PascalCase, which is when you smash together two or more words and use capital letters to improve readability, as in QuarterlySales or FirstName, LastName.

You can enter data into a database in one of two ways: directly by typing in cells or indirectly by using forms. *Forms* are preconfigured data entry files that help you input data (select Form on the Data menu). For instance, you can create a form in which you simply fill in the blanks that correspond to database column headings to populate rows with data.

Once data is entered, you can analyze it in myriad ways using Excel's built-in functions. Unlike other database systems, there is no need to extract data from Excel databases using complicated queries. Simply choose commands from the Data menu and then generate a report based on the results. It couldn't be simpler!

Summing Up

This chapter is mostly about saving you time and mouse clicks. Excel, for all its functionality, manages to keep from collecting a lot of gunk; even so, a few tweaks here and there can get it running even more efficiently. You can perform at least 10 simple configuration changes to increase your productivity. We showed you how to enable the built-in automatic save feature to keep from losing your data and how to use templates to your best advantage. Workspace files rescue you from a lot of setup and cleanup hassles by enabling you to open and save arranged groups of workbooks in one click. And you also learned several handy worksheet design principles, as well as how Excel can be used as a simple database creation and manipulation tool.

Degunking Microsoft PowerPoint

Degunking Checklist:

√   Tweak PowerPoint in 10 easy ways so you can use it more efficiently.

√   Apply design templates to standardize presentation appearance.

√   Use the slide-title master pair to make fast and global changes.

√   Discover why color schemes should be coordinated.

√   Make sure animations don't detract from content.

√   Discover presentation creation best practices.

√   Learn the different ways that presentations can be published.

P owerPoint is a high-visibility application. You use PowerPoint when you're giving a talk in front of your boss or your company's management team, or important clients, or your sales force, or your employees. It's important that your presentations are clear, clean, and gunk-free. There's nothing worse than having a PowerPoint presentation freeze up, discovering that your graphics aren't loading, or finding out that you've lost your fonts just before you present. What a nightmare! This chapter is intended to make sure that your PowerPoint presentations are constructed well and are as gunk-free as possible—minimizing the chance that they'll crash at the worst possible moment.

PowerPoint is a great tool that enables you to animate slides, create charts, insert sounds, play movies, and prepare for a presentation in an easy-to-navigate and fully featured application. You can compile presentations with automated narration, print out handouts for your audience, and publish a presentation on the Web. Developing presentation materials in PowerPoint can be many times faster than developing materials in Word because PowerPoint helps you streamline your thoughts with bullets, lists, charts, and pictures, whereas Word begs for complete sentences. Remember, most slides need to be prepared only with "talking points," and you provide the explanation of those points in your presentation. PowerPoint helps you do this.

Luckily, PowerPoint manages to stay relatively gunk-free. However, there are always ways you can increase efficiency by changing application-level settings and learning how to use the available features more effectively—and that's what we show you in this chapter. We'll give you our top-10 recommendations for quick degunking. We'll discuss the importance of templates and how to streamline presentation creation by using slide and title masters, color schemes, and animation effects. We'll then show you how to degunk presentation creation, and we'll include a section on design best practices. Next we'll discuss the various presentation methods. With this information under your belt, you can let PowerPoint make you a star at your next presentation.

Top-10 Changes to Make

PowerPoint is a specialized application and stays focused on the task at hand—how to make your presentations shine. You can, however, tweak the following 10 settings to make PowerPoint run even more efficiently:

1. Turn off fast saves.
2. Trim picture files.
3. Embed only the fonts you need.
4. Reduce the number of undos available.

5. Set the AutoRecover interval.

6. Turn off Automatic Layout for inserted objects.

7. Turn off background printing.

8. Review slide shows in a mini window.

9. Automatically start presentations in slide show view.

10. Optimize presentation performance.

Turn Off Fast Saves

In versions of PowerPoint earlier than PowerPoint 2002, fast saves are known to cause file corruption in certain circumstances. And although fast saves can save changes very quickly by appending only changes made during the current work session to the end of the existing file, they also increase file size very quickly because extra bytes of information are continually added to a file, making it grow and grow and increasing the likelihood of introducing problems. Fast saves seem to be a leftover feature from a time long ago when hard disks were small, processors were slow, and PowerPoint files were enormous; waiting for a full save to complete would disrupt your work flow. Turning off fast saves forces PowerPoint to remove the changes piled up at the end of a file the next time you save using Save or Save As on the File menu and can save you a lot of headaches down the road. To turn off fast saves, follow these steps:

1. In PowerPoint, close all presentation files; then select Options on the Tools menu.

2. In the Save tab of the Options dialog box, disable the Allow Fast Saves option, and click OK.

Changing this setting with no PowerPoint files open causes it to apply to all presentations you create subsequently; if you disable fast saves in an open presentation file, the setting applies only to that presentation. To streamline a particular presentation file, after you disable fast saves, save the existing file under a new name and then delete the original version.

Trim Picture Files

Snappy presentations include images and pictures to break up the text and add interest. Keep in mind, though, that image files can quickly bloat the size of your presentation file, creating a huge amount of gunk in your presentation. What you thought was just a little JPG file all of a sudden added 2 megabytes (MB) to your presentation's file size. And if you're including a dozen or so pictures in your presentation, this important file could quickly get bogged down in lots of unnecessary gunk.

Every image file has a resolution setting that determines the number of pixels displayed by the monitor screen or projector. The higher the resolution, the larger the image file size. Multiple large image files can slow presentation display. It's best to be sure that your image files use a resolution that optimizes viewing but doesn't go overboard adding unnecessary detail (and size) to the file.

Choosing a Resolution Setting

But how do you decide which resolution setting to use for images included in your presentations? Consider that most laptop computers and slide projectors these days commonly use a maximum 1024×768 resolution. Using 1024×768 as the maximum resolution setting for images that will take up a whole slide works best in most situations. A higher resolution won't improve viewing simply because of the limitations of the output device. If the image will take up only half or one-quarter of the slide area, you can easily decrease the image resolution to save kilobits without sacrificing viewability. You can use a simple formula to decide on image resolution:

1. Use 1024×768 resolution as the base maximum full-slide resolution for images.

2. Multiply the number of horizontal pixels in the resolution setting by how much space the image will consume on the slide. For instance, for an image that will cover one-half the slide, multiply 1024 horizontal pixels by 0.5 (indicating half the slide area). The result is 512 horizontal pixels.

3. Then multiply the number of vertical pixels in the resolution setting by how much space the image will consume on a slide. The image in our example is to cover one-half of the slide, so multiply 768 vertical pixels by 0.5.

4. The resulting resolution, 512×384 in this case, is a maximum resolution that will enable the image to be viewed without unnecessary file bloat.

You can use image-editing software to resave images at a lower resolution, or you can use built-in PowerPoint features. If you are using a version of PowerPoint earlier than PowerPoint 2002, follow these steps to reduce image file size:

1. Click the image to select it.

2. Choose Copy on the Edit menu.

3. Choose Paste Special on the Edit menu.

4. In the Paste Special dialog box, choose Picture (JPEG) from the As list, and click OK.

5. Delete the original image.

TIP: You can choose Picture (PNG) from the As list in step 4 if the image contains fine lines and small details that you don't want to lose by using JPEG compression.

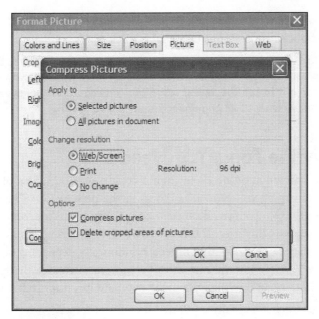

Figure 8-1

Choose how to compress images in the Compress Pictures
dialog box.

If you are using PowerPoint 2002 or later, a built-in feature can compress selected images for you. Follow these steps to compress an image:

1. Right-click the image, and select Format Picture from the context menu.

2. In the Picture tab of the Format Picture dialog box, click Compress.

3. In the Compress Pictures dialog box (see Figure 8-1), in the Apply To section, choose one of the following options:

   a. Choose Selected Pictures to compress only the selected image.

   b. Choose All Pictures in Document to compress all images included in the presentation. (If you choose this option, remember to review all of the compressed images in your presentation to be sure they are still easily viewable.)

4. In the Change Resolution section, choose one of the following options:

   a. Choose Web/Screen if your presentation will be viewed in electronic format.

   b. Choose Print if you will print the presentation.

5. In the Options section, select both the Compress Pictures and Delete Cropped Areas of Pictures options.

6. Click OK.

7. If the Compress Pictures warning box appears alerting you to the fact that compression might cause loss of picture quality, click Apply.

TIP: Slide images that contain a lot of detail might be more effective when displayed at a higher resolution. Experiment to see the lowest resolution setting that enables you to display such images clearly without adding unnecessary size to the file.

Embed Only the Fonts You Need

When the text in a presentation needs to look a certain way regardless of the computer used to display it, you can embed fonts in the presentation. This can ensure that basic fonts are not automatically substituted into your slides on computers that do not support the original fonts. Beware, though. Embedding fonts does increase presentation file size—sometimes astronomically, depending on the size of the font file. You can choose one of three ways to guarantee that your presentation text will remain unchanged no matter where it is displayed:

√   Use basic fonts, which are usually supported on any computer.

√   Package your presentation, which is described in Chapter 11, "Securing Office."

√   Embed fonts, which ensures that the proper font files travel with presentations.

Before you consider embedding a font, be sure there is not a built-in font that will work for what you want. More than 20 fonts come installed in most versions of Microsoft Office—surely you can find one that suits you. (Choose Font on the Format menu to see a list of fonts immediately available for use.) If not, consider packaging your presentation using either the Pack and Go or the Package for CD feature to include all files necessary to run the display; this will also protect your show from unauthorized tinkering. If neither of these options will work, attempt to embed only the font characters used in your presentation, not the whole font set (this is possible in PowerPoint 2003). You can embed any TrueType font. A TrueType font, designated by a double-T logo in the Font drop-down menu, is one that appears on-screen exactly as it will appear in printed form. What you see is what you get. To embed a TrueType font, follow these steps:

1. Be sure there are no license restrictions on the target font if it is not a Microsoft font.

2. Choose Options on the Tools menu.

3. In the Save tab of the Options dialog box, enable the Embed TrueType Fonts option (see Figure 8-2), and then do one of the following:

    a. Choose the Embed Characters in Use Only option to embed only specific characters.

    b. Choose Embed All Characters to embed a complete font set.

4. Click OK.

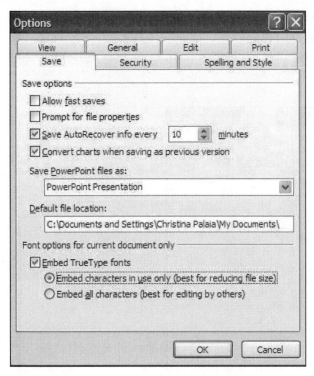

Figure 8-2
Choose whether you want to embed fonts in a presentation.

Notice that the font options apply only to the current document. If you plan to share your presentation with others and allow reviewers to make changes, it's best to embed the whole font set, even though this can increase file size enormously. Check the size of the font file before you embed it to be sure you can live with the results.

TIP: You can tell whether a font is TrueType, and hence whether you can choose to embed it, by looking in the Font dialog box. Select text or a text placeholder in an open presentation, and then choose Font on the Format menu. TrueType fonts have the TT TrueType icon next to them in the Font list.

Reduce the Number of Undos Available

Using the Undo command is a wonderful way to correct blunders during presentation creation—too bad more things in life don't have an Undo button! PowerPoint can enable an almost unlimited number of undos, but there's a trade-off: the more undos available, the higher the memory usage. Plus, high numbers of undos seem to confuse PowerPoint and you often won't get the results you expect by backtracking. To set the number of undos to a reasonable number, follow these steps:

1. Choose Options on the Tools menu.

2. In the Edit tab of the Options dialog box, use the up and down arrows to set the Maximum Number of Undos option as shown in Figure 8-3.

3. Click OK.

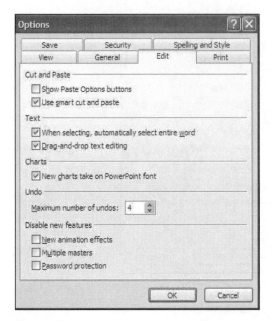

Figure 8-3

Limit the number of undos available to a reasonable number in the Edit tab of the Options dialog box.

Setting this to 4 or fewer seems like plenty—can you remember back further than that anyhow?

Set the AutoRecover Interval

For those times when the unavoidable happens—PowerPoint locks up or the electricity goes out and you are forced to close PowerPoint before you can save your file—it's good to know AutoRecover has got your back. When enabled, the AutoRecover feature automatically makes a background save of open PowerPoint files at a time interval that you set. To set the AutoRecover save interval, follow these steps:

1. Select Options on the Tools menu.

2. In the Save tab of the Options dialog box, enable the Save AutoRecover Info Every option if it is not already selected. Then use the up and down arrows to set a save interval as shown in Figure 8-4. A setting of 10 minutes

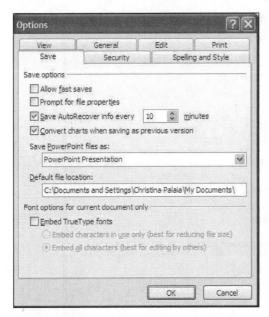

Figure 8-4
Set the AutoRecover interval in the Save tab of
the Options dialog box.

is usually adequate and provides a good balance between protecting your
work and optimizing application performance.

3. Click OK.

Remember, AutoRecover is not a substitute for regularly saving your work
using the Save and Save As commands.

Turn Off Automatic Layout for Inserted Objects

If you are using PowerPoint XP or later, the Automatic Layout for Inserted
Objects feature can cause no end of gunky little problems and seems to have no
practical value. So turn it off. Follow these steps:

1. In an open presentation, choose AutoCorrect Options on the Tools menu.

2. In the AutoFormat As You Type tab, clear the Automatic Layout for Inserted
   Objects option as shown in Figure 8-5.

3. Click OK.

Although this appears to be a presentation-specific setting, once you turn it off,
it will stay off.

Figure 8-5
Disable the Automatic Layout for Inserted Objects option in the
AutoCorrect dialog box.

Turn Off Background Printing

At first you might think that background printing, which enables you to continue working in a presentation while it prints, would save you time, but it
probably won't. Especially when printing image-heavy presentations, PowerPoint
returns control to you a little more quickly when background printing is turned
on, but because PowerPoint is sharing the processor with the printing process,
performance suffers all around. Overall, you'll realize several benefits by turning off background printing:

√ Presentations print faster.

√ You won't have to sit around waiting for PowerPoint to catch up to you
while you work in a presentation and a file prints in the background.

√ Your printouts will be higher quality because sometimes PowerPoint
misprints notes pages when background printing is turned on.

To turn off background printing, follow these steps:

1. Choose Options on the Tools menu.

2. In the Print tab of the Options dialog box, disable the Background Printing option as shown in Figure 8-6.

3. Click OK.

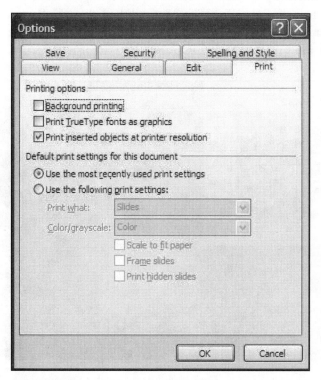

Figure 8-6
Turn off background printing to optimize both printing and editing.

TIP: You might also want to experiment with enabling the Print Inserted Objects at Printer Resolution option. This can improve your printouts of inserted objects such as pie charts.

Review Slide Shows in a Mini Window

How many times have you started a slide show for a practice run-through, only to notice some little detail that needs fixing? You have to stop the slide show, return to edit mode, make the fix, restart the slide show, and . . . darn! Something else needs a little touch-up.

Save yourself time and energy: hold down the Ctrl key while you click the Slide Show from Current Slide button in the lower left corner of the Slides or

Outline tab. PowerPoint displays your slide show in a small window rather than full screen (see Figure 8-7). Here's the good part: When you find something you'd like to change, click back in the main PowerPoint window. The mini show window minimizes itself into a button on the Windows Taskbar. Make your changes in the main PowerPoint window, and then click the PowerPoint Slide Show button on the Taskbar to resume your mini show right where you left off, with your most recent changes in place.

Figure 8-7
Display the slide show in a mini window to facilitate editing changes.

Automatically Start Presentations in Slide Show View

In Windows Explorer or My Computer, when you double-click a PowerPoint presentation file, PowerPoint opens the presentation in editing mode. Usually this is exactly what you want—unless, of course, you're about to give a presentation in front of an audience. Then it's a little tacky to make viewers sit there while PowerPoint launches, shows its splash screen, and finally opens your presentation in Normal view so you can start the real show.

It is so much more professional to launch directly into your presentation, and you can do that by saving your presentation as a PowerPoint Show, which uses the .pps file extension. Here's how to automatically start presentations in slide show view:

1. Open your presentation, and choose Save As on the File menu.

2. In the Save As dialog box, choose PowerPoint Show (*.pps) from the Save as Type drop-down list, and then click Save.

When you double-click a PowerPoint Show file in Explorer or My Computer, PowerPoint launches directly into the presentation without even a hint that you're running PowerPoint. Click, click—on with the show!

TIP: *When you know you'll want to launch directly into a presentation, you can save the original file as a PowerPoint Show or rename an existing file to use the .pps file extension. When you save as or rename to a PPS file in the first place, you will avoid having multiple copies of the same presentation on your PC.*

Optimize Presentation Performance

Several factors can contribute to a slow-running PowerPoint presentation, including disk free space, virtual memory usage, image resolution, and animation effects. By tweaking a few settings, you can improve presentation performance.

Two major factors in application performance, and hence PowerPoint presentation performance, are (1) how much free disk space your PC has and (2) the amount of RAM installed. If your hard disk has less free space than the amount of RAM installed, you'll need to free up some hard disk space by degunking your hard drive or upgrading to a larger hard disk. Check how much free disk space you have by following these steps:

1. Double-click the My Computer icon on your Desktop.

2. Right-click the C: drive and choose Properties from the context menu. The amount of free space is displayed graphically in the Properties dialog box as shown in Figure 8-8.

TIP: *A quicker way to see how much disk free space you have is to select the C: drive in My Computer and then read how much free space is available as it's displayed in the status bar.*

Once you determine whether you have adequate free disk space, unless your PC is swarming with RAM, you should turn on virtual memory to optimize overall PC performance. If you are running Windows 2000 and earlier, follow these steps:

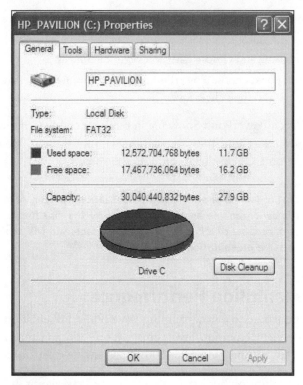

Figure 8-8
Check disk free space in the Properties
dialog box of your hard drive.

1. Close all open files and applications.

2. Click Start, select Settings, and then choose Control Panel.

3. In the Performance tab of the System Properties dialog box, click Virtual Memory.

4. Enable the "Let Windows manage my virtual memory settings (recommended)" option, click OK, and then click Close.

If you are running Windows XP or later, follow these steps to configure virtual memory:

1. Close all open files and applications.

2. Click Start, click Control Panel, and then double-click System.

3. In the Performance section of the Advanced tab of the System Properties dialog box, click the Settings button.

4. In the Virtual Memory section of the Advanced tab of the Performance Options dialog box, click the Change button.

5. In the Virtual Memory dialog box, be sure your main hard drive is high-lighted in the Drive list.

6. In the Paging File Size for Selected Drive section, choose the System Managed Size option (see Figure 8-9), click Set, and then click OK three times.

Configuring your PC to use virtual memory enables it to act as if it has more RAM installed than it actually does. To further improve the performance of your presentation, consider decreasing the resolution setting for the overall presentation, enabling hardware graphics acceleration, and reducing the number of colors your monitor displays.

Check to see whether your PC supports hardware graphics acceleration by following these steps:

1. Click Start and choose Control Panel.

2. Double-click the Display icon in Control Panel.

3. In the Settings tab of the Display Properties dialog box, click the Advanced button.

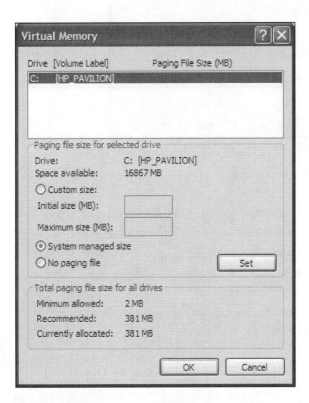

Figure 8-9

Let your PC manage virtual memory size to optimize performance.

4. In the Hardware Acceleration section of the Troubleshoot tab, check whether hardware acceleration is supported on your PC. The PC shown in Figure 8-10 supports hardware acceleration for graphics devices.

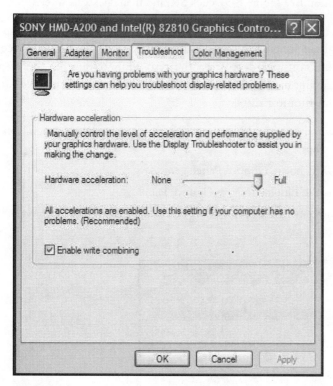

Figure 8-10

This PC supports graphics acceleration.

To reduce the resolution setting for the overall presentation, enable hardware graphics acceleration, and reduce the monitor color depth, follow these steps:

1. In an open presentation, choose Set Up Show on the Slide Show menu.

2. In the Performance section of the Set Up Show dialog box, select the Use Hardware Graphics Acceleration option to enable it, as shown in Figure 8-11.

3. Choose the "640x480 (Fastest, Lowest Fidelity)" option from the Slide Show Resolution drop-down list.

4. Click OK.

5. Click Start, click Control Panel, and double-click the Display icon.

6. In the Color Quality section of the Settings tab of the Display Properties dialog box, choose Medium (16-Bit) from the drop-down list. Click Apply, and then click OK.

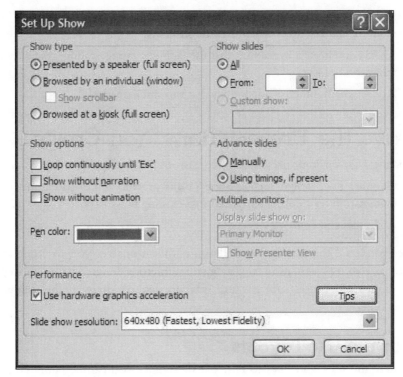

Figure 8-11
Optimize show performance in the Set Up Show dialog box.

If, after you change the resolution setting, the images in your show have changed unacceptably, use a different resolution setting in the drop-down list or choose Use Current Resolution. If, after enabling hardware graphics acceleration, you experience problems with the presentation display, use the slider button in the Troubleshooting tab shown in Figure 8-10 to decrease the acceleration setting by one notch, then run your presentation again. If the display does not improve as you tweak the acceleration setting incrementally, you might consider turning it off.

TIP: *After your presentation, you might want to change the monitor color quality back to the original setting if you were previously using a higher color quality. This is a system-wide setting.*

Images and animations are the greatest resource consumers in a presentation. When you're strapped for RAM or you need to further improve your presentation's performance, try to simplify them by using the following guidelines:

√ Reduce the size of text and graphics used in animations. (They use less memory and resources when they are smaller.)

√ Avoid complicated animations that use fading, rotating, scaling, gradients, or transparent objects.

√ Reduce the number of animations that run simultaneously.

Improve the Presentations You Create

Creating a PowerPoint presentation consists of two basic steps:

1. Choose a basic design, such as using a blank presentation or basing the presentation on a design template or an existing presentation.

2. Add slides and content.

The wonderful thing about PowerPoint is that it enables you to completely customize your presentation by giving you numerous design options for step 2. We discuss the various options and ways to degunk them in the following subsections.

Learn to Use Layouts

If you're the sort who likes to reinvent the wheel, you can certainly create a presentation using blank slides, manually adding text boxes, images, and shapes as you go along. Or you can degunk your slide creation process by using built-in layouts.

PowerPoint comes with over 20 different preconfigured arrangements called *layouts*. Layouts use placeholders to hold open space into which you'll add content later. Each time you add a new slide, you can choose from myriad built-in layouts so that slide creation becomes more like a fill-in-the-blanks question than a creative struggle.

You can view the available layouts by displaying the Slide Layout task pane. On the View menu, choose Task Pane, and then use the downward-pointing arrow in the top right corner of the task pane to select Slide Layout, as shown in Figure 8-12. Enable the Show When Inserting New Slides option at the bottom of the task pane to be sure that layouts are handy whenever you create a new slide.

You can drag and resize the placeholders in a layout arrangement to better suit the slide content. Also, if you have already created one or more slides and you'd like to apply a specific layout to them, select the slides in the Slides tab, point to the layout you want to apply in the Slide Layout task pane, and use the drop-down menu to choose Apply to Selected Slides.

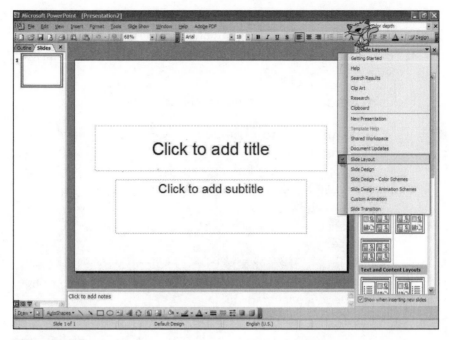

Figure 8-12
Display the Slide Layout task pane to make applying layouts easy.

Apply Design Templates

Applying design templates is another efficient way to modify the content of slides without having to handle each slide multiple times. A template is a cookie cutter, and you can apply a design template to the overall presentation or to individual slides within a presentation. Slides can have more than one template applied to them. But keep in mind that using numerous templates in one presentation can complicate rather than simplify presentation creation.

TIP: *The Blank Presentation design template, which is the default template for new presentations, differs from other PowerPoint design templates. It contains a slide master but no title master. (Read about slide and title masters in the section "Master Using Masters" later in this chapter.)*

To apply a preset design template to every slide in a new presentation, follow these steps:

1. Open a new presentation.

2. If the Slide Layout task pane is not showing, choose Task Pane on the View menu, and then use the downward-pointing arrow in the top right corner of the task pane to select Slide Design.

3. Choose a design template from those available. The last two items in the list of templates offer you the opportunity to install more templates.

4. Point to the template, click the drop-down menu, and choose Apply to All Slides.

Each new slide that you insert will use this template.

GunkBuster's Notebook: PowerPoint Design Best Practices

Here we've compiled a handy list you can refer to when you need to design a presentation. Applying these guidelines will help you create presentations easily and efficiently, and your end product will be not only effective, but professional in appearance.

√ **Organize information in a logical order.** Use the Outline tab to create an outline and arrange and rearrange slides so the information flows.

√ **Limit the number of slides in your presentation to 6 to 10.** Avoid overwhelming your audience with too much information. Use the slides to emphasize key points, and amplify on those key points as you speak.

√ **Take advantage of PowerPoint features to simplify presentation creation.** Use the slide master, title master, handout master, and notes master to simplify making global changes and maintain consistency throughout the presentation. Use built-in layouts to place content on slides. Apply design templates to standardize presentation design.

√ **Print slide notes to refer to during the presentation.** Printed notes sections will allow you to move around as you speak, rather than be planted in front of your laptop.

√ **Add numbers to slides.** Numbering slides will aid in presentation organization as well as navigation during your presentation.

√ **Choose text fonts wisely.** Use basic fonts to avoid bloating presentation file size by embedding specialty fonts. Consider that sans serif fonts, such as Arial and Tahoma, are usually easier to read and make for a less-cluttered screen appearance. Consider your presentation medium and choose fonts that are optimized for either electronic viewing (Verdana, Tahoma, Bookman) or printed presentation (Times New Roman). Choose fonts that have a larger x-height to improve readability (the x-height is literally the height of the x character; for instance, Tahoma has a larger x-height than Garamond).

√ **Limit the number of fonts you use to two or three.** Consider the material you are presenting and choose only a few appropriate fonts to avoid appearing amateurish. Also use bold and italic only for emphasis.

√ **Keep slide content concise.** Use bullet lists or short, punchy statements. Amplify on key points as you speak, and save the intricate details for handouts. Avoid overloading one slide with too much information; split one slide into two if necessary.

√ **Avoid letting presentation design detract from the information you're sharing.** Pick one or two simple transitions, and use them consistently. Avoid distracting animation effects. Ensure that font and image sizes are appropriate and easily viewable.

√ **Plan color schemes and backgrounds carefully.** Keep color schemes coordinated. Use a high contrast between background color and content. Consider how the chosen color scheme will look on the big screen; sometimes bright colors don't project well. Choose a background based on the room lighting: generally, choose a dark background with light text and graphics for a dark room, and choose a light background with dark text and graphics for a lighted room.

√ **Use meaningful images and graphics and sound.** Avoid cluttering your presentation with numerous images and sounds. Use them only when they emphasize the point you are making and add value. Be sure they're sized appropriately for easy viewing and so as not to bloat the presentation file size. Use only as much resolution as needed. Use labels and captions to be sure viewers understand what they are looking at. *Respect copyrights!*

These design guidelines can help you create an effective presentation with minimal stress.

Customize the Default PowerPoint Presentation

If you create many online presentations, you might have a standard layout that you typically use. Instead of starting from scratch each time you create a new presentation, create a blank presentation with all of the formatting and graphics that you normally use, and then save the presentation as the default for future presentations that you create. The default format might include a particular color scheme and a company logo, for example. You can also use an existing presentation and modify it as needed before saving it as the default.

To change the default presentation, follow these steps:

1. Configure the slides and components of the presentation as you want them to appear by default in new presentations; then choose Save As on the File menu.

2. In the Save as Type box, choose Design Template (*.pot), and then in the Name box, type **Blank Presentation**.

3. Click Save, and if you are asked if you want to replace the existing presentation, click Yes.

GunkBuster's Notebook: Why Don't the Slides in My Presentation Match the New Template?

Imagine this: You open an existing presentation and apply a new corporate template that includes the company logo and titles in Times New Roman font. Most of the slides in your presentation change their appearance to match the new template, but the logo is missing on one slide and another slide displays the title in Arial.

Inconsistencies such as these can occur when you have applied custom settings to slides. On the slide that is missing the logo, for example, a custom background that hides background objects has been applied. On the slide displaying the title incorrectly, the formatting for title text has been changed to Arial. These modifications to individual slides override the settings in the new design template.

Beware of custom settings applied to individual slides; they override template settings.

Master Using Masters

Usually, when a design template is applied, a slide master and a title master are automatically created. This is called the *slide-title master pair*. A *slide master* contains information about the font styles, placeholders, background, and color schemes used in your slides. You can view the slide master and then make changes to it that will affect each slide to which the associated design template is applied. For instance, if you'd like to change the bullet style for all bulleted lists throughout your presentation, you'd open the slide master and modify the bullet style to update all slides based on that master.

A *title master* contains information about the styles used on title slides in your presentation. Title slides contain placeholders for titles, subtitles, headers, footers, and any included images, as well as information on font style. Some people use title slides throughout their presentations to break slides into sections and subsections. You can view the title master and then make changes to it that will propagate to all title slides based on that master.

Using the slide master and title master to make global changes to your presentation goes a long way toward helping you maintain a consistent look and feel throughout your presentation, and it saves you enormous amounts of time. For simplicity's sake, and to keep presentation creation gunk free, avoid using too many different templates in your file. A slide-title master pair is created for each design template applied. When you want to make global changes, you must modify each slide-title master pair available. If you have applied 14 different templates, for example, you will have to modify 14 different pairs of masters, and that definitely does not follow a touch-it-once methodology!

A wonderful thing about masters is that you can modify them just as you would any other slide. Simply point to Master on the View menu, and then select Slide Master. A thumbnail of both the slide master and title master will appear in the left pane, as shown in Figure 8-13. Click the slide master thumbnail to be able to modify the following items on the slide master:

√ Font styles for title, body, and footer text

√ Placeholder positions for text and objects

√ Bullet styles

√ Background design

√ Color scheme

Click the title master thumbnail to modify the following items on the title master:

√ Font styles for title, subtitle, and footer text

√ Placeholder size and position for title, subtitle, and footers

---

TIP: *Handout and notes masters are also available to enable you to modify these presentation components. Point to Master on the View menu, and then choose Handout Master or Notes Master to view and modify these masters.*

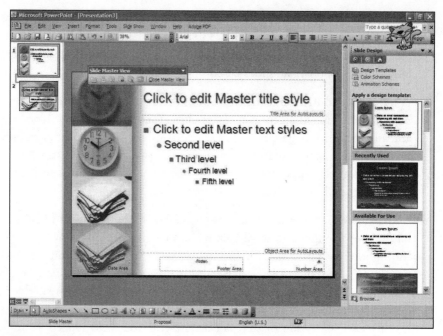

Figure 8-13

View the slide and title masters to make global changes. Here the slide master is selected and displayed.

Apply a Color Scheme

Each design template in PowerPoint has an associated color scheme. A color scheme is a group of eight related colors used throughout a presentation to color text, lines, shadows, fills, accents, hyperlinks, and the background. The color scheme becomes effective when a design template is applied. Whenever you add objects to a slide, PowerPoint uses the active color scheme to assign colors to the new objects. Color schemes are stored in the presentation file. You can modify or delete existing color schemes or add new color schemes to a presentation without affecting the template on which the presentation is based.

Color schemes apply to speaker notes and audience handouts, as well as to slides. When you modify or create color schemes for notes and handouts, the changes do not affect color schemes used for slides. However, when you delete color schemes for notes and handouts, the color schemes are deleted from the presentation file and are not available for slides.

Of course, you can modify a color scheme quite easily. To maintain a professional appearance, use colors that go well with each other and allow text and graphics to be easily viewed (most of the preconfigured design templates do a decent job of presenting an organized palette). Substituting extraneous tones or weird shades into a color scheme can disrupt the flow of your presentation and jar your audience's attention.

Use Animation

Using animation effects is the third way you can modify content in your presentation. PowerPoint offers numerous preset animation schemes, and you can efficiently apply animation effects to individual slides, as well as slide and title masters. We recommend using simpler animation effects for these reasons:

√   Less processor power is required to run a presentation.

√   Your presentation file size will be smaller, easier to handle, and more portable.

√   Your audience's attention will remain focused on the information you're presenting, not on the glitzy animation.

Animations can be fun additions to your presentation. For example, you can use them to introduce items in a list one by one as you address them. Just don't get carried away!

TIP: *Another good way to keep your audience's attention focused on the information is to blank the screen while you talk to keep them from reading ahead and, well, fazing out what you're saying. During a presentation, press the B key to turn the screen completely black, or press the W key to turn the screen white. When you're ready to move on and view the next slide, press any key and the presentation will reappear on-screen.*

GunkBuster's Notebook: Using Multimedia in PowerPoint Presentations

You can add sounds, music, movies, and animated GIFs to your presentations to enliven the show. Simply display the slide you want to add a multimedia file to, choose Movies and Sound on the Insert menu, and then choose the type of file you'd like to insert. You can add movies from the Clip Organizer or from a file, and you can insert sounds from the Clip Organizer, from a file, or from a CD; you can even record your own for playback. If you use sounds and movies, the PC that you use to make the PowerPoint presentation must be equipped with a sound card and speakers.

When you insert a multimedia file, either the sound icon, which looks like a tiny speaker, or a small movie screen is placed on the slide to represent the file. If sound files are more than 100 kilobytes in size, they are automatically linked to the presentation file, rather than embedded into the presentation file; otherwise, smaller sound files are inserted as embedded objects in the presentation. Movie files (including AVI, QuickTime, MPEG, WAV, MOV, QT, and MPG files) are automatically linked to your presentation. When you copy your presentation to removable media or to another PC, you must be sure to include all linked files so your movies and sounds can play properly.

You can customize how you want multimedia files to start and play during a presentation. You can have sounds or movies start automatically when a slide is displayed or after a specific time delay, or you can enable them to start upon a mouse click. Similarly, if you've looped a sound file, for instance, you can set the stop options. Right-click the multimedia icon on the slide to edit its features.

Be very wary that multimedia files can increase the size of your PowerPoint presentation file very quickly. Use them sparingly—remember, the slide show should not distract from your spoken presentation, but should enhance it.

There's More Than One Way to Present

Although PowerPoint presentations are ideally suited for computer projection systems, sometimes you might want to deliver a less-formal presentation. You can deliver a slide show in various formats without the use of a projection system.

Make a Hard Copy

PowerPoint presentations can be printed on paper with your choice of one, two, four, six, or nine slides per page. If you want to, you can suppress the slide backgrounds to make the slides more readable, especially when you print the presentation in black and white (grayscale). Printing a presentation is an easy way to provide handouts to all audience members—they won't have to take notes frantically to capture content and can listen to your presentation instead.

Publish as a Web Page

PowerPoint presentations can be published to the Web using the built-in Web Publishing Wizard. You can make your slide show instantly available to your immediate audience as well as the rest of the world! A key benefit of publishing a presentation as a Web page is that the complete slide show, including animations and sound, automatically works on the Web site.

Pack and Go

The Pack and Go Wizard can package your presentation to run on another computer. Packaged presentations include linked files, animations, TrueType fonts, and all other components that enable your presentation to run as you intended. You can also choose to include the PowerPoint Viewer, which enables the Pack and Go file to run on computers that don't have PowerPoint installed.

Send as an E-Mail Message

Of course, you shouldn't overlook the fact that presentations can be sent attached to an e-mail message directly to a recipient or group of recipients. PowerPoint provides this capability on the File menu as the Send To commands. You can e-mail a complete presentation to recipients; however, you cannot send a single slide unless you first send the presentation to Word (more information on Word and PowerPoint interoperability is given in Chapter 10, "Improving How Office Applications Work Together"). Beware of enabling recipients to review and modify presentations. Although the review process may be essential for collaboration, a few exchanges can make the file size enormous.

Summing Up

PowerPoint contains myriad features that enable you to create effective and professional presentations. You learned 10 ways you can configure PowerPoint at the application level to perform more efficiently. You also learned how to use design templates, masters, color schemes, and animation to the best effect. For you to refer to as you design and create new PowerPoint presentations, we've supplied a handy checklist that really degunks the process. Finally, you learned that you can publish your presentation in several different formats, including as printed pages, a Web page, or an e-mail attachment. Because PowerPoint is a specialized application and accumulates only minimal gunk, our goal in this chapter was to get you thinking of ways to enhance your interaction with the app, save time, and avoid frustration when you have to be creative.

Degunking Microsoft Outlook

Degunking Checklist:

√ Set up a mail folder hierarchy to group and organize your incoming mail.

√ Organize your contacts for quick information retrieval.

√ Use color-coding to stay organized.

√ Practice effective e-mail management.

√ Customize Outlook to work for you.

√ Create custom views to see what you want to see.

√ Learn what to do when your Calendar gets gunked up.

You probably open Microsoft Outlook whenever you sit down at your PC. You might even get a feeling similar to that sense of anticipation you experience walking toward your real mailbox. Opening Outlook can give you a hint of what the day holds in store. You can check your e-mail, view your appointments, check to see whether you've completed any tasks you can cross off your "to do" lists, review notes that you've made, and organize and view your contacts.

And then reality sets in: your Calendar might be all jumbled up with appointments, contact lists may be out of order, and you might need to wade through piles of junk e-mail to get to the important messages. But we can help. In this chapter, we'll show you how to degunk Outlook to make it operate at its full potential and we'll help you get your stuff organized. We'll focus on helping you customize and fine-tune the Outlook features that will help you reduce clutter, locate the information you need faster, and do a better job at tracking your important e-mails and other critical information. We'll also show you how you can degunk your work habits so that you can communicate with Outlook more effectively. Without realizing it, most of us waste a lot of time because we don't have good systems in place to manage all of the e-mail that we get. Once you become better organized, you'll be amazed at how much time you can save.

NOTE: *In this chapter, we'll be using the Outlook application that is included in Microsoft Office. Don't confuse Outlook with Outlook Express, which is a feature of Microsoft Internet Explorer. Their names are similar, but the two applications are quite different. For instance, it's tricky to back up Outlook Express data into an easily accessible form, whereas it's simple to back up Microsoft Office Outlook data using a quick copy procedure. Also, because it is stored in the Registry, Outlook Express gunk is nasty to clean up compared to Outlook's. Finally, Outlook Express offers fewer features to help you get organized, such as e-mail messaging, contact management, task management, and calendaring.*

Make These Changes After Installation

We'll start with the top 10 changes you can make to Outlook to make it work more efficiently:

1. Set up an e-mail folder hierarchy.
2. Set up an AutoArchive schedule.
3. Alphabetize contacts in last name-first order.
4. Organize your contacts by category.
5. Use color-coding to stay organized.

6. Automatically save copies of sent and unsent messages.

7. Enable the spell checking feature.

8. Choose the format for sending messages.

9. Set the mail checking period.

10. Change the folder Outlook opens in by default.

Set Up an E-Mail Folder Hierarchy

You probably have a jumbled mess of messages stored in your Inbox and can't find what you need when you need it. Therefore, you must take the time to degunk your e-mail and get it organized. Remember, the Inbox is not meant to be the permanent home for messages; it's just a temporary holding area until you can take action on messages, sort them into another folder for storage, or delete them.

Outlook uses separate folders to store each type of information. E-mail is stored in the Inbox folder, contacts are stored in the Contacts folder, and so on. Some Outlook folders and their shortcuts are already created for you on the Outlook Bar. You can add new folders and shortcuts as you need them, and you can work directly with the folder hierarchy by displaying the Folder List. It's wise to create folders in your Inbox over and above the default folders—the Inbox, Outbox, Deleted Items, Drafts, and Sent Items (plus Junk E-mail in Outlook 2003). Here are some tips to help you create folders and stay organized:

√ Don't go hog wild—try to keep the number of folders in your hierarchy limited to the amount that will fit on one screen in the All Mail Folders list (called the Folder List in earlier versions of Outlook).

√ Group related folders under a parent folder, and don't go too deep nesting folders or you will lose efficiency rather than gain it.

√ Create folders based on *topics* so that you can place all mail from any sender that is related to a certain topic in its folder.

√ Create folders for *time-delimited projects and events* so that you can place all mail related to an event or project in its corresponding folder and then retire that folder once the event has passed or the project is finished.

Taking time to set up a folder hierarchy may seem like an enormous task, especially if you have heaps of messages waiting to be sorted. Try to get organized in small chunks—10 or 15 minutes here and there will make a big difference. Follow these steps to begin moving messages out of the Inbox and into relevant folders:

1. Click the From or Subject column heading at the top of the Inbox message list. Outlook will display your messages sorted by sender or topic, respectively.

2. Start at the top of the list and decide whether the first message relates to a specific topic or a certain project. Make sure that your Inbox is highlighted in the All Mail Folders list in the Navigation Pane.

3. Choose New Folder from the File menu to create a folder with a name relevant to the first message.

4. In the message list, highlight the message and drag it into the new folder.

5. Follow steps 2–4 for each message in the message list. Because messages are grouped by sender or subject, you can select bunches at a time to move to a folder. Click adjacent messages while holding down the Shift key to select a contiguous group, or click various messages while holding down the Ctrl key to grab a noncontiguous group. Click the selected group, and then drag it to the appropriate folder.

Here are some additional tips to help you organize your e-mails and keep them organized:

√ Sift unwanted and unneeded messages into the Deleted Items folder as you go along.

√ Create a folder called Pending or Suspense to hold messages for which you must take some action before you can "put them away" into a more permanent folder.

√ An even easier way to deal with action items is to allow them to stay in the Inbox but with the explicit mind-set that items must be moved from the Inbox as soon as possible.

√ Keep only a few items in the Inbox that require your attention, and at the end of the day, check what's left in the Inbox.

√ When a project is completed, either delete the entire folder and its contents (if you are sure you will not need that information again) or archive the folder to get it out of the current Folder List. (More on archiving in the following section, "Set Up an AutoArchive Schedule.")

Set Up an AutoArchive Schedule

In Chapter 4, "Organizing Office-Related Files and Folders," we showed you how to manage mail folder size and tame attachments to keep Outlook optimized and of reasonable size. You probably guessed by now that Outlook must offer you a way to manage your mail folder size automatically. One feature that helps do this is called AutoArchive. It works by copying Outlook items (e-mail messages, Calendar events, meeting items, tasks, notes, and Journal entries) that meet certain criteria to an archive location and then removing the originals from the current folder. It also evaluates items to determine which items contain expired content and deletes those items instead of archiving them. You can totally customize how AutoArchive runs and whether it runs at all. It is turned on by default, and we think it is a handy item that, with a few configuration changes, can help you manage your older-but-worth-keeping Outlook items.

The archive file into which AutoArchive places items is a special PST data file. The .pst file extension is attached to Personal Folders files, which are files that store e-mail and other Outlook items on your hard disk. Your hard disk already contains a PST file for Outlook; the first time AutoArchive runs, it creates a second PST file in which to store older items at C:\Documents and Settings*username*\Local Settings\Application Data\Microsoft\Outlook\Archive.pst, where *username* is the name of the currently logged-on user. When items are archived, they are removed from their current folder location; however, folders that are empty of messages after they've been archived are allowed to remain in the main folder hierarchy.

Even after items are archived, you can still access them directly in the Archive Folders folder in the Folder List. If you open an Archive Folders folder, you can see that Outlook conveniently maintains your main folder hierarchy there.

The AutoArchive feature has two types of settings: global settings (defaults that apply to all Outlook folders) and per-folder settings (settings that enable you to customize how individual folders are archived). The default aging periods that AutoArchive uses to evaluate items for archiving eligibility are these:

√ Inbox, Drafts, Calendar, tasks, notes, and Journal items are allowed to age six months.

√ Items in the Sent Items and Deleted Items folders are allowed to age two months.

√ Outbox items are allowed to age three months.

You can change these defaults, however. Also, keep in mind the following three points:

√ Per-folder settings override global settings.

√ Archiving is not applied to contacts or recurring Calendar items.

√ You can manually archive items at any time (but why do that when you can set archiving as an automatic task?).

To customize the AutoArchive settings, complete the following steps:

1. Choose Options from the Tools menu.

2. Select the Other tab in the Options dialog box, and then click the AutoArchive button.

3. In the AutoArchive dialog box, shown in Figure 9-1, make sure a check mark appears in the Run AutoArchive Every check box; then use the up and down arrows to set the number of days. Running AutoArchive every 14 days is good practice.

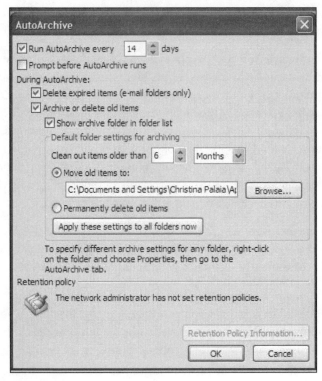

Figure 9-1
Customize the default AutoArchive settings to suit your situation.

4. Clear the check mark from the Prompt Before AutoArchive Runs option because you don't need to be bothered with such details—you're setting up the archiving schedule now just how you want it, so you don't need to personally authorize AutoArchive to run later.

5. Place check marks in the following check boxes as shown in the figure: Delete Expired Items, Archive or Delete Old Items, and Show Archive Folder in Folder List.

6. For the Clean Out Items Older Than option, use the up and down arrows to select the item age.

7. Be sure the Move Old Items To radio button is selected, and check the path name of the folder to which items will be moved. Usually, it's best not to change the default location of the archive PST file.

8. You can choose to run AutoArchive using these settings now by clicking the Apply These Settings to All Folders Now button, or you can wait till the next scheduled run of AutoArchive by clicking OK.

We mentioned that you can choose different archive settings for individual folders by creating per-folder AutoArchive rules. To do so, you must select and apply the AutoArchive settings to a folder's properties. Right-click the folder for which you want to customize the archiving settings, and then choose Properties from the context menu. In the Properties dialog box, select the AutoArchive tab, and then set the archive settings you want to apply. When you're finished, click Apply and then OK. From that point forward, that folder will be archived in the way you have specified.

Alphabetize Contacts in Last Name-First Order

The whole world functions on a last name-first basis for sorting names—except, of course, for Outlook, which by default lists your contacts in first name-first order. Fortunately, you can easily change the way Outlook orders new contacts that you add to the list. You can have Outlook sort by last-name-first order by following these steps:

1. Choose Options from the Tools menu. In the Preferences tab, click the Contact Options button to configure how the contact list is handled (see Figure 9-2).

2. For existing contacts, you may have to change the sort order manually by opening the contact and selecting the File As option of last name-first.

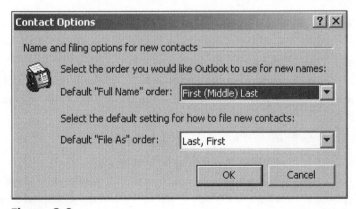

Figure 9-2
Choose Last, First as the file order for contacts.

Organize Your Contacts by Category

You can use the Categories feature in Outlook to organize your contacts list. For example, you can group your contacts into categories such as Family, Friends, and Business.

1. Select the contacts you want to assign to a category. Hold down the Ctrl key as you click contacts to select a group.

2. On the Edit menu, click Categories.

3. In the Categories dialog box, in the Available Categories box, check the name of the category you want to apply to the selected contacts. If an appropriate category isn't available, you can easily add a new category to the Master Category List by clicking the Master Category List button, typing a category name into the New Category box, and then clicking Add and OK. Click OK.

To view the contacts by category, on the View menu, select Current View, By Category.

Use Color-Coding to Stay Organized

It's amazing what a little bit of color can do: your eyes pick up various hues and can quickly associate them with a particular meaning. For example, you could use color on your Calendar to highlight your monthly mortgage payment due date in red. You can use color in three areas of Outlook:

√ You can change the color of overdue and completed tasks.

√ You can add color to appointment and meeting items in the Calendar.

√ You can add colored follow-up flags to e-mail messages.

Using color might seem really simple, but it can save you time.

Color-Code Your Tasks

It's helpful to color-code overdue tasks with a shade that will grab your attention and color-code tasks you've completed. To customize the color-coding for any task with a deadline, follow these steps:

1. Choose Options from the Tools menu.

2. Click the Task Options button in the Options dialog box.

3. In the Task Options dialog box, shown in Figure 9-3, use the drop-down lists to choose a color for the Overdue Task Color and the Completed Task Color options.

4. Click OK, and then click OK in the Options dialog box.

Color-Code Your Calendar Items

You can assign specific colors to appointments, meetings, and events manually, or by using rules. You can color regular appointments and meetings, as well as recurring appointments and meetings. And you can customize the labels of the colors you use to suit your situation. First, let's check to see whether the color

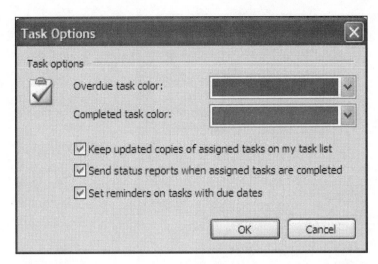

Figure 9-3
Color-code overdue and completed tasks in the Task Options dialog box.

labels need to be made more relevant to your situation by completing the following steps:

1. In the Calendar pane, on the Edit menu, choose Label, and then select Edit Labels from the submenu. You can also click the Calendar Coloring icon on the Standard toolbar, and then click Edit Labels.

2. In the Edit Calendar Labels dialog box, type the text you want to associate with a color in the corresponding text box as shown in Figure 9-4.

3. Click OK when finished.

You can use these 10 colors to code your appointments and meetings so you know at a glance what's coming up. To add color to a Calendar event individually, right-click an item, choose Label from the context menu, and then choose a color to add. To add color to a recurring appointment or meeting, complete these steps:

1. In the Calendar pane, double-click an appointment or meeting that recurs.

2. In the Open Recurring Item dialog box, choose the Open the Series option, and then click OK.

3. Use the drop-down arrow for the Label list to choose a color for the series, as shown in Figure 9-5.

4. Click the Save and Close button.

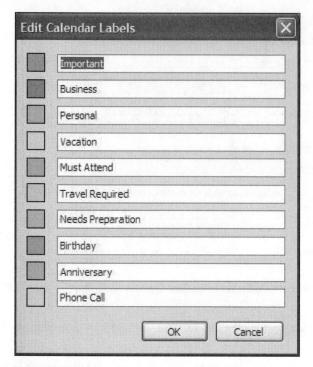

Figure 9-4

Edit the labels for Calendar colors in the Edit Calendar Labels dialog box.

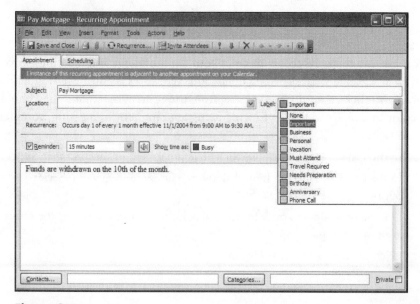

Figure 9-5

Choose a color for a series of recurring appointments.

GunkBuster's Notebook: Use Rules for Color-Coding

Having to color-code everything manually can be a pain, especially if your time is limited. You can automate this process by using simple rules. You set the conditions upon which color is applied and Outlook makes it happen. To create a rule to add color to specific appointments or meetings, complete these steps:

1. Choose Automatic Formatting in the Calendar pane on the Edit menu.

2. In the Automatic Formatting dialog box, click Add, and then type a name for the rule in the Name text box.

3. Use the drop-down list to choose a color for the Label option, then click the Condition button.

4. In the Appointments and Meetings tab of the Filters dialog box, specify conditions for which the color will be applied. Type specific words in the Search for Word(s) text box if you want Calendar items containing those words to be tinted with color. Use the drop-down list to choose in which fields the filter will look for the specified words for the In option.

5. Click the Organized By button to further refine the filtering by specifying the name of the person organizing the appointment or meetings, and click the Attendees button to specify the names of attendees. In both cases, you will be shown a list of your contacts from which to pick names.

6. Use the Time drop-down lists to specify times upon which to filter, then click OK twice.

Even if a Calendar item meets the filter conditions, it will not be colored according to the rule if you have manually assigned a color—manual color assignments override automatic coloring.

Mark Your E-Mails with Colored Flags

You can add flags to messages and contacts to remind you to take some action or to request a message recipient to take some action. Outlook makes it easy for you to mark action items by using flags. Flag a message for follow-up by completing these steps:

1. In the Mail pane, select the message in the message list.

2. Select Follow-up on the Actions menu. Then from the submenu, choose a colored flag to add to the message, or select Add Reminder from the submenu to set conditions for the reminder.

3. In the Flag for Follow Up dialog box, use the Flag To drop-down list to choose a reason for flagging the item, as shown in Figure 9-6. Your choices include the following:

√ Call

√ Do not Forward

√ Follow up

√ For Your Information

√ Forward

√ No Response Necessary

√ Read

√ Reply

√ Reply to All

√ Review

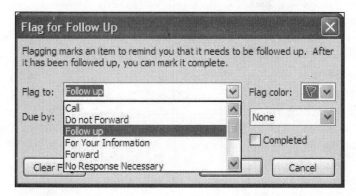

Figure 9-6

Choose a reason to flag an e-mail item in the Flag for Follow Up dialog box.

4. Use the Flag Color drop-down list to choose a flag color, and use the Due By drop-down lists to set a due date and time. Then click OK.

TIP: In Outlook 2003, copies of e-mail messages that you have flagged for follow-up automatically appear in the For Follow Up folder in the Search Folders folder in the Folder List. In earlier versions, a flag simply appears next to the message in the Flag Status column of the message list to prompt you. If you attach a flag to an outgoing message, a comment explaining the purpose of the flag as well as the due date, if any, appear at the top of the message when the recipient views it.

The color of the flag for messages that have passed their due date is automatically colored red because red is the default flag color. To change the default flag color, on the Actions menu, choose Follow Up, and then select Set Default Flag from the submenu and choose a new color from the list.

When you have followed up on a message, you can mark the flag as completed or remove the flag entirely. On the Actions menu, choose Follow Up, and then click either Flag Complete or Clear Flag, depending on your preference. For users of the latest version of Outlook, the For Follow Up folder is a convenient place to collect all action items. We know you'll feel great satisfaction as you clear items from this folder by completing the flags.

You can also set a flag on a contact to remind you to take some action: Follow Up, Call, Arrange Meeting, Send E-mail, or Send Letter as listed in the Flag for Follow Up dialog box for contacts. However, for contacts you cannot select the color of the flag—you're stuck with the default red. Keep in mind that flags are not readily seen in the Phone Cards and Detailed Phone Cards views of your contacts list. If you frequently flag contacts, use another view to enable the flags to grab your attention.

Automatically Save Copies of Sent and Unsent Messages

To generate an electronic paper trail and keep track of your correspondence, it's a good idea to make sure that Outlook is configured to save a copy of all messages you send in the Sent Items folder. To be sure this default setting has not been disabled, complete the following steps:

1. Select Options from the Tools menu.

2. Click the E-mail Options button in the Preferences tab of the Options dialog box.

3. In the E-mail Options dialog box, be sure the "Save copies of messages in Sent Items folder" option is checked, as shown in Figure 9-7.

Outlook kindly saves a copy of all unsent messages in the Drafts folder so you don't have to start from scratch re-creating messages you wrote before, but never had a chance to finish or send. This feature is turned on by default with a default time interval of three minutes between automatic saves. We find this a great help because we're constantly called away from the computer while we're in the middle of composing messages. We don't have to worry, though, because whenever we return, we see our message safely stored in the Drafts folder. If you've been using Outlook for a while, it's a good idea to double-check that this option has not been disabled for any reason. Also, you can change the time

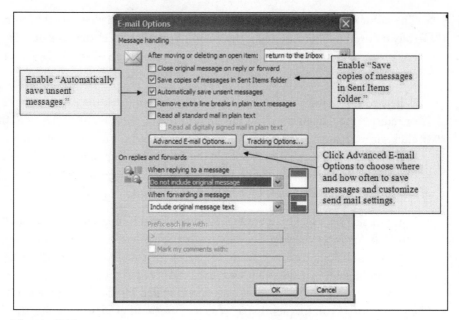

Figure 9-7
Configure how Outlook saves sent and unsent messages in the E-mail Options dialog box.

interval between saves and the location to which Outlook saves items by completing these steps:

1. Choose Options from the Tools menu.

2. Select the Preferences tab in the Options dialog box, and then click the E-mail Options button.

3. In the E-mail Options dialog box, be sure the Automatically Save Unsent Messages option is checked.

4. Click the Advanced E-mail Options button.

5. In the Advanced E-mail Options dialog box, use the Save Unsent Items In drop-down list to choose the folder where you want unfinished messages saved. The Drafts folder truly is a good place to keep your drafts.

6. Use the AutoSave Unsent Every text box to enter the number of minutes between automatic saves. (Three minutes is a comfortable interval, so accept the default value.)

7. Click OK to close all three dialog boxes.

TIP: When composing or replying to e-mail messages, you can easily rearrange the names of recipients by dragging their e-mail addresses between the To, Cc, and Bcc address fields. Just select the name or names you want to move and drag them where you want them. If you've deleted many addresses from one of the address fields and have leftover semicolons, you can remove them all by pressing Alt+K.

Enable the Spell Checking Feature

Most of us believe we spell pretty good, but revisit some of your messages, and when you examine them closely, we bet you'll find a lot of misspellings. Many of the misspellings are attributed to typos or the fast speed at which we dash off e-mails, but rather than risk embarrassing yourself and your team, enable the spell checking feature to check all your messages before they are sent:

1. On the Tools menu, click Options.

2. In the Options dialog box, select the Spelling tab, and select the Always Check Spelling Before Sending option as shown in Figure 9-8.

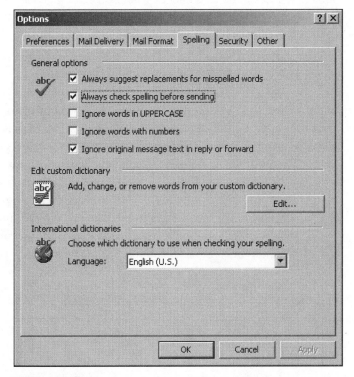

Figure 9-8
Enable spell checking of all messages before they are sent.

Choose the Format for Sending Messages

Did you ever open an e-mail message only to see text strewn all over and the page filled with unreadable characters? If so, you experienced the end result of receiving a message composed using an incompatible e-mail format: your viewer format was different from that of the message author's format. Here is a summary of the types of message formats Outlook offers:

√   **Plain text**. A message format that doesn't support text formatting such as bold, italic, or colored fonts. It also doesn't support pictures displayed directly in the message body (although images can be included as message attachments). All e-mail programs can display plain-text messages accurately.

√   **Hypertext Markup Language (HTML)**. A message format that supports text formatting, numbering, bullets, alignment, horizontal lines, pictures (including backgrounds), HTML styles, and Web pages. You can also use Outlook stationery and signature blocks with this format.

√   **Rich Text Format (RTF)**. A Microsoft format that supports text formatting, bullets, and alignment and also signature blocks with Outlook Rich Text. Outlook Rich Text can be read only by Microsoft Exchange Client versions 4.0 and 5.0, Outlook 97, Outlook 98, and Outlook 2000. (Outlook Express cannot read RTF.)

TIP: Outlook meeting requests and task requests are sent in RTF format.

The e-mail message format you use depends on your e-mail configuration and the recipient of your message. By default, Outlook wants to use Outlook Rich Text Format. In this day and age, this is fine because most e-mail viewers can display RTF; however, some Internet browser clients may lose your neat and meticulous text formatting and end up displaying a disfigured message. As high-speed Internet connections become the norm, HTML messages with embedded graphics and hyperlinks to Web sites can be used. But the bottom line is *know your audience*. If your recipient uses only a plain-text viewer, all the fancy formatting you might include becomes superfluous and may even keep your message from being displayed in readable format at all.

Follow these steps to choose a format for your outgoing e-mail:

1.   Choose Options in the Tools menu.

2.   In the Options dialog box, in the Mail Format tab, use the Send in This Message Format drop-down menu to choose a mail format, as shown in Figure 9-9. (In Outlook 2003, use the Compose in This Message Format drop-down menu.)

When in doubt, all e-mail viewers can display plain text, so this might be your safest bet.

Set the Mail Checking Period

You can set how often Outlook automatically checks the "post office" mail server to see whether you have any new messages:

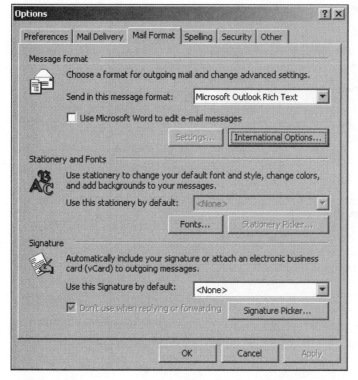

Figure 9-9
Choose a mail format for outgoing messages in the Mail Format tab.

1. Choose Options on the Tools menu.
2. In the Options dialog box, do one of the following:
    a. In Outlook 2003, select the Mail Setup tab and then click the Send/ Receive button. In the Send/Receive Groups dialog box, use the up and down arrows to set an interval for the Schedule an Automatic Send/ Receive Every option, shown in Figure 9-10. Click OK twice to exit.
    b. In earlier versions of Outlook, click the Mail Delivery tab and use the up and down arrows to set an interval for the Check for New Messages Every option. Click OK to exit.

Checking every 10 minutes is more than good enough. If you check more often, this could bog down your server. If you have an immediate need to know *right now,* you can force a check by clicking the Send/Receive button on the Standard toolbar.

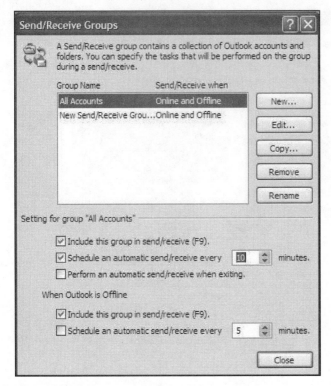

Figure 9-10
Schedule how often Outlook checks for new mail.

Change the Folder Outlook Opens In by Default

By default, Outlook is configured to start with the Outlook Today folder open; however, you can specify that a different folder opens when you start Outlook. For instance, if you prefer to go straight to your Inbox in the morning, you can set Inbox as the default folder. To change the default folder, follow these steps:

1. Select Options on the Tools menu.

2. In the Options dialog box, select the Other tab, and then click the Advanced Options button.

3. Click Browse and choose a folder from the list to specify which folder you want to appear when you start Outlook. Click OK.

Practice Effective E-Mail Management

E-mail messaging is one of the most important functions that Outlook performs. In this section, we'll show you how to optimize the following mail-related tasks to help you get better organized:

√   Use rules to sort incoming messages automatically into appropriate folders.

√   Eradicate junk e-mail using built-in filters.

√   Set up a backup schedule to ensure that your Outlook data files are secure from loss.

Use Rules to Sort Your E-Mail Messages

The Rules Wizard in Outlook enables you to get your PC to sort your incoming mail and meeting requests as you specify. For example, you can tell Outlook to place all messages from your manager in a folder named Important, or you can direct Outlook to send all messages from a distribution list to a Read Later folder. You can even make Outlook send a text message to your mobile phone whenever you receive an e-mail from a specific person, such as your mom. Think how wonderfully this will keep your Inbox degunked.

Once rules are turned on, they operate automatically until you turn them off. There are two primary types of rules: ones to help you stay organized and ones to help you stay up-to-date by displaying some sort of notification. Organization rules sort your mail for you; notification rules alert you to specific events. To create a new rule, follow these steps:

1. Go to the Mail pane and choose Rules and Alerts in the Tools menu.

2. Click the New Rule button in the Rules and Alerts dialog box to open the Rules Wizard.

3. Decide whether you'd like to create a rule based on an existing rule template or whether you'd like to start with a blank rule. You can usually customize the existing rule templates, so be sure the Start Creating a Rule From a Template option is selected.

4. Choose what kind of rule you are creating, an organization or notification rule, in the Step 1: Select a Template section. For this example, choose "Move Messages with Specific Words in the Subject to a Folder," as shown in Figure 9-11.

5. In the Step 2: Edit the Rule Description section, click the "specific words" link to specify which words Outlook should search on to apply the rule. In the Search Text dialog box, enter a word or phrase to search on, such as "Australia travel deals," click Add, then click OK.

6. In the Step 2: Edit the Rule Description section, click the "specified" link to select the folder to which you want messages moved. In the Rules and Alerts dialog box, click the name of an existing mail folder to which you want specified messages moved, or click New to create a new folder where designated messages should be moved, naming it, for example, Summer Vacation. Click OK.

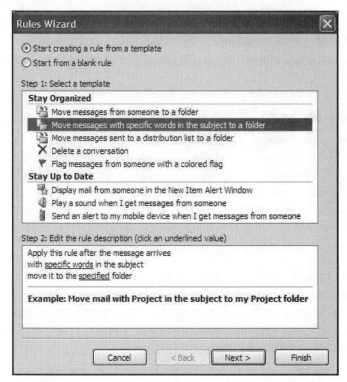

Figure 9-11

In the Rules Wizard, pick the type of rule you want to create.

7. In the Rules Wizard, click Next.

8. In the Step 1: Select Condition(s) section, insert a check mark before any condition you want Outlook to examine in applying this rule. For example, make sure the "on this machine only" option and the "with specific words in the subject" option are selected. Click Next.

9. In the Step 1: Select Action(s) section, insert a check mark before the actions that you want Outlook to take in applying this rule. For example, make sure the "move it to the specified folder" option is checked. Click Next.

10. In the Step 1: Select Exception(s) section, select any exceptions to the rule, such as "except if it has an attachment." Click Next.

11. Finish the rule setup by specifying a name for the rule in the Step 1 text box, and then enable the Run This Rule Now on Messages Already in the Inbox option and the Turn on This Rule option. At the bottom of this dialog box, you have one more chance to edit the rule description. Click Finish.

12. Outlook will quickly apply your rule to all messages in the Inbox. Click OK in the Rules and Alerts dialog box.

Your new rule is turned on. In this case, whenever a message arrives in your Inbox with the words *Australia travel deals* in the subject line, it will immediately be shifted into the Summer Vacation folder. Don't wait too long to book that trip! The point is, you can automate the way Outlook handles specified pieces of mail, including mail sent to a second e-mail account or from specific people, so that you don't have to do it manually.

Get Rid of Annoying Spam

Outlook can apply special rules to filter junk e-mail deposited in your Inbox before you even realize it's there. Outlook 2003 has a new feature called the Junk E-mail Filter that's completely dedicated to decimating spam. Earlier versions of Outlook also offer apt capabilities for sorting out unwanted messages. We want to show you how to put these functions to good use to reduce the amount of gunk you have to deal with—to nip the gunk in the bud, so to speak.

Eradicate Junk E-Mail with the Junk E-mail Filter

After installing Outlook 2003, the protection level for the Junk E-mail Filter is set to low. This might provide you with enough junk e-mail protection, but if it doesn't, you should alter the filter settings to be more stringent. It is a good idea to keep the filter setting as low as possible so that important messages aren't inadvertently sent to the Junk E-mail folder. To increase the protection level of the Junk E-mail Filter, follow these steps:

1. Go to the Mail pane and choose Options from the Tools menu.

2. In the Options dialog box, select the Preferences tab, and then in the "E-mail" section, click the Junk E-mail button.

3. In the Junk E-mail Options dialog box, in the Options tab, choose the protection level option you want to set.

4. Then, decide whether you want suspected junk e-mail that the filter catches to be permanently deleted. We do not recommend selecting this option because you might accidentally delete wanted messages with no safety net in place—when messages are permanently deleted, they are not detained in the Deleted Items folder for your possible review; they are zapped immediately.

5. Click Apply and then OK.

The Junk E-mail Filter works off the information stored in the Safe Senders, Safe Recipients, and Blocked Senders lists to figure out which mail most likely is junk. You can very easily add addresses to each of these lists to make the filtering more accurate and complete. You can do this proactively by adding addresses to the lists using the appropriate tabs in the Junk E-mail Options dialog box, shown in Figure 9-12. Or you can do this reactively by right-clicking individual messages, choosing Junk E-mail from the context menu,

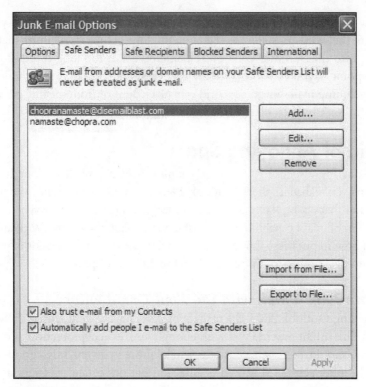

Figure 9-12
Add addresses to the Safe Senders, Safe Recipients, and Blocked
Senders lists using the tabs in the Junk E-mail Options dialog box.

and then selecting the appropriate action from the submenu: Add Sender to
Blocked Senders List, Add Sender to Safe Senders List, Add Sender's Domain to
Safe Senders List, or Add Recipient to Safe Recipients List (see Figure 9-13).

Filter Spam in Earlier Versions of Outlook

Earlier versions of Outlook enable you to customize junk mail filtering using a
slightly different procedure.

1. While in your Inbox or any of its subfolders, on the Tools menu, choose
   Organize.

2. Click Junk Mail in the Ways to Organize Inbox pane that opens.

3. In the first bulleted line, specify how you would like junk mail handled:
   choose the "move" option in the first drop-down menu to have it automatically moved. Choose "Junk E-mail" from the folder choices in the next
   drop-down list. Click Turn On.

4. In the Create New Folder dialog box, click OK to authorize Outlook to
   create the Junk E-mail folder in your Folder List.

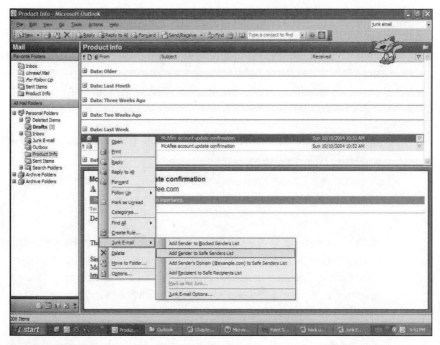

Figure 9-13
Add addresses to the Safe Senders, Safe Recipients, and Blocked Senders lists by right-clicking a message you want treated by the Junk E-mail Filter and using the context menu options.

5. In the Ways to Organize Inbox pane, in the second bulleted line, specify how you would like adult content mail handled: choose "move" from the first drop-down list, then choose "Junk E-mail" from the folder choices in the second drop-down list. Click Turn On.

6. Click the "click here" link to be able to add addresses manually to the Edit Junk Mail Senders and Edit Adult Content Senders lists.

7. When you are finished adding addresses, on the Tools menu, select Organize to close the Ways to Organize Inbox pane.

You can also add addresses to the filter lists by right-clicking messages and choosing Junk E-mail from the context menu.

Tune Your Filters

Beware that the Outlook filters are not infallible; occasionally, upon review of the Junk E-mail folder, you will catch a wanted message that accidentally got tossed. Right-click the message and add the sender to the Safe Senders list to prevent this in the future. At first, patrol your Junk E-mail folder regularly before deleting the contents to be sure no good messages are mistakenly being

filtered out; eventually, your filter lists will become sufficiently detailed to minimize mistakes, and you can download updates from the Outlook Web site to
improve filter functionality. Remember to empty your Junk E-mail folder regularly (perhaps add another recurring task to your Calendar) by right-clicking
the Junk E-mail folder in the Folder List and selecting Empty Junk E-mail
Folder from the context menu.

GunkBuster's Notebook: Reduce the Amount of Junk E-Mail You Receive

You *can* tell junk e-mail senders that there's nobody home, but
how? Following are several ways that you can reduce the quan-
tity of junk e-mail you receive.

Avoid sending a Read Receipt confirmation to sender.
Many senders of unwanted e-mail request a reply from you to
confirm that they've reached a working e-mail address. The best
practice is to discard these messages without responding and to
decline to return the requested Read Receipt. If senders perceive
your e-mail address is no longer valid, they might remove it from
their spamming lists, which could mean less junk e-mail for you in
the future.

Avoid replying with *Remove* in the subject line. Spam
messages sometimes include instructions on how to remove yourself from future mailings, such as to reply with *Remove* in the
subject line. Unfortunately, many spammers include such bogus
instructions to try to trick you into confirming that they've reached
a working e-mail address. Unless you are unsubscribing from a
mail distribution list that you signed up for or you know the message sender, the best practice is to discard spam messages without responding in any way.

Avoid sharing your primary e-mail address. Share your
main e-mail address only with friends, family, and known business associates. Consider using a second e-mail address when
filling out forms on the Internet, signing up for discussion lists, or
joining newsgroups so as to protect your primary e-mail identity.
Then set up a second e-mail account in Outlook with that address
and create a rule to move messages from that account into a
special folder, which you will scan periodically before deleting
junk messages.

Alter your e-mail address when posting to the Internet. Junk e-mailers are constantly on the lookout for new viable e-mail addresses, and they employ special software to scan Web pages and newsgroups to harvest e-mail addresses. If you list an e-mail address on a Web page or when posting to newsgroups, alter that address in such a way as to trick search programs but not confuse legitimate users. For example, if your e-mail address is natalie@southjersey.com, change it to natalieNOJUNKMAIL@southjersey.com. If users want to e-mail you, they will know to remove NOJUNKMAIL from the address, but search programs will not.

Make use of laws and consumer protection against unsolicited commercial e-mail (UCE). Some states now provide legislation against UCE. A good source of information is the state attorney general's office or the local consumer protection agency. The Direct Marketing Association (DMA) also offers a free service, similar to its program for telephone and postal mailing solicitations, enabling you to opt out of UCE. DMA members are required to remove from their mailing lists e-mail addresses of all consumers who have requested to be removed.

Set Up a Backup Schedule

Alas, Outlook does not come with a built-in backup feature, so you must set up a schedule and create backups of your Outlook data manually as part of your overall degunking strategy. All Outlook data is contained in one PST file or OST file. Theoretically, you can't just save individual e-mail messages or Outlook items to another folder on your hard disk as a means of backing up your Outlook data unless you export the items as TXT files, which causes them to lose formatting. There are three main ways for backing up Outlook data:

√   You can create a new PST file in your folder list, choose which Outlook items to drag and copy into it, and then copy the file to removable media, such as a CD.

√   You can export folders individually to a new PST file while maintaining the originals in the current Folder List.

√   You can set the AutoArchive feature to run on a specified schedule (see the earlier section called "Set Up an AutoArchive Schedule") and then copy the archive PST to removable media, such as a CD.

Because this backup strategy requires some manual effort on your part, we think keeping the whole process simple is the best way to ensure that you actually stick to a regular backup schedule to protect your data. Here are the steps to follow:

1. Choose New, Outlook Data File from the File menu.

2. In the New Outlook Data File dialog box, choose which type of PST file you would like to create based on compatibility with your version of Outlook. Click OK.

3. In the Create or Open Outlook Data File dialog box, name the new PST file, choose a save location (the default C:\Documents and Settings*username*\Local Settings\Application Data\Microsoft\Outlook location is handy), then click OK.

4. In the Create Microsoft Personal Folders dialog box, name the file, choose the encryption type (the default Compressible Encryption option is adequate), and then click OK. This new Personal Folders folder will appear in your mail folder hierarchy.

5. Locate the messages or mail folders you want to back up and copy them into the new PST file. To copy the messages and leave the originals in their original location, open a mail folder, select the messages you want to back up (hold down the Shift key or Ctrl key when clicking messages to select contiguous and noncontiguous groups, respectively), right-click the selected group, drag it to the new Personal Folders folder while holding down the right mouse button, and then select Copy from the context menu that appears when you release the mouse button. Repeat this procedure for all messages you'd like to back up.

6. Locate the Archive Folders folder in the folders list, right-click it, and drag it to the new Personal Folders folder while holding down the right mouse button. Choose Copy from the context menu.

7. Close Outlook, then click Start and choose Search. Click "All files and folders," and then enter **.pst** in the "All or part of file name" box. Click Search.

8. Locate the new PST file in the Search Results dialog box, right-click it, and select Copy from the context menu. Copy this file onto removable media, such as a CD.

9. Open Outlook, and then create a recurring task and a reminder to prompt you to complete this backup process once every three months.

The reason we suggest making a copy of the PST file rather than exporting the Outlook items you want to back up is because the copy procedure copies the data as well as folder customizations you have added, whereas the export procedure copies data only. What could make less degunking sense than having to recustomize Outlook in the event you actually have to rely on the exported data?

Customize Outlook to Work for You

With a few quick clicks, you can configure Outlook to work in exactly the way you find most convenient. Following are the items you can tweak to maximize your efficiency:

√   Empty the Deleted Items folder automatically.

√   Send documents as e-mail messages without even opening Outlook.

√   Place notes on your desktop for easy access.

√   View your Inbox and Calendar simultaneously.

√   Hide lengthy message headers when printing messages.

Empty the Deleted Items Folder Automatically

All kinds of things get shoved into the Deleted Items folder, including junk mail, messages with expired content, and sometimes even items you've received from unknown or suspicious senders. It's best to regularly empty this trash heap, and you can get Outlook to do this task for you so you can spend your time on other important things. To automatically empty the Deleted Items folder, complete the following steps:

1.   Click Options on the Tools menu.

2.   In the Options dialog box, in the Other tab, select the Empty the Deleted Items Folder Upon Exiting check box.

3.   Click OK.

Be aware that items you delete will be permanently removed from Outlook whenever you exit the application. You can set up a warning to alert you before Outlook permanently deletes items. In the Options dialog box, in the Other tab, click the Advanced Options button and check the Warn Before Permanently Deleting Items option.

Send an Office Document without Opening Outlook

Have you ever wondered whether there is a quicker and more expeditious way to send Word, Excel, and PowerPoint files by e-mail other than by creating a new message and browsing your file system to find the file to attach? Here's how you can do it without even opening Outlook:

1.   In the Office document, on the File menu, point to Send To, and then click Mail Recipient (as Attachment).

2.   Fill in the To, Cc, and Bcc fields and the Subject line, add message content if you'd like, and then click Send.

Voilà! You just sent an attachment without ever leaving the open document. You'll notice that it appears in your Sent Items folder, along with the date and time sent.

Place Notes on Your Desktop

Notes are the electronic equivalent of paper sticky notes. They are immensely useful and can be used just like note paper to jog your memory, jot down ideas, or post reminders. It's easy to create a note in Outlook:

1. On the File menu, point to New, and then select Note.

2. Type the text of the note.

3. Close the note by clicking the *x* in the upper-right corner.

For even quicker accessibility, you can make Outlook notes available on your desktop by completing the following steps:

1. If you do not already have a shortcut for Outlook on your desktop, create one by clicking Start, pointing to Programs or All Programs (depending on which version of Windows you are using), right-clicking Microsoft Outlook in the list of programs, and then choosing Send To, Desktop (Create Shortcut) on the context menu.

2. Right-click the desktop shortcut and choose Send To, Desktop (Create Shortcut) to create a copy of this shortcut.

3. Right-click the copy of the shortcut and choose Properties.

4. In the Shortcut tab, in the Target text box, add the following command-line switch to the end of the target path: **/c ipm.stickynote**. The Target box now reads as follows: "C:\Program Files\Microsoft Office\Office10\ OUTLOOK.EXE" /c ipm.stickynote. Make sure the command-line switch text is outside the quotation marks.

5. Click Apply, and then click OK.

Now when you double-click the shortcut, an Outlook note will appear on your desktop. You can add text to this note, and you'll find that when you open Outlook regularly, the note is also saved in the Outlook Notes folder. The notes will remain on your desktop as long as Outlook is open.

TIP: You can create a note quickly by pressing Ctrl+Shift+N from anywhere in Outlook.

View Your Inbox and Calendar Simultaneously

Instead of clicking all around, opening and closing panes in Outlook as you need them, sometimes it's easier to allow two features to be open side by side on your screen. To enable your Inbox and Calendar to be viewable at the same time, complete the following steps:

1. Close all documents and programs other than Outlook.

2. In Outlook, select Inbox in the Folder List to open it.

3. Right-click Calendar in the Folder List or Outlook Bar, and then select Open in New Window from the context menu.

4. Right-click an empty area of the Windows Taskbar and select Tile Windows Vertically from the context menu. Alternately, you can resize the Inbox and Calendar windows so they fit on the same screen.

To save your settings when you're finished for the day, close Outlook by clicking Exit on the File menu. This way, the next time you open Outlook, the Inbox and Calendar will open side by side as you left them.

Hide Lengthy Headers When Printing Messages

Frequently, you receive e-mail messages addressed to a large number of recipients so that the list of recipients is sometimes longer than the message itself. If you were to print these messages, the huge list of names would consume additional sheets of paper. Not good for the trees.

Outlook provides a few features that enable you to hide message headers, which include all the data contained in the To, Cc, Bcc, and Subject lines, so you don't needlessly waste paper when printing messages. You can do any of the following:

√ Copy the body of the message into a blank Word, WordPad, or Notepad file, and then print it from there. This is the easiest and quickest way, and we recommend it.

√ Save the message in a file format that you can open in Word, remove the unwanted headers, and then print. You risk generating gunk on your hard drive using this method.

√ Remove one or more fields from the message form in Outlook. This method can apply to all messages or simply to the open message.

TIP: While viewing a message, you can hide the message header by toggling the Message Header item on the View menu.

To remove header elements from the message form, do the following:

1. Open the message you want to print.

2. On the Tools menu, point to Forms, and then click Design This Form. (The Design a Form item enables you to change the message form in the Outlook Standard Forms Library, which affects all messages.)

3. Select the header field that you want to remove by right-clicking it (be sure to select the field, as shown in Figure 9-14, not the label), and choose Properties from the context menu.

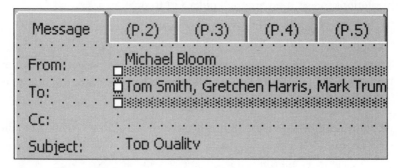

Figure 9-14
Select the header field that you want to remove.

4. In the Validation tab, clear the "Include this field for Printing and Save As" check box (see Figure 9-15).

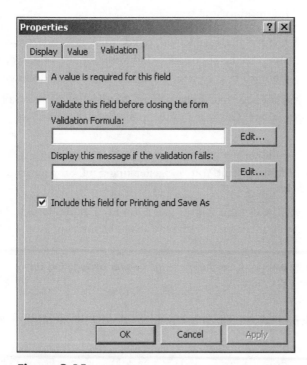

Figure 9-15
Disable the header element for printing and saving.

5. Click Apply, and then click OK.

6. Save the message and then print it.

You must repeat steps 3 through 5 for each header field you want to remove before printing, and these steps affect only the open message. Perhaps a bit of an effort, but you'll save yourself a lot of paper by leaving off cumbersome message headers.

Create Custom Views

Outlook offers numerous ways to slice and dice your Outlook items by using views and view filters. Applying a *view* to your data enables you to see it arranged in a particular order—all the data is present, but arranged as you have specified. A *view filter*, on the other hand, is a quick way to view and display only data that meet the criteria specified in the filter—data that does not meet the view criteria is not lost, it simply is not available to view while the filter is applied.

Using views and view filters is a good idea when you want to see only and all messages sent to you from your boss Susan between October 15 and October 31, for instance, or when you want to sort your appointments and meetings to display only non-work-related items. Views and view filters enable you to temporarily zero in on a particular data set while degunking extraneous information from display.

Each feature of Outlook comes with a bunch of standard views as shown in Table 9-1. In addition, you can customize a standard view or create your own unique views to sort data exactly how you need it.

Table 9-1   Standard Views Available for Outlook Features

Outlook Feature	Standard Views Available
Mail, Contacts, Tasks	Date
	Conversation
	From
	To
	Folder
	Size
	Subject
	Type
	Flag
	Attachments
	E-mail account
	Importance
	Categories

(continued)

Table 9-1   Standard Views Available for Outlook Features *(continued)*

Outlook Feature	Standard Views Available
Calendar	Day/Week/Month
	Day/Week/Month With AutoPreview
	Active Appointments
	Events
	Annual Events
	Recurring Appointments
	By Category
Notes	Icons
	Notes Lists
	Last Seven Days
	By Category
	By Color

View filters offer you an easy way to trim the fat and get right to the meat of the matter. Say you want to sift through all the messages in your Product Info folder to view only the ones received from your Internet service provider. You can apply a view filter to any mail folder by completing the following steps:

1.   Click the folder to which you want to apply a filter.

2.   On the View menu, select Arrange By, and then click Custom.

3.   Click Filter.

4.   In the Filter dialog box, select the filter options you want to apply. To filter using additional criteria, such as a category or importance level, click the More Choices tab and then select the options you want. If you select more than one option, only the items that meet all of the criteria will appear in the view.

5.   Click OK in both dialog boxes to apply the filter.

View filters remain applied until you turn them off by clicking Clear All in the Filter dialog box.

Use the Journal to Track Long-Distance Calls

The Journal Phone Call feature provides a handy way to keep track of the time you spend on the phone with various contacts. To track your calls in the Journal, complete the following steps:

1.   In Contacts, double-click the contact you are about to call.

2.   On the Actions menu, select New Journal Entry for Contact.

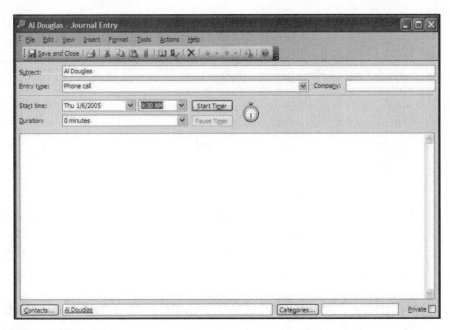

Figure 9-16
Use the Journal to keep track of how long you talk on the phone.

3. When you begin the phone call, click the Start Timer button (see Figure 9-16).
4. When you've hung up the phone, click Pause Timer, and then save your entry.

To view a list of all the phone calls logged in the Journal, open the Journal, and on the View menu, choose Current View and then click Phone Calls.

What to Do When Your Calendar Gets Gunked Up

Besides color-coding, Outlook provides several handy features that will help keep your Calendar gunk free.

Create Additional Calendars

When your Calendar gets so gunked up with entries you have difficulty finding appointments, you can degunk simply by creating an additional Calendar. First, create a way to categorize the types of appointments and Calendar events you keep. For example, if you are a member of a group or organization, you can create a Calendar that contains only that group's activities and events while allowing your work-related appointments to be tracked in the main (default) Calendar. Or you can create a separate Calendar that contains only the children's activities. Or keep a Calendar for each child! You can get as granular as you like sorting appointments and events into various Calendars, but the catch is (there's always a catch!) that meeting requests will appear only in your default (main) Calendar and you'll receive reminders only on items contained in your default Calendar folder.

Here's how you can create an additional Calendar in Outlook:

1. On the File menu, point to New, and then select Folder.

2. In the Name box, enter a name for the folder.

3. In the Folder Contains list, click Calendar Items, and then click OK.

The new Calendar will appear in the My Calendars section of the Calendar pane. You can add whichever entries you want to your new Calendar. You can even save a Calendar as a Web page and then post it to a Web site to publicize your group's events.

Display Nonconsecutive Dates in Your Calendar

The Calendar displays dates consecutively as you would expect. You can, however, force the Calendar to display several nonconsecutive dates, enabling you to view information associated with those dates. To view nonconsecutive dates, complete the following steps:

1. In the Date Navigator (the small calendar on the side of the screen that displays the current month), click the first date you want to view.

2. Hold down the Ctrl key and click any other dates you want to view simultaneously. To remove a date, click it again while the Ctrl key is still pressed.

Outlook will build a view of the selected days. You can display up to 14 nonconsecutive dates.

TIP: You can change the number of days that are visible in your Calendar view by pressing the Alt key and any number from 1 to 10. For example, to display a nine-day span starting with the date selected in the Date Navigator, type Alt+9. Use the number keys on the keyboard, not the numeric keypad.

Schedule E-Mail Responses in Your Outlook Calendar

At times, you will receive an e-mail that you don't have time to reply to immediately. Instead, so you don't forget about the message, you can easily add it to your Calendar to schedule a block of time when you will be able to respond. To turn an e-mail message into an item on your Calendar, complete the following steps:

1. Drag the message from your Inbox onto the Calendar icon on the Outlook Bar or onto your Calendar folder in the Folder List. This will create a new appointment item that contains the text of the message in the notes area of the appointment.

2. Select the date and time you want to reply, and specify any additional options such as a label or a reminder.

3. Click Save and Close to add the appointment to your Calendar.

It's not as easy to forget to reply to important messages when you add them to your Calendar in this way. Outlook enables you to drag items between all Outlook folders, including the Inbox, Tasks, Calendar, Contacts, Notes, and so on. Right-click an item as you drag it to see the options available when you release the mouse button.

Summing Up

Outlook is a supremely useful application for keeping you organized, on time, and in touch. In this chapter, we've showed you just the basics of how to customize Outlook to work more efficiently for you. When you're able to keep control over your incoming e-mail so your mail folders don't get out of hand, organize appointments into categorized Calendars, and sort contacts into logical groups for easy viewing using the tips in this chapter, you'll feel like you're keeping chaos at bay and we bet your days will go more smoothly. This is just the start, though. Poke around, push buttons, and explore Outlook to find even more configuration options to keep you productive.

Improving How Office Applications Work Together

Degunking Checklist:

√ Discover several of the myriad ways Office applications work together.

√ Choose the best way to transfer data from one program to another.

√ Learn the advantages and disadvantages of linked and embedded objects.

√ Send e-mail and Office data from the various Office applications.

√ Perform a mail merge without losing your sanity.

Microsoft Office applications can interoperate with each other and other programs in nearly unlimited ways. For example, you can readily copy data in one application and paste it in another. But if you are not careful, you can create a lot of gunk in the process.

In each of the Office applications you can accomplish any of the same basic tasks: you can send an e-mail directly from Excel, for example, or use Word to create the outline for PowerPoint slides. In Office, you're confronted with choices. Knowing which program is best suited to your particular project is the trick to keeping the gunk down while you work. Use Table 10-1 to match what you want to do with the most efficient way of accomplishing it.

Table 10-1   Methods of Sharing Data between Files

Task	Method
Make a copy of information that appears in one program and paste it into another program.	Use the Office Clipboard to copy and paste.
Quickly copy or move information between two open files.	Use drag-and-drop editing.
Copy from another file information that you can keep up-to-date with changes made to the original source file.	Create a linked object.
Copy from a file information created in another program that you can edit in the source program without leaving the current document.	Create an embedded object.
Create a way to jump to information in another program by clicking specially formatted text or a graphic.	Create a hyperlink.
Share a file with others so they can review and make comments.	Route a file in e-mail.
Share a file with others.	Send a file as an e-mail attachment.
Use a file created in another program.	Import the data from the other program.

In this chapter we'll explain the Office interoperability features listed in Table 10-1 to give you an idea of the ways the Office applications complement each other.

Transfer Data between Your Applications

The beautiful thing about working in electronic format is that you can easily switch around content and the order of text, graphics, or any other item to your heart's content without wasting a lot of time or paper. As usual, Office offers several ways to do this. Using one method instead of another in certain situations can really help you simplify and degunk the process. You can use the

Office Clipboard to cut, copy, and paste items betweens files (or within the same file); you can create linked or embedded objects; you can use drag-and-drop editing; or you can insert a hyperlink to jump you to another location. In this section, we'll show you the best way to use these methods.

Understand the Office Clipboard

In Office, one of the chief tools you use to move data about is the Office Clipboard. It's an area that temporarily stores the items you gather by copying or cutting until you're ready to paste one or all to a destination. This ingenious feature was introduced in Office 2000. Frankly, these days we can hardly imagine working without it!

To gather multiple items, you must first open the Office Clipboard. In Office 2003, choose Office Clipboard on the Edit menu to open the Clipboard task pane. In earlier versions of Office, choose Toolbars on the View menu and then click Clipboard to open the floating Clipboard toolbar, shown in Figure 10-1.

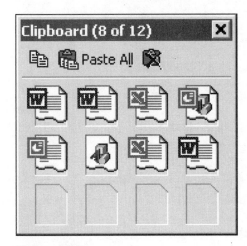

Figure 10-1
The floating Office Clipboard holds things
until you're ready to paste them.

The Clipboard is automatically invoked in the following situations:

√   You copy or cut two different items consecutively.

√   You copy the same item two times in a row.

√   You copy one item, paste it, and then copy another item in the same application.

The Clipboard does not function in views or in programs where the Cut, Copy, and Paste commands are not available.

The Office 2003 Clipboard holds an amazing 24 items (earlier versions hold 12 items). You can choose to paste these items one by one or all at once. The Clipboard displays each item with an icon representing the application from which it was gathered (if recognized). The first 50 characters of textual items are shown to help you identify the item. Graphical items are represented by a thumbnail. (In earlier versions of Office, hover the pointer over the Clipboard item to see the text or thumbnail.) The Office 2003 Clipboard task pane shown in Figure 10-2 is holding textual and graphical items gathered from various locations, including PowerPoint, Excel, Word, and the Web.

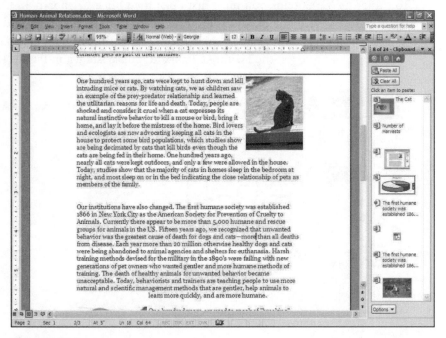

Figure 10-2
The Office 2003 Clipboard task pane can contain a variety of items.

The smartest way to work with the Clipboard is to enable the Smart Cut and Paste option in the Edit tab of the Options dialog box (from the Tools menu). This feature degunks your cut and paste operations by automatically removing superfluous spaces around target items. Also, in the Edit tab, you can specify that the Insert key be used for paste operations as a keyboard shortcut.

Windows supplies the system Clipboard, which is a relative of the Office Clipboard. The two have somewhat similar functionality. When you copy multiple items to the Office Clipboard, the last item is automatically copied to the system Clipboard as well, to make it available to paste in non-Office files. When you clear items from the Office Clipboard, you simultaneously clear the system Clipboard. And when you choose the Paste command on the Edit menu, click the Paste icon, or press Ctrl+V, sneakily enough you're actually pasting the last item copied off of the system Clipboard.

Office Clipboard Behavior

The Office Clipboard has the following quirks:

√   It can hold up to 4 megabytes (8 MB in Office 2003) of data or 12 items (24 items in Office 2003), whichever limit you reach first. If you attempt to copy a selection that is larger than 4 or 8 MB, you receive an error message and will be prompted to clear the Clipboard or close it.

√   In Excel, you cannot paste a formula to the Office Clipboard, only cell values.

√   If the Office Clipboard is not visible or is turned off, it behaves like the Windows system Clipboard.

√   If the Office Clipboard is not visible or is turned off, selections that you copy using the Copy command or Ctrl+C overwrite any previous item copied to the Clipboard.

√   The data stored in the Office Clipboard is stored in Hypertext Markup Language (HTML) format.

√   The contents of the Office Clipboard are deleted when the current work session ends. If you have only one Office program running, the contents of the Office Clipboard are deleted when you close that program. If you have multiple Office programs running, the contents of the Office Clipboard are deleted after you close the last Office program.

√   There is no Microsoft Visual Basic for Applications object model for the Office Clipboard, so there is no way to manipulate the Clipboard programmatically. You can't customize it.

√   If the same item is copied twice in succession, the Office Clipboard does not store the item twice because the calculated value of both items is identical. For example, if you enter the value 1 in cell A1 and the formula =A1 in cell A2 and then copy cell A1 and then cell A2 using the Office Clipboard, only one copy of the item is placed on the Clipboard. If you copy the same item twice, but not in succession, two copies of the item are stored on the Office Clipboard.

Format of Information Pasted from the Clipboard

Information you cut or copy is pasted to another program, if possible, in a format that program can edit. For example, data from Excel worksheets is pasted into Word as Word tables, complete with column widths and font formatting. Text separated by tab characters copied from Word is pasted into Excel in rows and columns. This is an Office feature that helps you keep the paste operation gunk free.

If the item is not converted directly into a form the destination program can edit, the item is pasted as an embedded object (for more information on embedded objects, see the next section, "Linking and Embedding Objects"). You can then use the source program to edit the embedded object. If the copied item can't be embedded, it is pasted as a static image that cannot be edited. To avoid gunked-up paste results, consider controlling how information is pasted by using the Paste Special command on the Edit menu. Figure 10-3 shows the Paste Special dialog box, which offers you a list of paste formats, each described in the Result area. The options available in the As list are dependent on the type of item to be pasted.

Linking and Embedding Objects

When you want to share information between applications, you can insert the information as a linked object or an embedded object. The main differences

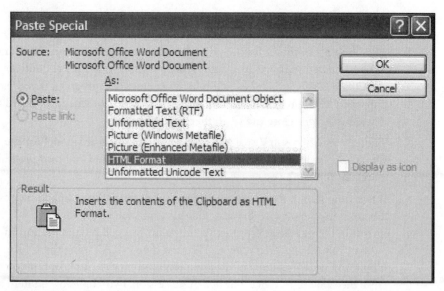

Figure 10-3

The Paste Special dialog box offers several choices, enabling you to control how Clipboard items are pasted.

between these two object types are where the object data is stored and how you update the object after placement. Whereas both types of objects are useful, to reduce gunk, certain situations call for the use of one type of object rather than the other. In Office, an *object* is any discrete bit of data that you can manipulate, such as a word, a paragraph, an image, a chart, or a file. When you're working with linking and embedding objects, each object has a *source file,* the file in which it was created and from where it originates, and a *destination file,* the location where you copy to or link the object. A linked object has these characteristics:

√   It maintains a connection to the source file.

√   It can be updated by editing the source file version.

√   You can specify how and when the object is updated.

In reality, the destination file displays only a representation of the linked object for viewing convenience. Because the destination file contains only location information pointing to the source file, and not the object itself, linked objects do not greatly increase destination file size, which is good from a gunk-busting perspective. However, when you want to share files containing linked objects, you must also be sure to send along all the associated source files so that the links can be maintained and the linked objects displayed properly.

TIP: *Be sure that you enable automatic updating of linked items in Word and Excel. In Word, choose Options on the Tools menu, and then in the General tab be sure the Update Automatic Links at Open option is selected. In Excel, choose Options on the Tools menu, and then in the Edit tab, select the Ask to Update Automatic Links option.*

An embedded object, on the other hand, has these characteristics:

√   Once placed, it becomes part of the destination file.

√   It is not automatically updated when the source file is modified.

√   It can be updated manually in the source application (the program used to create the object).

Objects are embedded in your file when you paste them. They become static images if you do not have a program installed that can edit them, or they become data that is editable in the source program if you have the source program or similar software installed. Beware, though. Embedded objects can greatly increase the size of the destination file depending on the object's size, and that's not good from a gunk-busting perspective. If you can keep file size under control, using embedded objects does make it easier to share files with other users because all data is contained in one file and you don't have to worry about sharing source files too.

Creating and Editing Linked Objects

To insert a linked object into an Office file, follow these steps:

1. Open the source file, select the information you want to insert as a linked object, right-click the selection, and choose Copy on the context menu.

2. Open the destination file, move the cursor to where you want to insert the object, and choose Paste Special on the Edit menu.

3. Select the Paste Link radio button, choose a type of formatting for the object from the As list, and then click OK.

By default, linked objects are updated automatically in Office files. This can save you a lot of time editing an object to be sure it's up-to-date with the latest data. You can also use the Links dialog box, shown in Figure 10-4, to customize the update process using the following options:

√ Specify that the object be updated automatically by choosing the Automatic Update option.

√ Specify that the object be updated manually by choosing the Manual Update option.

√ Prevent updates by choosing the Locked option.

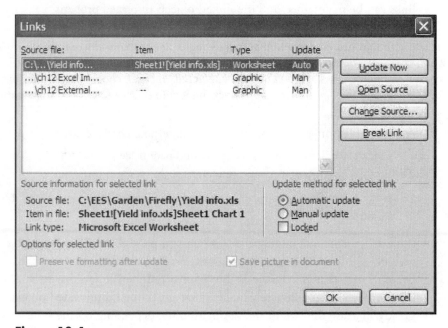

Figure 10-4

Change the update options for a linked object in the Links dialog box.

√   Manually update the object by clicking the Update Now button.

√   Edit or review the source file by clicking the Open Source button.

√   Link the object to a different source by clicking the Change Source button.

√   Disconnect the object from its source file by clicking the Break Link button.

You can also update a linked object whenever you print the document that contains it. Choose Print on the File menu, and then click the Options button. Enable the Update Links option in the Print dialog box, as shown in Figure 10-5, to be sure the linked objects in the document are using the latest information contained in the object source files.

To edit a linked object, open the source file and make the necessary changes. These changes will be reflected in the destination file object according to the update behavior you've configured.

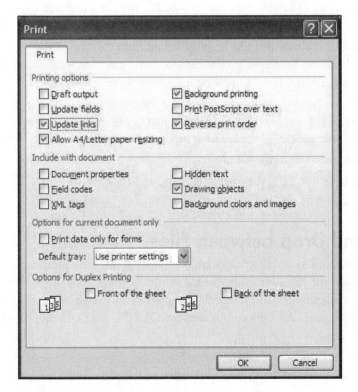

Figure 10-5

Choose the Update Links option in the Print dialog box to be sure your linked objects are current.

Creating and Editing Embedded Objects

You create an embedded object every time you paste an object or image into the destination file by using the Paste command or clicking the Paste button on the Standard toolbar. You can also use the Paste Special dialog box to create an embedded object with specific formatting that you choose. Follow these steps:

1. Copy the object from the source file.

2. In the destination file, choose Paste Special on the Edit menu.

3. Be sure the Paste option is selected, choose a format for the object from the As list, and then click OK.

Even though embedded objects are pasted as static objects, meaning they will not be updated when the original source information is changed, you can edit the data they contain. Double-click the embedded object to open it in the source program, and edit the object as you like. When you close the source program, the embedded object in the destination file reflects the changes you made. Of course, the source program in which the object was originally saved or a compatible application must be installed on your PC for this to work. If you do not have the source program installed, you can convert the object to another file format that you can edit by following these steps:

1. Select the embedded object and choose *ObjectName* Object from the Edit menu, where *ObjectName* is the name assigned to the embedded object. This option usually appears as the last item on the Edit menu.

2. Choose Convert from the submenu.

3. Choose an option from the Object Type list, and click Convert To.

4. Click OK.

Drag and Drop between Files

There's a quick and easy way to move objects between files and programs—just drag and drop. Both the source file and the destination file must support object linking and embedding (OLE), which is a protocol for sharing information between applications. All Office apps support OLE. To drag and drop objects, follow these steps:

1. Arrange your screen so that the source file is open, showing the object you want to link, and the destination file is open to the place where you want to insert the object.

2. Select the object—a range of cells in Excel, a slide in PowerPoint, or an image in another program—right-click the selection, and hold down the right mouse button as you drag the object to the destination file.

3. At the proper location, release the mouse button and choose one of the following options from the context menu:

a. Choose Move Here to cut the object and paste it into the destination file as an embedded object.

b. Choose Copy Here to copy the object and paste it into the destination file as an embedded object.

c. Choose Copy Here as a Document to copy the object and paste it as an embedded doc in the destination file.

d. Choose Link Document Here to insert the document as a linked object in the destination file.

e. Choose Create a Hyperlink Here to insert the object's address, or the path to where it resides in your folder system, as a hyperlink in the destination file.

f. Choose Create a Shortcut Here to insert an alias for the object that points to the source file.

Create a Hyperlink

Previously, hyperlinks were the magical little tools that jumped you instantaneously from one location to another as you surfed the Internet. These days, hyperlinks are used in so many different ways to make navigation a snap, not only on the Internet, but also in your own file system and documents. If you've enabled automatic formatting of hyperlinks in the AutoFormat as You Type tab of the AutoCorrect dialog box in Office apps, the Web addresses and e-mail addresses you type will be automatically formatted as hyperlinks. Otherwise, you can manually create hyperlinks in your files to link to new or existing documents or specific locations in other files or the current file. Using hyperlinks can help you keep your files as streamlined and gunk-free as possible—all the necessary data is just an easy jump away without increasing file size too much.

Link to a New or Existing Document

To link to another document or file on your PC, follow these steps:

1. In the destination file, select the text or image that will become the hyperlink, and choose Hyperlink on the Insert menu.

2. Type the path to the file you want to link to in the Address box, or use the Look In file hierarchy to navigate to the target file as shown in Figure 10-6. Click OK.

If you have not yet created the file to which you want to link, select Create New Document in the Link To area of the Insert Hyperlink dialog box. You can then name the new file and decide whether to edit it (create it) now or later.

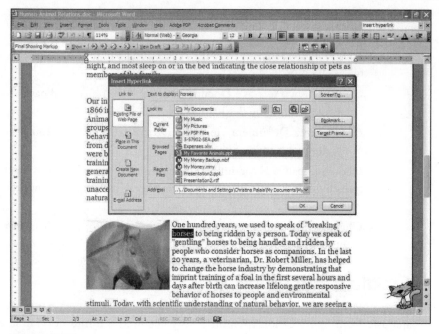

Figure 10-6
Navigate to the file you want to link to in the Insert Hyperlink dialog box.

Link to a Specific Location in a File

For Word files and Web pages, you can link to a specific location in another file
or the current file by using bookmarks. Follow these steps:

1. In the file that you want to link to, select the text or data that you want the
    hyperlink to jump to, and choose Bookmark on the Insert menu.

---

*TIP: To link to a location in the current file, bookmark that location as described here, and
choose Place in This Document in the Link To section of the Insert Hyperlink dialog box.*

---

2. Type a name for the bookmark in the Bookmark Name box, and then click
    Add. Remember, bookmark names must begin with a letter and can contain
    no spaces. Use an underscore to separate words if necessary.

3. In the destination file, select the information that you want to represent the
    hyperlink, and choose Hyperlink on the Insert menu.

4. Choose Existing File or Web Page in the Link To section, navigate to the file
    that contains the bookmark, select the file, and then click the Bookmark button.

5. Select the bookmark from the list in the Select Place in Document dialog
    box, and then click OK.

6. Click OK in the Insert Hyperlink dialog box.

TIP: *To link to a place in the current document, you can also use the built-in Word heading styles, Heading 1 through Heading 9, instead of a bookmark. At the location you want to jump to, format the text as a heading using one of the built-in styles. When you create the hyperlink using the Insert Hyperlink dialog box, choose Place in This Document in the Link To section, and choose a heading from the list.*

To link to a specific location in an Excel worksheet, you must first create a named range in the sheet (see Chapter 7, "Degunking Microsoft Excel," for more information on creating named ranges). Then when you create the hyperlink, type *#DefinedName* at the end of the hyperlink address in the Address box in the Insert Hyperlink dialog box, where *DefinedName* is the named range in the Excel worksheet. Don't forget to precede the name of the range with the number sign (#) as shown in Figure 10-7.

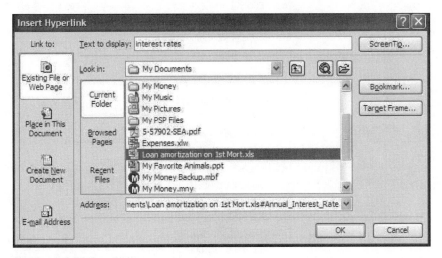

Figure 10-7
Use the name of the named range in the hyperlink address to refer to a specific part of an Excel worksheet.

You can use a similar technique to refer to a particular slide in a PowerPoint presentation: append *#SlideNumber* to the end of the hyperlink address, where *SlideNumber* is the number of the target slide. Don't forget to include the number sign (#) before the slide number!

You can also create a hyperlink by using drag-and-drop editing, as described earlier in this chapter. And yet another technique is to copy an object and then choose Paste as Hyperlink on the Edit menu in the destination file.

Degunk Sharing Information by E-Mail

You might be wondering about all the different options of the Send To command on the File menu in Word, Excel, and PowerPoint. Some of the commands are self-explanatory, but you might not realize the conveniences the others offer. Each is just right to use in specific situations, depending on your goal. One of the best things about the Send To command is that it enables you to communicate by e-mail from within the current document—no need even to switch to Outlook. Table 10-2 lists the available commands, and we explain some of the more useful options in the following sections.

Table 10-2   Options Available for the Send To Command

Application	Send To Options
Word	Mail Recipient
	Mail Recipient (for Review)
	Mail Recipient (as Attachment)
	Routing Recipient
	Exchange Folder
	Online Meeting Participant
	Recipient Using a Fax Modem
	Recipient Using Internet Fax Service
	Microsoft Office PowerPoint
Excel	Mail Recipient
	Mail Recipient (for Review)
	Mail Recipient (as Attachment)
	Routing Recipient
	Exchange Folder
	Online Meeting Participant
	Recipient Using Internet Fax Service
PowerPoint	Mail Recipient (for Review)
	Mail Recipient (as Attachment)
	Exchange Folder
	Online Meeting Participant
	Recipient Using Internet Fax Service
	Microsoft Office Word

Send to Mail Recipient

Use this option to send a new or existing Word or Excel file to a recipient or group of recipients. Choosing this option in a Word document inserts the document as the e-mail message body. By default, the Subject line of the message is the Word file's name. You can fill in the To and CC fields, and then click the Send a Copy button to distribute the Word doc to recipients.

In Excel, when you choose the Send to Mail Recipient command, you are given a choice to send the entire workbook as an attachment or to send the currently selected sheet as the message body. If you choose to send the workbook as an attachment, the Subject line by default contains the name of the workbook file, the workbook is attached, and you can fill in the To and CC fields and send the message to multiple recipients. If you choose to insert the current sheet as the message body, the Subject line contains the name of the workbook file by default. You can fill in the To and CC fields, add descriptive text in the Introduction box, and then click Send This Sheet.

Send to Mail Recipient (for Review)

This Send To command option helps degunk the collaboration process for Word, Excel, and PowerPoint files. When you choose this option, a review request is automatically created that contains a link to the target file (if the file is stored in a network location) or the target file as an attachment. The e-mail message is automatically flagged for follow-up. You can fill in the To and CC fields and send the message. Reviewing tools, including Track Changes, are automatically enabled for recipients, and when the files are returned to you, you'll be prompted to accept or reject changes.

TIP: In Excel, you must first save a shared version of a workbook to send it for review.

Send to Mail Recipient (as Attachment)

This is a quick and easy way to shoot off an e-mail with the current Word, Excel, or PowerPoint file attached. You simply fill in the To and CC fields, write a message body if you like, and click Send.

Send to Routing Recipient

In Word and Excel, you can choose to route files to recipients, which sends the target file as an attachment to an e-mail message that each recipient gets in turn. This is a useful option if you'd like to send a workbook or document to recipients one at a time so that each reviewer can make changes to the file in a cumulative fashion. If you've enabled Track Changes in the file, each reviewer will be able to see the changes and comments inserted previously. Routing a file through a number of reviewers this way enables you to track the status of the file. Recipients will receive the file as an attachment with a routing slip attached. The routing slip provides directions for how the document should be reviewed and then routed, such as this: "The attached document has a routing slip. When you are done reviewing this document, choose Next Routing Recipient from the Microsoft Office Excel [or Word] Send To menu on the File menu to return the document to its sender."

Send to Recipient Using Internet Fax Service

If you've signed up with a fax service provider, you can use this Send To command to fax a document. An e-mail message is automatically opened for you with the target file attached as a TIF file, which is an image format. Simply fill out the address fields and send; the file will be faxed to the recipient. If you've saved the recipient's fax number in your Outlook Contacts list, you can insert it from there. For you to send the fax, Outlook must be open on your PC. If it is not open, when you click Send, the fax message will be stored in your outbox until the next time you open Outlook and send outgoing mail.

Send to Recipient Using a Fax Modem

To send a Word document as a fax from your PC, you must have your fax modem set up as a printer. The Fax Wizard will open to step you through the process.

Send to Microsoft Office Word

You can send a complete PowerPoint presentation to Word by choosing the Send to Microsoft Office Word option on the File menu in a presentation file. You can choose how you'd like the slides to be laid out in the Word document in the Send to Microsoft Office Word dialog box, as shown in Figure 10-8.

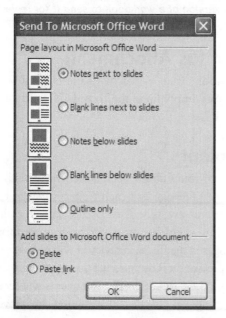

Figure 10-8

Choose how slides should be set on the page in a Word document using the Send to Microsoft Office Word dialog box.

Use the Notes Next to Slides and Notes Below Slides options to send along your presentation notes to Word. Use the Blank Lines Next to Slides and Blank Lines Below Slides to send along handouts. Choose Outline Only to send your presentation outline to Word.

Also in the Send to Microsoft Office Word dialog box, you can choose whether you want to insert the slides as embedded objects by selecting the Paste radio button or as linked objects by selecting the Paste Link radio button. (See the section "Linking and Embedding Objects" earlier in this chapter for more information on linked and embedded objects.)

Make Word. Excel. PowerPoint. and Outlook Work Together

It's easy to trade information back and forth between the Office applications. In the following sections, we'll discuss some of the more useful ways you can degunk your work processes so you can accomplish tasks with greater ease. We'll show you how to save yourself time by using built-in Office interoperability features to do the following:

√   Create a PowerPoint presentation from a Word outline

√   Write a letter to an Outlook contact using Word

√   Use Word as your e-mail editor

√   Import text files into an Excel worksheet

√   Use Outlook as an information manager

Create a PowerPoint Presentation from a Word Outline

When you must create a PowerPoint presentation, you can save yourself time by using an existing Word document to develop the slides. To prepare the Word document for conversion into slides, be sure that you have used the built-in heading styles Heading 1 through Heading 9 to format the text. PowerPoint converts the Word heading styles into outline-style text on the slides. For example, all text styled as Heading 1 in Word becomes the title of a new slide. Text styled as Heading 2 in a Heading 1 section becomes the first-level text on that slide. Text styled as Heading 3 becomes second-level text, and so forth. To use a Word document to create slides, open the Word document, choose Send To on the File menu, and point to Microsoft PowerPoint.

Write a Letter to an Outlook Contact Using Word

Instantly creating a letter to an Outlook contact couldn't be easier. In your Outlook contacts list, select the contact for whom you want to draft a letter, and then choose New Letter to Contact on the Actions menu. A new Word document will open, and the Letter Wizard, shown in Figure 10-9, appears to walk you through the four-step process.

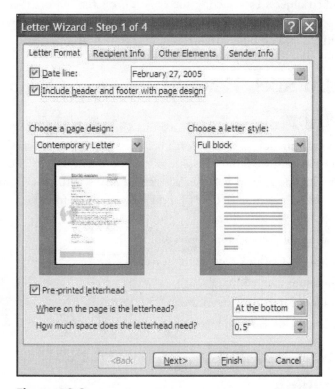

Figure 10-9

Use the Letter Wizard to write a letter to an Outlook contact.

You can customize the letter by configuring the following options:

√   Choose to autoinsert the date.

√   Include header and footer space.

√   Choose a design from an installed Word template.

√   Choose a letter style.

√   Leave space for preprinted letterhead design.

√   Choose recipient's name and contact information from Outlook contacts.

√   Choose a salutation.

√ Choose to include a reference line, mailing instructions, attention line, or subject line.

√ Choose to provide courtesy copies to other Outlook contacts.

√ Include the sender name and return address.

√ Select a closing.

Use Word as Your E-Mail Editor

Configuring Word to be your e-mail editor in Outlook enables you to take advantage of the following Word features when you create e-mail messages:

√ AutoCorrect

√ Bullets and numbering

√ Tables

√ Spelling and grammar checking

√ Themes

√ AutoFormat

√ Hyperlink and e-mail address formatting

To enable Word as your e-mail editor in Outlook, choose Options on the Tools menu, and choose Use Microsoft Word to Edit E-mail Messages in the Mail Format tab.

Import Text Files into an Excel Worksheet

At some point it might save you time to use the data contained in a text file (with the .txt file extension) to populate an Excel worksheet. If the data in the original text file changes periodically, you can import the file into Excel as a database query so that it can be updated (refreshed) whenever the original text file changes. On the other hand, you can simply convert the text file contents to static numerical data in Excel that you will not refresh later.

To import a text file as a refreshable range in an Excel worksheet, follow these steps:

1. Click the cell where you want to put the data from the text file. To ensure that the external data does not replace existing data, choose a cell that has no data below or to the right of it.

2. Point to Import External Data on the Data menu, and then click Import Data (depending on the version of Excel you are using, you might see Get External Data on the Data menu and then click Import Text File).

3. Navigate to and select the text file you want to import in the Select Data Source dialog box, and then click Open.

4. Follow the steps in the Text Import Wizard to select the formatting for the imported data (see Figure 10-10). Click Finish.

5. Click Properties in the Import Data dialog box to set formatting and layout options for how the external data range is brought into the Excel worksheet and also to set the refresh options. Click OK.

6. Click OK in the Import Data dialog box.

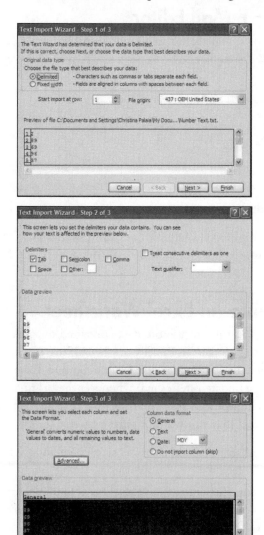

Figure 10-10

The Text Import Wizard leads you through the process of converting a text file into Excel data.

Converting Non-numbers to Actual Values

Sometimes when you import data into Excel from other programs, the data is formatted as text, which means it cannot be used in calculations. You can try to reformat the data as numbers by selecting columns or cell ranges and using the commands on the Format menu, but this often does not work. Eventually you find the only way to convert the data into numerical form is to manually edit each individual cell. The good news is, if you're using Excel 2002 or later, Excel can identify the troublesome non-numeric cells for you to correct. If you're using an earlier version, follow these steps to save yourself time and energy converting text data to numerical form:

1. Select any empty cell and type 1 in it.
2. Select the cell in step 1, and choose Copy on the Edit menu.
3. Select all the cells containing data that needs to be converted to numerical form, and choose Paste Special on the Edit menu.
4. In the Paste Special dialog box, select the Multiply option, then click OK.

This multiplies each cell by 1 and in the process converts the cell contents to a number value!

Use Outlook as an Information Manager

Outlook provides many useful features to help you manage activity in your files. For instance, from within Word, Excel, or PowerPoint, you can add a task to the Outlook Task list to remind yourself to perform some action on the file. You can also track the status of an Office file in the Outlook Journal, as well as link tasks, e-mail messages, and Journal entries to a particular Outlook contact to track activity.

Add a Task for an Office File

If you have to do something in or to an Office file by a certain date, such as review the document or forward updates to another person, you can remind yourself by adding a task to the Outlook Task list. Follow these steps:

1. In the Office file, be sure the Reviewing toolbar is open (choose Toolbars on the View menu, and click Reviewing).
2. On the Reviewing toolbar, click Create Microsoft Office Outlook Task.

TIP: *In Office 2003, you might have to add the Create Microsoft Office Outlook Task command to the Reviewing toolbar. Be sure the Reviewing toolbar is displayed, and then choose Customize on the Tools menu. In the Commands tab, choose All Commands from the Categories list. Drag the Create Task command to the Reviewing toolbar to add a button for it.*

---

3. Fill in the information about the task, including the due date, start date, status, priority level, and completion percentage as shown in Figure 10-11.

4. Click Save and Close.

In Outlook, you will see the task appear in your to do list.

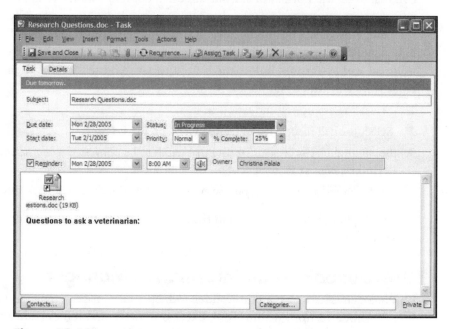

Figure 10-11
Create a task associated with a document to remind you to take action.

Use the Journal to Track Files and Items

You can have the Outlook Journal track specific Office files, as well as Office files and Outlook items associated with particular contacts. This way, from the timeline view in the Journal, you can easily tell when you created or modified a tracked document, or you can view all files and items associated with a particular contact. First, you must enable Office file tracking in the Outlook Journal. Follow these steps:

1. In Outlook, choose Options on the Tools menu.

2. Click the Journal Options button in the Preferences tab.

3. In the Also Record Files From section, place a check mark beside each of the Office applications for which you'd like to enable activity tracking, as shown in Figure 10-12. You can also associate particular contacts with the recording activity.

4. Click OK twice.

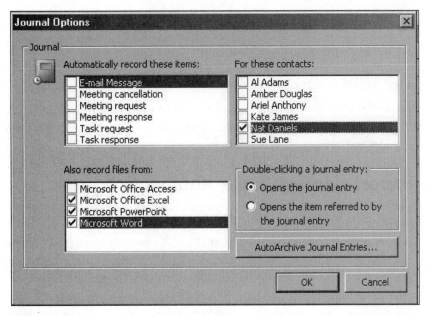

Figure 10-12
Enable files from other Office applications to be tracked in the Journal Options dialog box.

To track activity for a particular Office file, follow these steps:

1. In Outlook, open the Journal.

2. Use Windows Explorer or My Computer to navigate to the file you want to track.

3. Arrange the screen so that you can see both the Journal and your PC's folder hierarchy.

4. Click and drag the file from Windows Explorer or My Computer into the Journal. When you release the mouse button, a journal entry is created.

As mentioned earlier, you can associate a particular contact with Office files and Outlook items so that you can view, all at once, the files and items related to that particular person. First, you must link the file or Outlook item to the contact. Follow these steps to link an Office file to a contact so that you can track activity in the file:

1. In Outlook, open the contact for whom you'd like to link and track files.

2. Choose Link on the Actions menu, and then click File.

3. Navigate to the target file in the Choose a File dialog box, and click Insert.

4. Configure any other options in the Journal entry, and then click Save and Close.

To link Outlook items, including e-mails, tasks, appointments, and notes to a contact, choose Link, Item on the Actions menu in a contact and then select the item or items to track.

View all activities associated with a contact by doing the following:

1. In the Outlook contact list, double-click a contact to open it.
2. In the Activities tab, choose Journal from the Show pull-down list. Tracked files and items are listed for you to review.

Import Contacts from Another Program

Outlook provides an easy way to import contact information from another program: simply use the Import and Export command. For instance, you can import contact information from ACT!, a Personal Folders (PST) file, a text file, or a database as shown in Figure 10-13. Before you import anything, be sure to back up your Outlook data. Then choose Import and Export on the File menu, and follow the steps in the Import a File dialog box. For some file types, you might have to install the proper converters, such as the Microsoft Office Outlook Translator, if required. When the import process is finished, check to see whether the contacts were imported successfully.

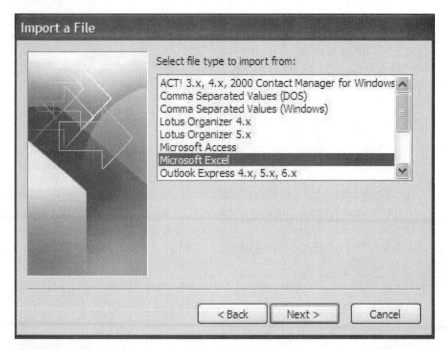

Figure 10-13

Outlook provides a variety of file types from which to import contact information.

To import contact information into Outlook from Excel, you must first name the range of cells that contains the contact data. In Excel, select the range of cells, and choose Name, Define on the Insert menu. Then, in Outlook, in the import process, choose Microsoft Excel as the type of file to import from, and then navigate to and select the Excel file containing the named range to import the data into Outlook.

To export contact information to Excel, when you want to perform a mail merge, for instance, follow these steps:

1. In Outlook, choose Import and Export on the File menu.

2. Choose Export to a File, and then click Next.

3. Select Microsoft Excel from the Create a File of Type list, and then click Next.

4. Choose Contacts in the Select Folder to Export From list, and click Next.

5. Name the new Excel file and choose a location for it in the Save Exported File As box. Click Next.

6. In the Export to a File dialog box, click the Map Custom Fields if you'd like to customize the way the contact information is exported to Excel.

7. Click Finish.

Perform a Mail Merge Easily

When you have a mass mailing to do, you might think the only way to personalize all the letters and address all the envelopes is to type them by hand. Whoa! There's a better way, and it's *not* too complicated for you to master easily. A *mail merge* is a way of creating documents that are mostly the same but that contain some unique elements such as different names and addresses or personalized greetings. You can draw the unique elements from a data source, such as an Excel database, your Outlook contacts file, or a text file, and insert them at appropriate places in a master document, which contains placeholders for the unique data. Word automates the merge process so that many unique documents can be produced quickly and easily, saving you from the tiresome task of manually creating, editing, and personalizing each unique file. Using a mail merge saves time, *enormous* amounts of time. You simply have to have faith in the process.

Do you believe us when we say that sending hundreds of personalized letters to everyone on a mailing list can be accomplished with ease in eight basic steps? Word provides a wizard that guides you through the process. Besides form letters, you can even use this process to create mailing labels or envelopes, e-mail messages, and faxes. All you need to get started is the main form document and a data source file containing the unique data elements—and even if you don't have these, the Word Mail Merge Wizard makes it easy to create them.

Let's say you need to create a mass e-mail message to send to a set of your contacts. To start from scratch, follow these steps:

1. Open a blank document in Word, select Letters and Mailings on the Tools menu, and then click Mail Merge.

2. Choose E-mail Messages from the Select Document Type section. Click Next.

3. Choose Use the Current Document from the Select Starting Document section. Click Next.

TIP: *You can also choose to base the starting document (the main form document) on a template or to use an existing file.*

---

4. Choose Use an Existing List from the Select Recipients section. Click Next. In the Select Data Source dialog box, navigate to the data source file, and click Open. Select which recipients to include in the mail merge in the Mail Merge Recipients dialog box as shown in Figure 10-14. Click OK, and then click Next in the wizard.

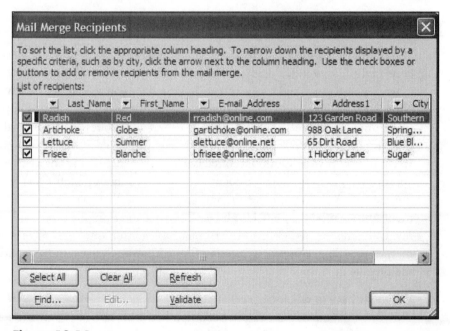

Figure 10-14
Select the recipients from the data source in the Mail Merge Recipients dialog box.

TIP: *You can choose to select recipients from your Outlook Contacts list or to create a new list as a data source. If you create a new list, that file is saved as a mailing database (MBD) file.*

5. Write the e-mail message. Where appropriate, insert the placeholders (fields) for information from your data source by selecting from the list of links in the Mail Merge Wizard and then customizing each item as shown in Figure 10-15. Click the More Items link for additional options. Fields are contained in double angle brackets in the main document. Click Next.

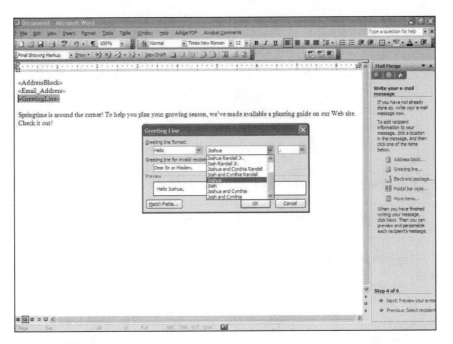

Figure 10-15
Insert fields into the main document by clicking the links provided in the Mail Merge Wizard.

6. Preview the merge. Use the arrow buttons in the wizard to page through the messages for each recipient. You can also choose to exclude a particular recipient or edit the recipient list. When you are satisfied that all the information is correct, click Next to perform the merge.

7. Click the Electronic Mail link in the wizard to set up the merge for e-mail messages. Be sure the label for the column containing recipient e-mail addresses in the data source is displayed in the To field of the Merge to E-mail dialog box. Insert a subject line if you wish, select a format for the message, and then click OK. Word immediately merges the messages and sends them from Outlook.

8. If you plan to use this form document again, save the file by choosing Save As on the File menu.

And that's that. It's not as complicated as you imagined because the Mail Merge Wizard makes it easy to perform a merge operation. All you need to do is experiment a little to find ways to customize your merge in each step of the wizard.

TIP: *Display the Mail Merge toolbar to have easy access to the appropriate commands. Choose Toolbars on the View menu and then click Mail Merge.*

Use Excel as a Mail Merge Data Source

It's easy to set up an Excel file to act as the data source for a mail merge. Follow these steps:

1. In Excel, make sure the data is in list form: each column has a label in row 1, no blank columns or rows are included in the list area, and the range of cells containing the list information is named (select the cells and choose Name, Define on the Insert menu).

2. Be sure the column labels clearly identify the data they contain, such as First_Name, Last_Name, Email_Address. Remember to modularize the data as much as possible, which maximizes the ways you can insert data into the form document. Make sure there's a separate column for each discrete piece of data you'll insert as a field in the form document.

3. Save and close the workbook.

In the Mail Merge Wizard, when it's time to choose a data source (see step 4 in the preceding section) in the Select Recipients section, choose Use an Existing List. In the Select Data Source dialog box, navigate to the Excel file, and click Open. Select the named range of the Excel list to point the Mail Merge Wizard at the correct data.

Summing Up

In this chapter, we discussed several of the many ways Office applications work together to help you get work done efficiently. You learned about the various ways you can transfer and share data between programs using the Office Clipboard, linked and embedded objects, drag-and-drop editing, and hyperlinks. We discussed how you can send Office-related data by e-mail from within Word, Excel, and PowerPoint to streamline the process. We also showed you how to import and export information in Office files and how to use Outlook as an information manager. Finally, we degunked the mail merge process so that you don't avoid using such a handy feature for your next mass mailing.

Securing Office

Degunking Checklist:

√ Implement the best security practices to secure your Office installation.

√ Use Microsoft resources to keep current with new security threats and learn how to fight them.

√ Apply our 10 easy-to-incorporate techniques for controlling who has access to your Office files and how they can modify them.

√ Follow the handy checklist to prepare your documents so that they can be safely shared with others.

√ Apply a few additional techniques to better secure your Word and PowerPoint documents.

√ Protect your system from macro virus infection.

√ Understand how virus-scanning software teams up with Office to protect your stuff.

Security is an important topic these days. After all, there are numerous ways to lose information, steal data, violate privacy, penetrate computer systems, and spread malicious code—more than ever before. In fact, almost every day on the news you hear of a new type of security breach, worm virus, or Web site defacement. Not to scare you, but there are people out there who know a lot more about computers than you do and who wish to harm your PC if they catch you when your back is turned. In this chapter, we'll show you how to batten down the hatches and make your Office installation as impervious to security violations as possible. We'll also show you how to remove personal information from your documents, protect your work from unauthorized changes, tighten security on Office apps, and ensure that files you send and receive do not contain viruses.

Tightening security is just the next step on the road to gunk-free living. Putting in place a solid security plan makes good degunking sense because prevention is the best medicine. Just think of the gunked-up mess you'd have to deal with if your PC were invaded by spyware, malicious code, or a virus; you'd have a lot of frustrating cleaning, repairing, and reinstalling to do.

Incorporate Security Best Practices

Office takes the business of protecting your data and systems seriously. Your installation of Office comes with numerous security defaults already in place to provide at least a minimum amount of data security, document integrity, and virus protection. It's generally not a good idea to reconfigure your PC to use less-secure settings than the defaults; instead, we'll show you how to enhance security to fit your particular situation. Above all else, the two very important security procedures that you should make a habit of following are these:

√   Back up your important data regularly. This will help you recover if you happen to suffer data loss or virus infection. (We'll give you detailed information on how to back up and protect your data in Chapter 12 "Backing Up and Restoring Office.")

√   Install and run up-to-date antivirus software on your PC. Make sure that the antivirus software is actually enabled and running (not just installed with a subscription that has run out) and that it updates itself regularly to stay current with the latest virus signatures.

Use Microsoft Resources to Bolster Your Defenses

Microsoft dedicates major resources to helping Office users practice secure computing. Take advantage of these resources to keep abreast of the latest security threats and download the latest security patches and critical updates to augment your defenses. Here are just a few of the Microsoft-sponsored Web sites that can help:

√ The Microsoft Security and Office site at **http://office.microsoft.com/ en-us/assistance/HA010957811033.aspx**

√ The Microsoft Security at Home site at **www.microsoft.com/athome/ security/protect/default.aspx**

√ The Windows Update site at **http://v5.windowsupdate.microsoft.com/ v5consumer/default.aspx?ln=en-us**

√ The Office Update site at **http://office.microsoft.com/en-us/ officeupdate/default.aspx**

√ The Microsoft Security Updates site at **www.microsoft.com/security/ bulletins/default.mspx**

Follow the Top 10 Ways to Secure Office

You can implement a few simple but very important methods to avert disaster. Here are 10 ways you can ensure that data you send and receive remains safe and secure:

1. Download documents only from trusted sources.
2. Don't open suspicious-looking e-mail messages or file attachments.
3. Verify document authenticity by examining attached digital certificates and digital signatures.
4. Remove personal information from your documents.
5. Make sure deleted information is completely removed.
6. Erase "invisible" information.
7. Review revision marks for tracked changes.
8. Snap a lock on your documents using protection features.
9. Require a password to open or modify sensitive documents.
10. Recommend opening your documents as read-only.

Files that you create using Office apps contain personal and hidden information that you probably prefer to keep private. Documents that you share with other users can be edited and changed without your knowledge so that you lose control of content. Several useful Office features, such as Track Changes, fast saves, comments, versions, AutoText, and field codes, use this personal information and store content changes. To make your Office files more secure, you'll need to enable some security features on a document-by-document basis using the following tips.

Download Documents Only from Trusted Sources

Avoid copying information or downloading files, scripts, or applications from suspicious-looking Web sites. Use sites maintained by well-known companies. If you have no way of knowing whether a source is legitimate, err on the side of safety and don't download from it. If you must save files from a questionable source, take the extra step of downloading them to removable storage media, such as disks or CDs, instead of storing them on your hard drive. If you later find the file contains malicious code, you can easily keep it quarantined from your file system.

TIP: *Consider saving a restore point in Windows XP before opening suspicious files (we show you how in Chapter 12, "Backing Up and Restoring Office"). If something goes haywire, you can revert back to a point prior to when you opened the suspicious file.*

Don't Open Suspicious-Looking E-Mail Messages or File Attachments

If you receive a message from an unknown source or one tagged with a bogus subject line such as "ILOVEYOU" and you don't know the sender, don't open it. You can unwittingly expose your system to a nasty virus. Outlook security defaults strip executable file attachments from messages in your Inbox, but almost any other type of file attachment can contain a virus or worm or mischievous code. It's best to delete a message and attachment you don't trust rather than run the risk of exposing your system to malware. Ensure that the Deleted Items folder in Outlook and the Windows Recycle Bin are emptied, too. And then run your virus-scanning software just to make sure your file system remains uninfected.

TIP: *Many viruses are distributed as EXE files because they need to run to wreak havoc. Also, many virus-spreading messages contain "RE:" in the subject line to trick you into thinking the phony message is really a reply to an earlier inquiry of yours. More details on viruses are given later in this chapter in the section "Use Virus-Scanning Software to Detect and Remove Macro Viruses." See Chapter 9, "Degunking Microsoft Outlook," for more information on e-mail security.*

Verify Document Authenticity by Examining Attached Digital Certificates and Signatures

In Office 2003, a *digital certificate* is the electronic equivalent of that seal of authenticity stamped on the bottom of your Norman Rockwell matched coffee mugs: when a digital certificate is attached to a document, it provides information about the document, such as the name of the author and where the document originated, that can assure the recipient that the file comes from a reputable source and has not been tampered with in transit. To be issued a valid digital certificate, a source must apply to a trusted third-party certification authority, which in effect vouches for the reputability of the source. A *digital signature* is the electronic equivalent of a handwritten signature; it is an encrypted key that is attached to a document and assures that the document originated from the signer and has not been changed since signing. To examine a file's digital certificate or signature, do the following:

1. Choose Options from the Tools menu.

2. Select the Security tab in the Options dialog box.

3. Click the Digital Signatures button. If a digital certificate or signature has been attached to the file, it will appear in the Digital Signatures dialog box.

4. Examine the Signer, Digital ID Issued By, and Date information to decide whether you trust the source and to ensure that the certificate is still valid.

5. For more detailed information, select a certificate or signature from the Signer list, and then click the View Certificate button to see details.

6. Click OK three times to close the dialog boxes.

Remove Personal Information from Your Documents

Before you share Office files in electronic format, you should review their content as well as the associated file properties to be sure the information is appropriate to disseminate. Some personal information that is contained in a Word document, for instance, is the name of the author, manager, company, and the person who last saved the document; names, dates, and times associated with comments; routing slips; contact information in the message header for a message generated by clicking the E-mail button on the Standard toolbar; and the name of the person who saved the file (stored under Saved By in the file properties). To remove this information from a Word, Excel, or PowerPoint file, complete these steps:

1. Click Options on the Tools menu.
2. Click the Security tab in the Options dialog box.
3. Select the Remove Personal Information from File Properties on Save check box; then click OK.
4. Save the document.

TIP: *In previous versions of Office such as Office 2000, you can save a document as a text file (.txt) using the Save As command on the File menu. This will strip out personal information. Then, open and save the text file as a Word document.*

Once you have stripped the personal information from the file properties, you will notice that the name associated with any comments inserted in the document has been changed to "Author," as has the name associated with Track Changes edits. When you hover over the file's icon in Windows Explorer, no author name is listed in the information that appears in the ScreenTip.

Make Sure Deleted Information Is Completely Removed

If you save a document with the Allow Fast Saves check box selected (Tools menu, Options dialog box, Save tab) and then open the document as a text file, you will find that the document can contain information that you previously deleted. This happens because a fast save appends the changes you make to the end of the document so that all changes can be saved quickly without interrupting the document's availability for editing. This could be embarrassing, at the very least, when you think you've safely deleted the section of your document in which company secrets and sensitive issues are discussed in detail. This situation occurred recently when the British government posted a read-only Word file to a public Web site reporting solid intelligence validating U.S. arguments about the existence of weapons of mass destruction inventories in Iraq. But hidden, undeleted text embedded within the file, which could be viewed with a text editor, exposed the fact that the report was based on a U.S. intelligence report speculating on the Iraqi inventories. Both governments were obviously embarrassed.

To quickly remove deleted information from a document, do the following:

1. If you opened the document as a text file, close the text file and open the document as a regular Word document.
2. Click Save As from the File menu, and then click Save.

Although saving the document as a text file (.txt) removes any hidden text and personal data, it also removes all formatting and pictures. Instead, try the copy and paste method when you want to preserve formatting:

1. Open the document as usual, accept all changes (Tools menu, Track Changes, Accept or Reject Changes).

2. Copy all to a new document (Edit menu, Select All, Copy).

3. Remember to attach templates as appropriate.

TIP: *You can enable the fast saves option in PowerPoint too, so be sure to check your presentations for previous changes that you would rather not share. In both Word and PowerPoint, you can turn off fast saves by choosing Options on the Tools menu, clicking the Save tab, and then clearing the Allow Fast Saves check box.*

We recommend disabling the Allow Fast Saves option (Tools menu, Options, Save tab) if information security is an issue. Waiting the extra second or two for a full save to complete is worth avoiding the embarrassment of exposing sensitive data.

Erase "Invisible" Information

To reduce on-screen clutter in a document you create, you can hide some information from view. Some examples of things to hide might be revision marks for tracked changes, comments, and hidden text. Before you give others a copy of the document, it's best to view this invisible information and decide whether it's appropriate to share. (Recipients of your documents can easily make visible this supposedly invisible text with just a few mouse clicks.) You might want to omit this information in the printed version of the document or remove the information altogether before you distribute the document online.

In Word, here are the steps you should follow:

1. Open the Security tab in the Options dialog box (choose Options on the Tools menu), and be sure that the Make Hidden Markup Visible When Opening or Saving option is selected.

2. Before you close the Options dialog box, select the View tab, and make sure that the Hidden Text option is selected in the Formatting Text section.

3. Scan your document for comments, formatting, or any text that has been designated as hidden, which is indicated by a dotted underline, and decide whether you'd like to include it when you send your document.

> ### GunkBuster's Notebook: Easy Way to Locate and Delete Hidden Text
>
> Here's an easy way to locate hidden text and delete it: Use the Find feature or the Replace feature on the Edit menu to search for every instance of a hidden font (text) and replace it with nothing to delete it. Otherwise, hidden text can be edited and deleted just like normal text. If you plan to print your document and do not want the hidden text printed, open the Options dialog box again, click the Print tab, and then clear the Hidden Text check box in the Include with Document section.
>
> Similarly, you should review comments or delete them before you distribute Office documents. You can view all the comments in a document or comments from only a specific reviewer. To view comments, choose Comments (in earlier Office versions) from the View menu or Markup (in Office 2003). You can choose to delete or hide comments before you print a document. An easy way to locate comments and delete them is to use the Find feature or the Replace feature on the Edit menu to find every instance of a comment mark (use the options under the Special button in the Find and Replace dialog box) and replace it with nothing to delete it. To print a document without printing the comments, choose Options on the Tools menu, select the Print tab, and then clear the Comments check box under Include with Document.

Review Revision Marks for Tracked Changes

Unless you are in the midst of a collaborative project for which it is important to keep track of editing changes made to Word or Excel files, it's often best to share only the final version of a document with recipients. To get rid of this gunk, point to Track Changes on the Tools menu, click Highlight Changes on the submenu, and then select the Highlight Changes on Screen check box in the Highlight Changes dialog box. (In Word 2003, view revision marks on-screen by choosing Markup on the View menu.)

You can simply hide revision marks in a document you plan to print without accepting or rejecting them. Choose Print from the File menu, and then in the Print dialog box, make sure that Document is selected in the Print What drop-down list as shown in Figure 11-1. Also, in the Highlight Changes dialog box, clear the Highlight Changes in Printed Document check box.

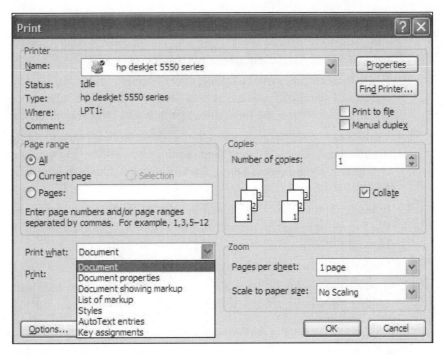

Figure 11-1
Hide tracked changes in a printed document by choosing not to print markup.

Snap a Lock on Docs Using Protection Features

If you find you cannot make changes to a Word document or Excel spreadsheet, the file might be locked for editing, it might be password-protected, or you might be trying to modify a document or text in a file that is protected.

TIP: You cannot edit a document that is open in Word Viewer, but you can copy text to the Clipboard to paste into other applications.

If you see a message similar to this, "**This modification is not allowed because the document is locked,**" at the bottom of the application window when you try to modify a file, the file is protected using the Protect Document or Protect Workbook/Sheet feature. Menu commands and styles also might be unavailable, depending on the type of protection applied.

Protect Word Documents

You can restrict changes made by users to allow only tracked changes, comments, or changes to form fields. In Word 2003, you can apply formatting restrictions and editing restrictions as well as exempt particular parts of the document from protection. To protect a document in Word 2003, do the following:

1. Choose Protect Document from the Tools menu.

2. In the Protect Document task pane, under Formatting Restrictions, check the Limit Formatting to a Selection of Styles check box, and then use the Settings link to select the styles for which you will allow modifications.

3. Under Editing Restrictions, select the Allow Only This Type of Editing in the Document check box, and then use the drop-down menu to choose either No Changes (Read Only), Tracked Changes, Comments, or Filling In Forms.

4. In the Exceptions area, choose whether you'd like to exempt certain parts of the document or certain users from the protection settings, as shown in Figure 11-2.

5. Click the Yes, Start Enforcing Protection button.

6. Type a password in the Enter New Password (Optional) box, and then confirm the password. Click OK.

To protect a document in earlier versions of Word, use the File menu Save As feature (File menu, Save As, Tools, General Options) and enter a password to enable editing, as shown in Figure 11-3.

Figure 11-2

In the Exceptions section, you can exempt certain users from the protection applied to parts of the document.

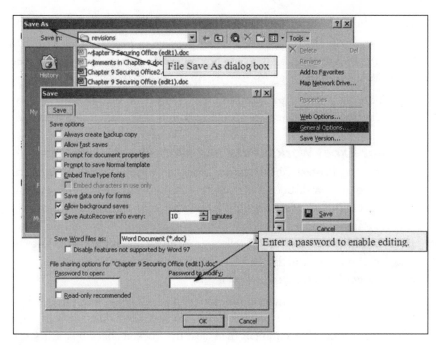

Figure 11-3
Use the method demonstrated here to protect a document in Word 2000.

If you've selected Tracked Changes, for example, you'll notice that the Track Changes feature is automatically turned on in the document and any insertions a recipient makes in the document are tracked; the recipient cannot turn off the Track Changes feature without knowing the password.

Protect Excel Workbooks

You can protect an entire workbook file by restricting who can open and use its data and by requiring a password to view or save changes to the file (see "Require a Password to Open or Modify Sensitive Documents" later in this chapter for more information on applying passwords to workbooks).

An Excel workbook is the overall file that stores your individual worksheets. When you use the Protect Workbook feature, you can lock down either the structure of the workbook or the windows, or both. Protecting a workbook prevents users from adding, deleting, moving, renaming, or hiding worksheets. When you protect the workbook windows, you prevent users from resizing and repositioning the windows. You have the option of assigning a password to workbook protection so that only users who know the password can unprotect the document. To protect a workbook, complete these steps:

1. On the Tools menu, point to Protection, and then choose Protect Workbook.

2. In the Protect Workbook dialog box, select the options to protect: Structure or Windows.

3. Optionally, supply a password in the Password text box. (Remember to store the password in a safe place and share it only with authorized users.)

Protect Excel Worksheets and Worksheet Elements

By using the Protect Sheet feature, you can apply protection to particular worksheets and worksheet elements. You can prevent users from inserting, deleting, changing, or reformatting the contents of locked cells. You can also exempt certain cell ranges or certain users from the applied protection. When you apply worksheet protection, all cells are locked by default; if you wish to unlock cells, you must do this by hand before you apply worksheet protection. To protect a worksheet, do the following:

1. If you wish to allow users to modify specific cells in the worksheet, select the cells to unlock: On the Format menu, choose Cells. In the Format Cells dialog box, select the Protection tab, then clear the Locked check box. Click OK.

TIP: If the **Cells** command is not available, parts of the worksheet might already be locked. On the **Tools** menu, point to **Protection**, and then click **Unprotect Sheet**.

---

2. If you would like certain users to be able to modify the worksheet in ways other than the protection feature will allow, you must exempt those users from protection. Choose Protection from the Tools menu, and then select Allow Users to Edit Ranges. Specify the ranges you would like unlocked when users supply the correct password and click the Permissions button to add the names of specific users to the exemption list. Click Apply and then OK.

3. On the Tools menu, point to Protection, and choose Protect Sheet.

4. In the Protect Sheet dialog box, be sure the "Protect worksheet and contents of locked cells" option is selected. Then select from the list the actions you would like users to be able to do in the protected worksheet. Optionally, type a password for worksheet protection. Click OK.

TIP: If you do not apply a password for the **Protect Sheet** feature, any user can turn off protection.

After protection is applied, users will be issued a warning message any time they try to modify a workbook or worksheet in ways the protection features disallow.

TIP: Take worksheet and workbook element protection for what it is: a way to keep recipients of your workbooks from changing or moving specific data accidentally or on purpose. It provides a way to protect the integrity of your data; however, it cannot take the place of file security measures you can apply to protect your Excel files through password protection (see the next section).

Require a Password to Open or Modify Sensitive Documents

When you password-protect a document, Office encrypts the document so that only you or people you share the password with can decrypt and view the document contents. You can apply password protection on a file-by-file basis for Word docs, Excel workbooks, and PowerPoint presentations. To require a password to open a document, workbook, or presentation, follow these steps:

1. Open the document.

2. Choose Options from the Tools menu.

3. Select the Security tab in the Options dialog box.

4. Enter a password in the Password to Open text box as shown in Figure 11-4. Then click OK.

5. In the Confirm Password dialog box, type the password again, and then click OK.

TIP: Word encrypts the whole password-protected document; Excel and PowerPoint encrypt only the password using strong encryption.

TIP: When you create a password, write it down and keep it in a secure place. (Do not write it on a sticky note and tape it to your monitor!) If you lose the password, you cannot open or gain access to the password-protected document.

GunkBuster's Notebook: Protecting Your Documents from Being Modified

You can limit whether users are allowed to make changes to your document by requiring a *password to modify*. Only users who know the password can modify a document. Although this option does not encrypt the document—the document can be opened and read by anyone—you can use it in combination with a password to open so that recipients are prompted for both passwords when they attempt to view the document. To require a password to modify a document, in the Save tab of the Options dialog box (choose Options on the Tools menu), enter a password in the Password to Modify text box.

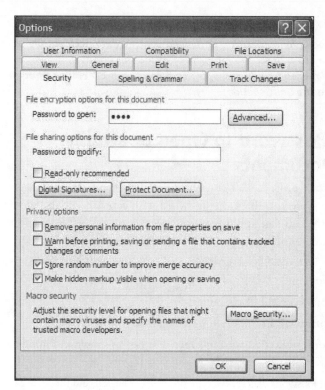

Figure 11-4

Use the Security tab of the Options dialog box to require a
password to open this Word document.

> *Tip: If you have applied a password to modify a document and a user
> who does not know the password makes unauthorized changes to
> the document, that person can save the changes only by saving the
> document using a different file name.*

There's a quick way to apply these settings when you save a file:

1. Choose Save As from the File menu.

2. In the Save As dialog box, click the Tools button, and
   choose General Options or Security Options (in Word
   2003) from the drop-down menu.

3. In the Password to Open text box and/or the Password to
   Modify box, type a password, and then click OK.

4. In the Confirm Password dialog box, type the password
   again, and then click OK.

5. Click Save.

Recommend Opening Your Documents as Read-Only

You can suggest, but not require, that users open a Word document or Excel workbook as read-only. Making this recommendation can emphasize the fact that you think the file contents are important and should not be changed without authorization. Although you have no way of forcing document recipients to acquiesce, you can have Word and Excel recommend to readers that they open a document as read-only by completing the following steps:

1. Open the document.

2. Choose Options from the Tools menu.

3. In the Options dialog box, select the Security or Save tab.

4. Select the Read-Only Recommended check box, and then click OK.

Users can open and copy a read-only document, but they cannot change or save it—if they make a change, they can save the document only by using a different file name.

Prepare Documents for Review

Now that you know how to apply some techniques to better secure your documents, let's continue with our security degunking by developing a checklist for preparing your documents for distribution and review by others. We've indicated in parentheses which types of files each step applies to. Here are the steps you should follow to prepare a file so that you can safely share it with others:

1. Open the file you want to prepare for review *(Word, Excel, and PowerPoint)*.

2. Check whether the file contains multiple versions (see the section "Use Versions to Trace Changes Made to a Document" later in this chapter for more information). If multiple versions exist, save the current version as a separate document using a different file name, and use it as the review copy *(Word)*.

3. Check the file's contents for hidden text and comments to be sure they are appropriate to share *(Word, Excel, and PowerPoint)*.

4. Review tracked changes and accept and delete revisions so that you can save a final draft *(Word and Excel)*.

5. If necessary, remove personal information from the file by stripping it from the file properties *(Word, Excel, and PowerPoint)*.

6. Protect the file from unauthorized changes by using the Protect Document or Protect Workbook/Sheet feature; assign a password to the protection feature *(Word and Excel)*.

7. Assign a password to open the file, and then share this password only with authorized recipients *(Word, Excel, and PowerPoint)*.

8. Assign a password to modify the file contents, and share this password only with users authorized to make changes *(Word, Excel, and PowerPoint)*.

9. Recommend that the file be opened as read–only *(Word and Excel)*.

10. Save and close the file, distribute the passwords to appropriate recipients, and then distribute the document.

GunkBuster's Notebook: Use Security Settings for an Entire Project

An easy way to apply security to an entire project, no matter whether that project encompasses a mix of workbooks, documents, presentations, or shared folders, is to select two or three project-specific passwords. For each project, do the following:

* Designate one password (password to open) to apply file-level security to all project files to control who can access the project.

* Choose a second password (password to modify) to control who can make changes to the project files.

* Use a third password to make file security even more granular by controlling exactly who can make what changes in protected documents.

Apply these passwords consistently to all related project files, and share passwords with team members on a need-to-know basis, allowing them just enough access to do their jobs. This is called the *principle of least privilege*. We know it sounds pretentious, but for the sake of your data's security, it's best to limit the permissions you extend to users by sharing passwords so that you can feel sure that unauthorized users are prevented from making unauthorized changes. For example, for this project, we use ********** as the password for file-level security, which allows both of us to open, modify, and save different chapter files as well as Excel scheduling sheets and PowerPoint art files; we share a password to modify, ******, with our editors, but we cleverly neglect to share with them the password to unprotect our documents! We find we have a lot less rewriting to do this way.

Securing Word Documents for Distribution

Because many of the files you create in Office will be Word documents, let's spend a little more time looking at how these documents can be made more secure. In addition to the 10 security measures we discussed previously, you can do the following:

- √ *Prevent users from changing a form.* You can assign a password for changing the content of a form.
- √ *Use versions to trace changes made to a document.* Keep modifications made to a document sorted out by storing versions—snapshots—of documents at different stages of their development and after distribution.

Prevent Users from Changing a Form

A form contains fill-in-the-blank areas just as Mad Libs do (see Figure 11-5). As with Mad Libs, a user is required to insert a specific type of information into each of the form fields (the blanks) so that the end result "makes sense."

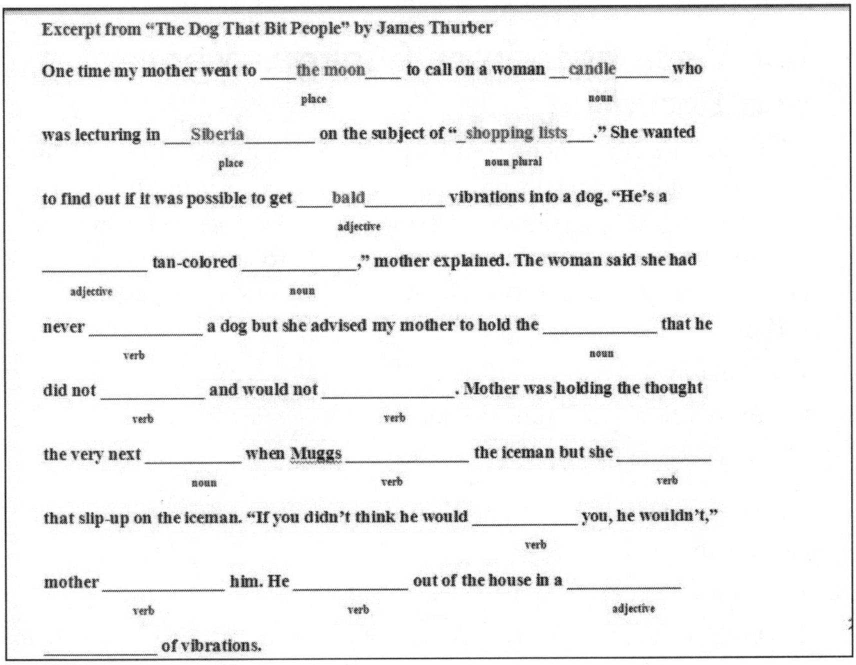
Excerpt from "The Dog That Bit People" by James Thurber

One time my mother went to ___the moon___ to call on a woman __candle_____ who
place noun
was lecturing in ___Siberia_______ on the subject of "_shopping lists___." She wanted
place noun plural
to find out if it was possible to get ___bald________ vibrations into a dog. "He's a
adjective
__________ tan-colored __________," mother explained. The woman said she had
adjective noun
never ___________ a dog but she advised my mother to hold the ___________ that he
verb noun
did not __________ and would not ____________. Mother was holding the thought
verb verb
the very next _________ when Muggs ___________ the iceman but she _________
noun verb verb
that slip-up on the iceman. "If you didn't think he would __________ you, he wouldn't,"
verb
mother ___________ him. He __________ out of the house in a ___________
verb verb adjective
___________ of vibrations.

Figure 11-5
Forms contain fill-in-the-blank areas just as this Mad Lib does.

You've probably filled out numerous forms online—inserting your name, address, and phone number, and getting yelled out in large red print when you've entered too few numbers in your ZIP code. You've also probably noticed that you can insert information into the designated form fields but you cannot make changes to the display content, including the form text and form field labels. You can set up your forms the same way—to accept only proper input in designated areas and prevent users from changing the display content. To do so, after creating a form, you must protect it:

1. Select Protect Document from the Tools menu.

2. Select the Forms radio button, or choose Filling in Forms from the drop-down list in Word 2003.

3. You can assign a password to the form so that users who know the password can remove the protection and change the form. Users who don't know the password can still enter information in the form fields. Type a password in the Password text box.

4. To protect the entire form, click OK. In earlier Word versions, to protect only parts of a form, those parts must be in separate sections. Click Sections, and then clear the check boxes of the sections you don't want to protect.

5. Click OK.

Use Versions to Trace Changes Made to a Document

When you are concerned about keeping track of changes made to documents after distribution, using document file versions is a quick and easy way to maintain control. Using versions makes good degunking sense too, because it saves disk space: Word saves only the changes made to a document, not the whole document, each time a version is saved. There are several ways you can save a version of a document:

√ Manually

√ Automatically each time the document is closed

√ As a separate file

You can take a snapshot of a document in its current state by directing Word to create a version right now:

1. Choose Versions from the File menu.

2. In the Versions in *Document Name* dialog box, click the Save Now button.

3. In the Save Version dialog box, enter any comments you wish to use to describe this version. Then click OK.

4. Click Close.

You can have Word automatically save a version of your document each time the document is closed:

1. Choose Versions from the File menu.

2. In the Versions in *Document Name* dialog box, select the "Automatically save a version on close" check box.

3. Click Close.

TIP: You won't be able to save a version automatically upon close when you save a document as a Web page.

GunkBuster's Notebook: Saving a File Version as a Separate File

After you've saved multiple versions of a document in one file, you might decide that you want recipients to see only a particular version. You can direct Word to save a specific version as a separate file. This is useful when you want to prevent users from seeing previous versions. You can also use this technique when you want to compare an earlier version to a later version using the Compare Documents command (on the Tools menu, choose Track Changes, Compare Documents; or choose Compare and Merge Documents on the Tools menu in Word 2003). To save a version of a document as a separate file, complete these steps:

1. Choose Versions from the File menu.
2. Select the version of the document you want to save as a separate file.
3. Click Open.
4. On the File menu, click Save As.
5. In the File Name text box, enter a name, and then click Save.

Prevent Reviewers from Opening Previous Versions

If you specified that Word save one or more versions of your document in the same file, those versions are saved as hidden information in the document file so that you can retrieve them later. Because versions of a document are available to others and because they do not remain hidden if you or someone else saves the document in another format, you might want to remove the versions before you share the document.

√ If you want to keep the previous versions, save the current version as a separate document, and then distribute only that document.

√ If you don't want to keep the previous versions, delete the unwanted versions, and then distribute the document.

Securing PowerPoint Presentations for Distribution

PowerPoint provides a few more app-specific features to help you secure your presentations.

Use Pack and Go

Use the Pack and Go feature to compile your presentation into a runtime version (.pps) that does not require the PowerPoint application or the PowerPoint Viewer application to be seen (and enjoyed, hopefully).

Pack and Go is also a good feature to enable you to take the finalized version of your presentation on the road. The resultant file is compressed and contains all embedded and linked objects; it's a self-contained file that allows you to take everything necessary to open and view your PowerPoint presentation no matter where you end up.

Use PowerPoint Viewer

Microsoft provides as a free download, a viewer application program for each version of PowerPoint. If you are posting your PowerPoint documents to a Web page, provide a PowerPoint Viewer download link in the event the user does not have PowerPoint (or your version of PowerPoint) installed. This allows you to be reasonably certain viewers will see your presentation as you meant it to be seen. Be aware, however, that presentations you have protected with a password to open or password to modify can still be opened and viewed in the PowerPoint Viewer.

Keep Macro Viruses at Bay

A computer virus is a little program that can infiltrate a system by inserting copies of itself into legitimate programming code. Usually this invasion has unwelcome side effects such as data loss, application failure, or negative impacts on performance. Viruses attack the software of a computer—the operating system, usually—and try to damage or destroy programs or data. Viruses must be run, or executed, to have any effect, and that's why many viruses are written in executable form using the .exe file extension and why they insert themselves into runnable code. By hitchhiking along with legitimate code, viruses assure themselves of being run so they can spread infection.

TIP: *Files that your PC sees simply as data and that contain no runnable code, such as TXT (.txt) files or plain-text e-mail messages, cannot contain viruses (which need to associate with executable code), and so plain data files cannot harm your PC.*

A type of virus has emerged, unfortunately, that is specifically designed to affect your Office applications and document data: the macro virus. A *macro* is a set of commands that you can package together to automate tasks in Office apps and is written in Microsoft Visual Basic for Applications (VBA) language. A *macro virus* is a virus that uses an application's own macro programming language (VBA for Office) to propagate and distribute itself covertly while being disguised in the host application's own functions, for example, in Word or Excel templates and documents. Macro viruses are stored in macros and can run automatically when you open an Office file—just as some legitimate macros do—unless you have security procedures put in place to screen macros.

TIP: *Leaving your PC exposed to virus infection from any source is yet another form of gunk, or more accurately, it's a critical gap in your degunking strategy that opens you to needless exposure—like forgetting to pay the annual premium to maintain your home security system.*

When you open a document or template that contains a macro virus, the virus infects your system and spreads to other documents and templates on your system. In many cases, macro viruses don't actually cause damage to your data but propagate themselves over and over, adding unnecessary payload to ordinary documents. In other cases, some malicious macros have been written specifically to damage your work. Unlike operating system viruses, macro viruses do not infect programs (files with the .exe extension) or the operating system boot sector; they specifically target documents, templates, workbook files, or any application that uses a programming language, as well as potentially threaten the operating system. Some macro viruses are annoying but not harmful; others can be very destructive. You can unwittingly be participating in their spread of infection unless you are aware of them and take steps to block them. Here we discuss macro virus protection techniques that apply specifically to the Microsoft Office environment.

You also must be aware that macro viruses can spread across platforms; for example, a macro virus can infect files on a computer that runs the Windows operating system and then can hitch a ride across the Internet, for example, to infect files on a Macintosh computer. However, macro viruses do not travel independently over the Internet or any other medium (for example, by disk or over a network connection); they are transferred only when a document or template in which they reside is opened. Macro viruses also cannot be transferred by e-mail unless an affected document is attached to the e-mail message and the recipient opens that attachment without proper protections in place.

TIP: *To view frequently asked questions about macro viruses, see Microsoft Knowledge Base article 211607: "Frequently Asked Questions About Word Macro Viruses" at the site http://support.microsoft.com/kb/211607.*

Determine Whether You Have a Macro Virus

It is not always easy to determine whether you have a macro virus. There is no telltale red rash or fever with chills (although there might be a headache). If you are familiar with the macros installed on your system, you can look through them for ones that you do not recognize. One or more of the unfamiliar macros may be part of a macro virus that has infected your system. Examples of this type of macro might be named AAAZAO, AAAZFS, AutoOpen, FileSaveAs, and PayLoad.

Some other symptoms to look for include these:

√   Unexplainable behavior occurs on your system. For example, you might be prompted for a password on a file that you know does not require a password, or your document might unexpectedly be saved as a template.

√   Unusual or unexplainable messages appear in a dialog box.

√   Your documents undergo unusual changes; for example, a macro virus might unexpectedly move three words and then insert the word *WAZZU* at random locations.

√   Menu items might be missing from menus; for example, the Macro or Customize commands no longer appear on the Tools menu.

√   When you try to save a document, Word, Excel, or PowerPoint lets you save the document only as a document template (*.dot, *. xlt, or *.pot).

√   The icon for a file looks like a template icon rather than a document icon.

√   When you point to Macro on the Tools menu and then click Macros, nothing happens.

√   New macros appear in the list of installed macros. For example, macros with names such as AutoOpen, AutoNew, AutoExec, or FileSaveAs might mysteriously show up. If your system already saved macros by these names, the original macro contents might be changed by the macro virus or your macro might have been renamed.

TIP: *A macro virus can cause one or more of the preceding symptoms as well as other symptoms not listed. Be alert for unusual behavior.*

How to Deal with a Macro Virus

For a long-term solution to macro viruses, install antivirus software that is specifically designed to detect macro viruses. Other than that, don't feel too bad if you're infected; just use the following four methods to resolve macro virus problems.

Method 1: Press Shift When You Open a File

If your system does not exhibit any of the symptoms described earlier when you start an Office app but you want to be sure you prevent infection, hold down the Shift key when you open a file that you suspect might contain a macro virus. Pressing and holding down Shift when you open a document or template (or pressing Shift when you start an Office app) prevents any auto macros from running; therefore, if a macro virus is present, it will not be loaded.

Method 2: Delete the Macro and Recover the Document

If you have experienced any of the symptoms listed earlier, or if you suspect that you have a macro virus that is not described here, use the following steps to remove the macros and correct the affected documents (remember, this is only a temporary solution; these steps might not work because new macro viruses appear every day):

1. Close whichever Office application you are working in; let's assume it's Word in this example.

2. Rename the Normal.dot template file. For example, rename Normal.dot to Normal.old.

3. Make a copy of the infected document or template.

4. Start Word.

5. Choose Open from the File menu, and navigate to the folder containing the affected file. Click to select the file.

6. Press and hold down the Shift key, and then click Open. Continue to hold the Shift key until the affected file is open in Word.

7. To remove a suspected macro virus, follow these steps:

   a. On the Tools menu, point to Macro, and then choose Macros from the submenu.

TIP: If nothing happens when you click Macros, try to use one of the other three methods.

---

   b. In the Macros In list, click "All active templates and documents."

   c. Select the suspected macro, and click Delete. Click Yes when asked whether you want to delete the macro.

   d. Repeat step c for all suspect macros.

   e. Click Cancel to close the Macros dialog box.

8. To recover the text of an infected document, follow these steps:

   a. Press Ctrl+End to move the insertion point to the bottom of the document.

b. Press Ctrl+Shift+Home to select the entire document except the last paragraph mark.

c. On the Edit menu, click Copy.

d. On the File menu, click New. Select the template you want to use, and click OK.

e. On the Edit menu, click Paste.

f. Repeat step 7 to ensure that the virus-containing macros have not again replicated.

g. Save your recovered document.

Repeat these steps for any document that you suspect might contain a macro virus.

Method 3: Use the Organizer in Word

Use the Organizer to clean up a suspected macro virus. Remember that if you've opened other files after you open the infected file, the other files most likely are infected as well. One caveat: Do not use this method if your global template (Normal.dot in most cases) contains macros that you want to keep. To use the Organizer, follow these steps:

1. Close all documents except a new blank document. If an infected document is open, it can easily re-infect your global template.

2. Click Templates and Add-Ins on the Tools menu, and then click Organizer.

3. On one side of the Organizer, open the global template (Normal.dot).

4. Click the Macro Project Items tab, and then rename or delete each of the following macros. If other macros are also listed, rename or delete them also.

   √ NewMacros

   √ AutoClose

   √ AutoExec

   √ AutoOpen

   √ FileExit

   √ FileNew

   √ FileOpen

   √ FileSave

   √ FileSaveAs

   √ Macros

   √ ToolsMacro

5. Click Close File to close the global template. When you are prompted to save the changes to the file, click Yes.

6. Click Open File, and open the document that contains the suspect macros.

7. Repeat step 4 and rename or delete each of the suspect macros.

8. Click Close File to close the document. When you are prompted to save the changes to the file, click Yes.

9. Click Close to close the Organizer.

Method 4: Insert the File into a New Document

Before you use this method, rename your global (Normal.dot) template. Follow these steps to insert a suspected macro–virus–infected document into a new file:

1. Start Word with a new blank document.

TIP: If the Macro, Customize, or Templates and Add-Ins commands are not on the Tools menu, use one of the other three methods to deal with macro viruses.

---

2. Choose File from the Insert menu, navigate to the folder containing the affected file, select the file, and then click Open.

3. To check whether any macros are contained in the new document (there should not be any), follow these steps:

   a. On the Tools menu, point to Macro, and then click Macros.

   b. In the Macros In text box, select "All active templates and documents."

   c. There should not be any macros listed in the Macro Name list. If macros are listed, you will have to use a different method.

   d. Click Cancel.

4. Save the new document with a different file name, and then delete the infected file.

Only *You* Can Prevent Macro Viruses

Not only must you be sure you are not inadvertently attaching an infected macro to documents you plan to share, you must be doubly certain that any file with attached macros that you open is completely virus-free before you open it.

One very low-tech and very simple way to prevent macro virus infection first and foremost is to *know where you've gotten a document*. If someone sends you a document or file, be sure you can trust that person. Is it someone you work with? Is it the obnoxious practical joker from your bowling league? Would this person send around files that have been obtained from untrustworthy sources?

If you are unsure whether the document is safe, contact the person who created the document and interrogate that person on the source of the macros (in a dank and subterranean room using the classical methods of information extraction).

Here are some other ways you can prevent your system from being attacked by a macro virus:

√ Use built-in Office macro virus protection.

√ Enable warnings to remind you macros are being loaded.

√ Favor macros that have been digitally signed.

√ Maintain a list of trusted sources.

√ Use virus-scanning software to detect and remove macro viruses.

We explain these preventive methods in the following sections.

Use Built-in Office Macro Virus Protection

In each Office program—Word, Excel, PowerPoint, and Outlook—make sure that you have macro virus protection turned on. Set virus protection to High or Medium to automatically screen which macros are accepted by your system. Here's how:

1. Choose Macro from the Tools menu, and then click Security.

2. In the Security dialog box, in the Security Level tab, select High or Medium, and then click OK.

Table 11-1 shows the various Office macro security levels, and Figure 11-6 shows the Security Level tab in the Security dialog box.

Table 11-1   Macro Security Levels

Security Level	Description
High	You can run only macros that have been digitally signed and ones that you confirm are from a trusted source. Before trusting a source, you should confirm that the source is responsible and uses a virus scanner before signing macros. Unsigned macros are automatically disabled, and Word opens the document without any warning.
Medium	A warning is displayed whenever Word, Excel, or PowerPoint encounters a macro from a source that is not on your list of trusted sources. You can choose whether to enable or disable the macros when you open the document. If the document might contain a virus, you should choose to disable macros.
Low	If you are sure that all the documents and add-ins that you open are safe, you can select this option, which turns off macro virus protection. At this security level, macros are always enabled when you open documents.

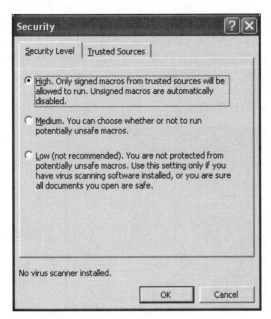

Figure 11-6
Select High or Medium as the security level for
macro virus protection.

Office 2003 adds an even more stringent security level to the list called Very
High. This type of security allows only macros installed in trusted places to be
run; all other macros, regardless of whether they are digitally signed or not, are
disabled automatically with no warning.

Enable Warnings to Remind You Macros Are Being Loaded

Research shows that most macro viruses are designed to run, or attack, when
you first open the file containing the infected macro, thereby preempting any
chance you have to stop them. It doesn't matter how you open the file: if the
file is opened into its related application, the macro virus executes. In some
cases, damage does not appear right away. By the time you realize that a macro
virus has attacked you, the virus has either spread to other documents on your
computer or—*yikes!*—to other computers.

Office applications can detect whether a document you attempt to open contains a macro before you open it. When you have the macro security level set to
Medium, you are automatically presented with a warning to remind you that
you are about to load a file containing macros. Such a warning forces you to
pause before opening a file to think through whether you know and trust the
document source enough to believe the macros could pass a health check. This

macro virus protection feature prompts you to either enable or disable the macros as you open the document. With warnings enabled, when you receive a workbook attached to an e-mail message, for instance, and you double-click to open it, you are first presented with the macro virus protection dialog box shown in Figure 11-7.

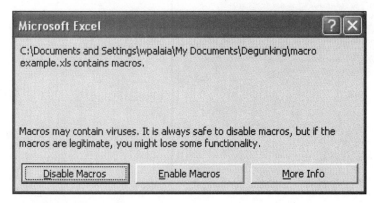

Figure 11-7
A macro warning dialog box in Excel gives you a chance to decide whether to enable or disable macros.

The dialog box gives you three choices:

√ *Disable Macros.* Choose this command if you are unsure of the source of the document, but you still want to open it.

√ *Enable Macros.* Choose this command if you know who created the document and trust that the macros are free of viruses.

√ *More Info.* Choose this command to be sure the document does not open. If you are completely unsure whether the document is free of macro viruses, you should not open the document but contact the document source to determine whether the document is safe (follow the interrogation procedure mentioned earlier).

TIP: To learn more about viruses and computer security in general, visit the Microsoft Security Advisor Web site at www.microsoft.com/security/default.mspx. To learn about macro security for Office 2000, download the "Microsoft Office 2000 Macro Security" white paper (http://office.microsoft.com/Downloads/2000/o2ksec.aspx); for info on macro security in Office 2003, see the article titled "Macro Security Levels in Office 2003" at www.microsoft.com/office/ork/2003/seven/ch23/SecA02.htm and also the info at www.microsoft.com/technet/prodtechnol/office/office2003/operate/o3secdet.mspx.

If you don't share files or disks with others or download files from the Internet, you might be tempted to disable this warning feature by setting the macro security level to Low. After all, macro warnings slow the file-opening process and require input from you—and, of course, you know all your macros are safe. However, Microsoft does not recommend setting the macro security level to Low because it offers you no virus protection whatsoever, and as we mentioned, macro viruses are stealthy.

Favor Macros That Have Been Digitally Signed

By accepting digitally signed macros from trustworthy sources, you can ensure that macros have not been tampered with or infected along the way in their journey from their creator to your system. Key to this macro virus protection feature is determining whether a source is *trustworthy;* it's a judgment call. When you open a document containing a macro with a digital signature on your computer, the digital signature shows up on-screen as a digital certificate. You should examine this certificate closely to be sure it is valid, originates from a trusted source, and is vouched for by a trustworthy third-party certification authority. If, after examining the certificate, you remain wary of the source and the safety of the macros, disable the macros. On the other hand, if you deem the source as trustworthy, you can add the name of the originator to your list of trusted sources, explained in the next section.

Maintain a List of Trusted Sources

Once you have verified that a macro is virus-free and a source is trustworthy and possessed of a valid digital certificate, you can add the name of the macro supplier to a list of sources that is automatically trusted by your system. This way, any time a trusted source sends you a file, your computer will automatically accept and enable any embedded macros without even alerting you (no warning message is provided that macros are being loaded). You can add sources to the Trusted Publisher list only for macros that have been digitally signed. To add a source to the list, do the following:

1. With your macro security level set to High or Medium, open the file containing the digitally signed macro that originates from the source you want to add to the list.

2. When the Security Warning dialog box appears, select the "Always trust macros from this publisher" option. Click OK.

Use Virus-Scanning Software to Detect and Remove Macro Viruses

Virus-scanning software can detect and often can remove macro viruses from documents before the viruses have a chance to execute. Most modern virus-scanning programs that you can install on your computer support Office macro virus scanning, which checks files for infected documents and templates. When you attempt to open a document in Word, Excel, PowerPoint, or Outlook, the document is checked by the virus-scanning program before it is opened (this is called scan-on-launch). When you install a virus-scanning program, it is registered on your computer in the Windows Registry, and this Registry setting enables the Office apps to determine how to pass the documents through the scanning program before the documents are opened.

To rely on antivirus software, you must verify whether it is registered on your computer and supports Office. On the Tools menu, point to Macro, and then click Security. If no virus-scanning program is registered to scan Office documents, the Security dialog box indicates "No virus scanners installed" as shown earlier in Figure 11-6. (It's a good sign if you don't see this message at the bottom of the Security dialog box because it means your antivirus software extends its coverage to Office.) If a virus-scanning program is not registered on your computer, you should obtain a virus-scanning program that supports Office macro virus scanning or discuss the issue with your network administrator.

As a long-term solution to macro viruses, install antivirus software that is specifically designed to detect macro viruses (Symantec Norton AntiVirus, McAfee VirusScan, Alwil Avast! 4). After you install any type of antivirus software, you must keep it updated to ensure that new macro viruses are detected and removed—new viruses are written daily. Today, most antivirus software vendors offer you the option of subscribing to an automatic update service so that your virus protection programs keep up-to-date.

As you know, macro viruses can infiltrate the global template of an Office application: Normal.dot, Book.xlt, Sheet.xlt, or Blank Presentation.pot. From that point on, every document you open could be automatically infected with the macro virus. For this reason, you can choose to lock the global template by changing the file attributes to read-only in File Manager or using a password on the template as a way of providing macro virus security:

1. On the Tools menu, point to Macro, and then click Visual Basic Editor.

2. In the Visual Basic Editor, click to select *ThisDocument* in the Project window, where *ThisDocument* is the name of the Office file you have open. If the Project window does not appear, click Project Explorer on the View menu.

3. On the Tools menu, click Project Properties.

4. In the Protection tab (see Figure 11-8), select the Lock Project for Viewing check box.

5. Type a password in the Password box.

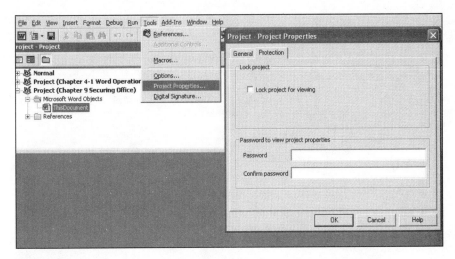

Figure 11-8
In Visual Basic Editor, lock a project using a password.

6. Type the same password in the Confirm Password box.

7. Click OK.

8. On the File menu, click Close, and return to Word, Excel, or PowerPoint.

9. In the Office application, hold down Shift as you choose Save All on the File menu.

10. If the following message appears, click Yes: "Changes have been made that affect the global template, *Template Name*. Do you want to save those changes?"

TIP: *For more information about locking your Microsoft Visual Basic for Applications project, in the Visual Basic Editor, click Microsoft Visual Basic Help on the Help menu, type* **protection tab** *in the Office Assistant or the Answer Wizard, and then click* **Search** *to view the topic.*

Summing Up

Security is a complicated and ever-changing topic. You must be vigilant to protect your data and Office resources from loss, change, and infection. When you implement the security best practices and other methods we recommend in this chapter, we're sure you'll find you're sleeping better at night.

Backing Up and Restoring Office

Degunking Checklist:

√ Learn why it is essential to make regular backups of your Office-related data.

√ Discover exactly which files and folders you should back up.

√ Compress your data before you archive it.

√ Learn how to make a backup manually and by using built-in tools.

√ Create a backup schedule that you can adhere to.

√ Make sure you know how to restore your data in case of an emergency.

You've heard it all before: you should back up all your important data files and folders and images, blah, blah, blah. But are you doing it? Are you actually making copies of your important stuff on a regular basis and in an organized fashion and storing it someplace safe? We don't mean to sound like your know-it-all neighbor or the geeky computer guy at work, but *backups are essential,* not only as an integral step in the degunking process but as insurance against data loss and disaster. These days, with cheap external storage and built-in tools available, no longer are there any excuses for failing to implement a backup and recovery strategy. Trust us; it's not as complicated or time-consuming as you've imagined it to be!

As we've mentioned throughout this book, weird things happen around computers all the time. Applications fail for no good reason; hard disk drives fry at inopportune times; lightning strikes the unprotected; viruses sneak past firewalls; laptops get stolen; home accidents happen every day; data gets deleted accidentally. These are all good reasons to have a backup and restore strategy in place. A backup and recovery strategy is as important as your data and your time. Back up according to how much data you can stand to lose and how much effort and time you are prepared to expend to manually restore it. Even if, for instance, you have hard copies of all your crucial information and feel safe, you will still need to spend time re-entering the information into your PC if something goes wrong.

In this chapter, we'll show you how to implement a convenient and easy-to-use backup and recovery strategy. We'll discuss which data you should back up and where you should store it. We'll show you how to use built-in Microsoft Windows and Office utilities to make the recurring task of backing up your data even simpler. We'll discuss how often you should make a backup and how to protect the resulting archive files. And finally, we'll show you how to use a backup to restore missing or corrupted data to a usable form. Major data loss is *completely* avoidable—it all depends on having a sound backup plan in place.

Determine What You Should Back Up

Back up anything that you cannot replace easily. Here's a basic checklist:

√   Files you've created and stored in the My Documents folder and its subfolders: My Music, My Downloads, My Pictures, and so forth

√   Custom templates stored in the Templates folder

√   Personal project folders stored in My Documents or elsewhere outside your user profile

√   E-mail messages, your address book, and calendars

√   Digital photos and images that you want to keep

√   Software you've purchased and downloaded from the Internet

√   Music files you have purchased and downloaded from the Internet

√   Financial information files and bank records

√   Microsoft Internet Explorer Favorites

√   Office application customizations and other preferences saved in the Registry

---

TIP: *In this chapter, we are going to concentrate on showing you how to back up Office-related stuff—the things you'll find in the My Documents folder and subfolders and elsewhere in your user profile. For more information on protecting other essential items on your PC, see Joli Ballew and Jeff Duntemann's book* **Degunking Windows** *or Jesse Torres and Peter Sideris's* **Surviving PC Disasters, Mishaps, and Blunders** *(both from Paraglyph Press).*

You don't need to make backups of the Office applications themselves, or other software that you purchased from a store, because these applications can be reinstalled from the CDs.

TIP: *It's a good idea to make a copy of any custom templates you've created, strip the macros out of the copies, and then store and back up these "clean" templates. This way, if a macro virus infiltrates your system and attacks a macro in one of your templates, you can remove the corrupted template and replace it with a clean copy.*

Make a personal checklist naming the specific files and folders that you want to back up. Keep the list handy during the actual backup so that you can keep track of which data you are copying. It's also convenient to have the list around for when disaster strikes so that you know immediately what you do and do not have backup copies of. Table 12-1 lists, by file extension, file types that you might want to back up.

Table 12-1   File Types to Back Up

File Type	File Extensions	Location
Word files	.doc, .rtf	My Documents folder, user-created folders
Word templates	.dot	My Documents folder, Templates folder, user-created folders
Text files	.txt	My Documents folder, user-created folders
Excel workbooks	.xls	My Documents folder, user-created folders
Excel templates	.xlt	My Documents folder, Templates folder, user-created folders

(continued)

Table 12-1   File Types to Back Up (Continued)

File Type	File Extensions	Location
Excel toolbars	.xlb	C:\Documents and Settings*username*\Application Data\Microsoft\Excel
PowerPoint presentations	.ppt	My Documents folder, user-created folders
PowerPoint Shows	.pps	My Documents folder, user-created folders
PowerPoint templates	.pot	My Documents folder, Templates folder, user-created folders
AutoCorrect lists	.acl	C:\Documents and Settings*username*\Application Data\Microsoft\Office, C:\Program Files\Microsoft Office
Customized dictionary files	.dic	C:\Documents and Settings*username*\Application Data\Microsoft\Proof
Outlook Personal Folders files	.pst	C:\Documents and Settings*username*\Application Data\Microsoft\Outlook
Outlook shortcut options	.fav	C:\Documents and Settings*username*\Application Data\Microsoft\Outlook

TIP: Once you commit to implementing a regular backup plan, you'll find that it's much easier if all your files are in order to begin with! The steps of the degunking strategy we explain in the first and second parts of this book, especially in Chapter 4, "Organizing Office-Related Files and Folders," will go a long way toward getting you organized so that backing up can be a snap.

Storage Options for Backed-Up Data

The next step is to decide where you're going to store the data that you're backing up. A multitude of storage solutions is available these days. One thing is certain: you can't use floppy disks anymore. Today's data files are so humungous that you'd need an unwieldy stack of 1.44-megabyte-capacity floppies to store it all. Plenty of other viable and inexpensive options exist. To decide on which one to use, compare the various solutions on cost, capacity, and ease of use. You can choose from the following storage media:

√   External hard disk drives

√   CD-RWs or DVD-RWs

√   Zip drives and Zip disks

√   Online storage facilities

√   Tape drives

External Hard Disk Drives

An external hard disk drive can be attached to your PC using a Universal Serial Bus (USB) port or high-speed port such as FireWire or USB 2.0. They can be easily detached from your PC and stored off-site without too much bother. You save stuff to the external disk, and then you detach the disk and take it with you. External disks range in capacity from 20 to 400 gigabytes (GB) of data (most internal PC hard disks can hold about 80 GB).

Most external hard disks are immediately recognized by the Windows operating system and will appear in My Computer or Windows Explorer when connected. When comparing different brands and models, consider the speed of information transfer (dependent upon transmission medium—FireWire or USB) and speed of writing data (given in revolutions per minute, or rpm, ratings). External hard disks have ample storage capacity and can transfer information relatively quickly, but it's a bit more of a hassle to plug in, back up, unplug, and transport the hard disk off-site as compared to, say, CDs, DVDs, or Zip disks.

CD-RWs or DVD-RWs

Compact discs and DVDs do make convenient little packages for storing and transporting your backup data. The *RW* stands for *read write,* which means that you must have a CD or DVD writer drive installed in your PC to be able to transfer data to discs. Most new PCs come with CD-RW and DVD-RW drives these days. If yours does not include one, you can purchase an external CD or DVD burner and attach it to your PC using a high-speed cable or USB port.

TIP: *If you are running Windows 2000, Windows XP, or Windows Server 2003, beware that the Backup utility (explained later) does not recognize internal CD-R, CD-RW, and DVD-RW drives as legitimate backup devices. To store your backups on CDs or DVDs, you will have to make a manual backup to a file and then write the file to disc.*

CDs can hold between 650 and 700 megabytes of data, and DVDs can hold several gigabytes. Backup time depends on the speed of the drive writer, but it normally takes only a few minutes to burn a backup disc. CDs and DVDs are ultimately transportable and easily filed and stored without taking up too much space.

TIP: *One way to keep your backup media degunked is to label your CDs or DVDs clearly. Include the date and time of the backup and a name for the contents of the disc. Once you pick a disc-labeling scheme, stick with it.*

Zip Drives and Zip Disks

The Iomega Corporation produces Zip drives and Zip disks for storage. You can attach an external Zip drive to your computer to extend your original hard drive storage capacity by 100 MB, 250 MB, or 750 MB, depending on the model you purchase. Zip drives enable you to save data by writing it onto removable Zip disks, which have a capacity of 100 MB, 250 MB, or 750 MB. An added bonus is that backup software comes with the Zip drive and can help you automate and organize a backup strategy employing the drive and Zip disks. You can use the Zip disks for storage of your backups—they are small and portable enough to be an attractive and convenient option.

Online Storage Facilities

Services are available that will store your data in an online storage facility for a monthly fee. This storage solution enables you to access your backups over the Internet anytime and from any place. Transferring backup data to the storage location can take substantial amounts of time depending on the amount of data to be sent and the speed of your Internet connection—although this process can be done in the background. If you have a dial-up Internet connection, think twice before enrolling in an online storage service because transfers could tie up your phone lines for hours. Also, if the storage company's or your own organization's servers go down or the storage company goes out of business, you might not be able to access your data. Furthermore, if you are transferring personal or sensitive information, you must employ an encryption methodology or use a secured transport medium (virtual private network or a tunneling protocol) to keep the data protected while in transit. Be sure to research the company's privacy policy and the security of its servers so that you don't wake up at night worrying whether your backups are being hacked without your knowledge.

Tape Drives

Tape drives are storage solutions used mostly by large organizations to back up their hard disks. Tape drives write data to magnetic tape cartridges, and although the tape cartridges have huge capacity, they are relatively expensive, as are the tape drives. We'll take a guess and predict that you won't be using magnetic tape to store your backups because so many other inexpensive and convenient methods are available.

TIP: *We recommend using an external hard drive or CDs for your backup strategy. These two types of media are readily available, easy to use, and very portable. Plus, they are the least-expensive backup methods for regular use.*

Where to Store Your Backups

To keep your data safest, it's best to store it on a medium that is located away from your PC—in another room, on another floor, or at an altogether different location. This way, if Hurricane Sue manages to flatten your PC, you at least have your data kept safe and sound in the part of town still standing. And although it's rare for such cataclysmic events to destroy both your computer and your backups, the lesson is to consider storing your backed-up data away from your computer—at least on a high shelf in a closet in another room.

Also, consider the data. Treat your backups as you would important papers or valued possessions. If you keep birth certificates or property deeds and jewelry in a safety deposit box, you can stash your backup CDs or DVDs there too. If you keep family photos and mementos in a fireproof box or safe, use that device to store your backup media or removable hard drive when it's not in use.

If, alas, you are unable to make a backup to an external device, consider at least backing up your data to a second internal hard drive or hard drive partition. *Any* type of backup is better than none. Just know that if your PC becomes disabled, you most likely will lose your internal backups too.

Use File Compression

File compression software can convert a large data file that takes up a lot of space into a new data file that contains a description of the original data based on the patterns of bits and bytes it contains. Amazingly, data compression can save 10 to 50 percent of the space used by the original file and *no data is lost in the compression process!* When you uncompress the file, it appears as the original. File compression is degunking nirvana.

The Windows operating system has a built-in file compression capability called, simply, Compressed (zipped) Folder. With this feature, you can "zip" files and folders into compressed packages that take up less storage space and take less time to transfer to your storage medium. Use the Compressed (zipped) Folder feature to reduce the size of Office-related files and image files such as bitmaps (BMP files) before you save them as backup copies to optimize the space available in the backup location. Note that image files such as JPG and GIF files, for instance, are already in a compressed format when saved so will benefit little from being zipped.

TIP: *You can apply encryption to compressed files by using the Compressed (zipped) Folder feature. If you subscribe to an online file storage service, encryption can be invaluable for protecting your sensitive data from unauthorized access.*

There are two ways you can use the Compressed (zipped) Folder feature:

√   You can create a zipped folder and then use drag and drop or cut and paste to move items into it.

√   You can right-click an item you want to compress and send it to a zipped folder that you create for it.

A compressed folder has a zippered folder icon. Compressed folders can be moved, copied, and stored just like regular folders. You can choose to open files directly from the compressed folder or extract them first before accessing them.

Many other versions of compression software exist, including ArchiveXP, PKZip, StuffIt, and WinZip. You can take advantage of the free 30-day evaluation period that most of these applications offer to try them out before you decide which one to purchase. Proprietary compression software applications usually include many more features than the Windows utility. Many integrate with Windows Explorer to make zip commands available when you right-click items. Others also integrate with Outlook to make it super easy to send zipped files as e-mail attachments.

TIP: *You can also zip file attachments to send EXE and other file types that are normally blocked by Outlook for security reasons. On the flip side, be very wary of downloading and opening zipped files because they can, for the aforementioned reason, contain unsafe or infected files that have bypassed default Outlook security. Trust the source before you accept zipped files through e-mail.*

File compression is a smart way to reduce the size of your backups. Be aware, though, that if for any reason you must restore your system using a compressed file, you must have the compatible compression application available to uncompress the data before it is usable.

How to Create a Backup

We're going to show you two basic (and very easy!) methods to back up your important data:

√   Create a backup manually, a method available to all versions of the Windows operating system

√   Use the Backup utility, a method available if you are running Windows XP or later

You can create a manual backup no matter which version of the Windows operating system you are running—you simply must have a CD-RW, DVD-RW, or Zip drive available, or an external hard disk. You can also customize and automate the backup task by using the Backup utility, which is available in

Windows XP and later versions. If you are running Windows XP Home Edition, the Backup utility is not enabled by default as it is for Windows XP Professional. We'll describe how to add and enable the Backup utility if it doesn't appear on your system. Additionally, we'll show you how to save your Office-related preferences and application customizations.

Create a Manual Backup

Making a manual backup of your important things is as easy as copying and pasting. If you plan to store the backup on a CD or DVD, follow these steps:

1. Insert a blank CD into the CD-RW or DVD-RW drive.

2. Open My Computer.

3. Right-click Start, and choose Explore.

4. In Windows Explorer, navigate to the folder or file that you want to back up. To choose multiple files or folders, hold down the Shift key or Ctrl key as you click items. Then right-click one of the selected items and choose Copy from the context menu.

TIP: *A CD can hold about 700 MB of data; a DVD can hold between 1 and 4.7 GB. As you select files to back up, keep a rough count of the total space they use so you do not overrun the capacity of your storage device.*

---

5. In My Computer, right-click the CD-RW or DVD-RW drive and choose Paste from the context menu.

6. Windows will alert you that you have files ready to be written to the storage disc. Click the ScreenTip to open the Files Ready to Be Written window. If more space is available, continue copying and pasting files from your PC onto the CD-RW or DVD-RW drive. Stop when the disc is about 95 percent full.

7. In the Files Ready to Be Written window, choose Write These Files to CD/DVD on the File menu as shown in Figure 12-1.

8. On the Welcome to the CD/DVD Writing Wizard page of the CD Writing Wizard, type in a name for the disc. Using the date and time as the disc name is handy for organizational purposes. Click Next.

9. When the device is finished writing the files to the CD or DVD, the Completing the CD/DVD Writing Wizard page will appear. Click Finish.

TIP: *If you plan to set up a double-backup system as explained later in this chapter, select Yes, Write These Files to Another CD/DVD in the Completing the CD/DVD Writing Wizard page to make another backup copy. Also, to conserve space, consider copying the files you want to back up to a single folder on your hard disk, compressing the folder, and then copying that folder to the CD or DVD.*

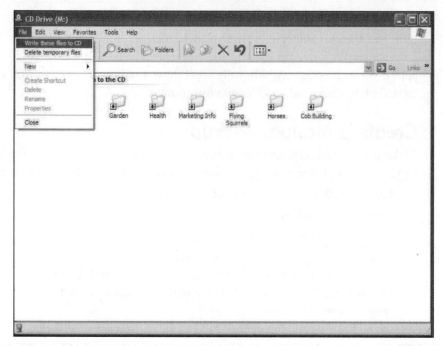

Figure 12-1
After you've copied all necessary files and folders to the device, burn the backup using the Write These Files to CD/DVD command.

If you are using an external hard disk drive or a Zip drive for backups, follow these steps:

1. Make sure that the external drive or Zip drive is connected to your computer. If you wish to save the data to a Zip disk, be sure a Zip disk is inserted in the Zip drive.

2. Open My Computer.

3. Right-click Start, and choose Explore.

4. In Windows Explorer, navigate to the folder or file that you want to back up. To choose multiple files or folders, hold down the Shift key or Ctrl key as you click items. Then right-click one of the selected items and choose Copy from the context menu.

5. In My Computer, right-click the external drive or the Zip drive, and choose Paste from the context menu.

6. For external hard disks or Zip drives, if necessary, disconnect the device from your computer using the proper ejection technique. Eject the Zip disk if necessary.

7. Store the device or Zip disk in a safe place away from your PC.

So that you don't forget to back up your data regularly, add a recurring item to your Outlook Task list as a reminder. When Outlook is open, you will be prompted to make a backup at the scheduled time.

Use the Backup Utility

If you are using Windows XP or later, you can let the Backup utility do the (minimal) work of creating your data backups. First, check whether the Backup utility is installed on your system: click Start, and point to All Programs and then Microsoft Office Tools. If Backup does not appear in the list of tools, it is not installed on your PC.

Install the Backup Utility

You can easily install the Backup utility by following these steps:

1. Insert the Windows XP installation CD into the CD drive. If the wizard does not start automatically, double-click the CD drive icon in My Computer.

2. On the Welcome to Microsoft Windows XP page, select the Perform Additional Tasks option, shown in Figure 12-2.

3. On the What Do You Want to Do page, click Browse This CD.

4. In the window that opens, double-click the ValueAdd folder, double-click the Msft folder, and then double-click the Ntbackup folder.

5. Double-click Ntbackup.msi to install the Backup utility.

6. Click Finish on the Completing the Windows Backup Utility Installation Wizard page.

Understand Backup Options in the Backup Utility

Before you run the Backup utility, we want to explain a few of the different decisions you'll have to make so you can think about them ahead of time. First, of course, is deciding where you will store the backup: on a CD, DVD, or Zip disk or an external hard disk drive or online storage facility.

Next decide which kind of backup you want to create. The Backup tool will offer to do five different types:

√ *Normal.* Backs up the selected files and marks each file as backed up. This is the default type of backup and the one you will use to create your initial backup of your system and Office-related files.

√ *Copy.* Backs up the selected files but does not mark them as backed up.

√ *Incremental.* Backs up the selected files but only if they were created or modified since the last normal or incremental backup. The advantage is that this backup file is smaller than a normal backup and takes less time to complete. The disadvantage is that to restore from an incremental backup,

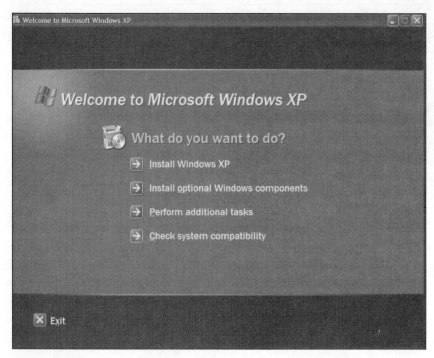

Figure 12-2
Choose Perform Additional Tasks to install the Backup utility from the installation CD.

you'll have to restore the latest normal backup and then each incremental backup taken since that full backup, which can be a hassle.

√ *Differential.* Backs up the selected files only if they were created or modified since the previous normal or incremental backup, but does not mark them as backed up. Differential backups are normally smaller and faster than normal backups, but file size can grow astronomically. Because the files are not marked as backed up, they are again eligible for backup at the next scheduled differential backup and the backed-up data is duplicated in each differential backup until the next normal backup is completed. They are, however, somewhat easier to restore from than incremental backups are because you restore only the latest normal backup and the latest differential backup.

√ *Daily.* Backs up only the files that were created or modified that day.

A strategy of using periodic normal backups supplemented by daily backups will keep your data safe if you use your PC every day for work and important personal business. Make a normal backup four times a year—say, on the first day of spring, summer, autumn, and winter—and then make daily backups. Archive (or store over the long term) the normal backups for up to a year, and

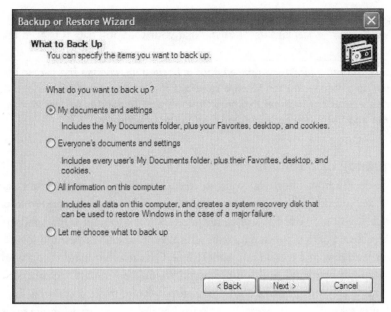

Figure 12-3
Choose what you want to back up on the What to Back Up page.

keep copies of the last month's daily backups before you start writing over that data. If you use your PC less frequently, make a normal backup whenever you add important data to your PC that you would not like to lose.

Then decide exactly which files and folders to back up at each scheduled backup. The Backup utility in Wizard Mode will offer the following four options (they are shown in Figure 12-3):

√ *My Documents and Settings.* This option includes your My Documents folder and its subfolders, your Microsoft Internet Explorer Favorites, your Desktop settings, and cookies.

√ *Everyone's Documents and Settings.* You can choose this option if you share your PC with other users. It will back up each user's My Documents folder, Internet Explorer Favorites, Desktop settings, and cookies.

√ *All Information on This Computer.* This is the whole shebang. It creates a complete backup of everything on your PC and creates a system recovery disk that you can use to restore your system after a major disaster (knock on wood). If you've installed lots of software or downloaded heaps of music or image files from the Internet, the size of this backup file can be gigantic.

√ *Let Me Choose What to Back Up.* This option enables you to choose exactly which folders and files you will back up. This is useful when you want to protect data you've stored outside of your user profile (C:\Documents and Settings*username*) and for ensuring that your Outlook data is backed up.

TIP: To be sure that all your Office-related data is backed up, choose the Let Me Choose What to Back Up option, and then be sure to select the My Documents folder and its subfolders, as well as the Internet Explorer, Outlook, and Templates folders in C:\Documents and Settings\username\Application Data\Microsoft.

Frequency of Backups

Finally, decide how often you want to make a backup. To do this, think about how often you use your computer and how much data you can stand to lose. For instance, if you use your PC only a few times a week to send e-mail and upload digital pictures, back up your data once a month or whenever you add something to your hard disk that you do not want to lose. On the other hand, if you work on the computer every day and want to avoid wasting inordinate amounts of time duplicating previous effort if something goes wrong, make a daily backup and supplement it with a full normal backup four or five times a year for safe measure.

TIP: The average home user can make a full normal backup of all Office-related data once a week to protect their stuff. Business users or multimedia buffs should make daily backups and supplement these with a full normal backup four or five times a year.

Run the Backup Utility

The Backup utility not only simplifies the backup operation but gives you myriad options on how to make a backup. Here's how you can use the Backup utility in Wizard Mode, which leads you easily through the procedure:

1. Close all applications and files.

2. Click Start; point to All Programs, Accessories, System Tools; and click Backup.

3. The Welcome to the Backup or Restore Wizard page in the Backup or Restore Wizard opens. Click Next.

4. Select the Back Up Files and Settings option, and then click Next.

5. On the What to Back Up Page, choose one of the following options (see the preceding section for a fuller explanation of what these options include in the backup):

   a. My Documents and Settings

   b. Everyone's Documents and Settings

   c. All Information on This Computer

   d. Let Me Choose What to Back Up

If you choose options a, b, or c, click Next and move on to step 6. If you choose Let Me Choose What to Back Up, click Next and then select what to back up. On the Items to Backup page, place a check mark in the box next to My Documents. Then double-click My Computer in the left pane, navigate to C:\Documents and Settings*username*\Application Data, and place a check mark beside the Microsoft folder. This will ensure that your Office-related settings, Outlook data, Internet Explorer settings, and Office data, including custom templates, custom dictionary files, and AutoText lists, are included in the backup. Click Next.

6. On the Backup Type, Destination, and Name page, select Let Me Choose a Place Not Listed Here from the Choose a Place to Save the Backup drop-down menu or click the Browse button to pick a destination location. If you plan to back up to an external drive or Zip drive, be sure the device is properly connected to your PC. If you plan to back up to a Zip disk, be sure the disk is inserted into the drive. If you plan to back up to a CD or DVD, create an interim save location on your hard disk to hold the backup data until you write it to the CD or DVD. Navigate to the destination in the Save As dialog box.

TIP: *By design, the Backup utility does not recognize internal CD-R, CD-RW, and DVD-RW drives as legitimate backup devices. To store your backups on CDs or DVDs, you will have to make a backup to a folder location on your hard drive and then manually write the folder to disc later.*

---

7. Type a name in the File Name box, and then click Save.

8. On the Backup Type, Destination, and Name page, verify that the backup destination is correct and that the proper name appears in the Type a Name for This Backup box as shown in Figure 12-4. Click Next.

9. On the Completing the Backup or Restore Wizard page, click the Advanced button.

10. On the Type of Backup page, choose which type of backup you'd like to perform. Choose from Normal, Copy, Incremental, Differential, and Daily, as shown in Figure 12-5. Click Next.

11. On the How to Back Up page, ensure that the Verify Data after Backup and the Disable Volume Shadow Copy options are not selected. Although verifying the data after a backup sounds like a good idea, it cannot assure you that you will be able to restore from the backup; we'll show you how to do that later in this chapter. Also, the Volume Shadow Copy service enables backups to be made of open files and files in use, which is very useful when you are running Backup in the background and plan to continue working on your PC. Click Next.

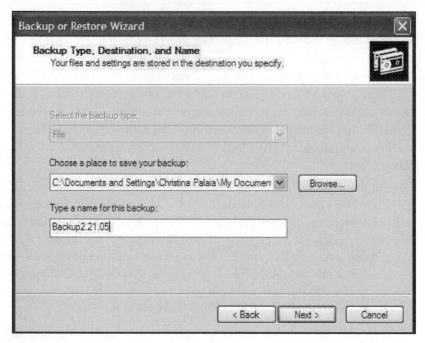

Figure 12-4

Verify that the save location and backup file name are correct.

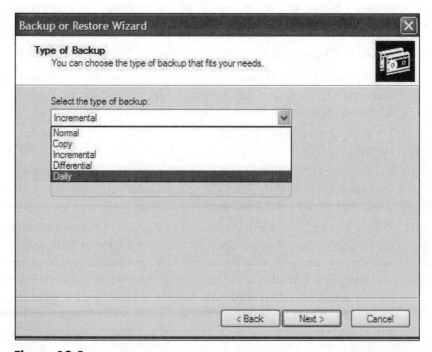

Figure 12-5

Choose the type of backup you want to create.

12. On the Backup Options page, choose whether this backup will overwrite previous backups stored on the storage medium or whether this backup will be appended to the end of the other backup files. Click Next.

13. On the When to Back Up page, choose whether you'd like to perform the backup now or schedule it for a later time. Click Next.

14. To close the wizard and start the backup, click Finish on the Completing the Backup or Restore Wizard page.

Using Advanced Mode

You can use the Backup utility in Advanced Mode for greater control over the backup process. For instance, you can choose exactly which files and folders you want to back up. This is an excellent way to ensure that your Outlook data, including e-mail messages stored in Personal Folders files and your calendars and address book, is saved. (When you choose the My Documents and Settings option as described in the section "Run the Backup Utility," Outlook data gets overlooked.) To choose exactly which data to back up, follow these steps:

1. Close all applications and files.

2. Click Start; point to All Programs, Accessories, System Tools; and click Backup.

3. On the Welcome to the Backup or Restore Wizard page, click the Advanced Mode link.

4. In the Welcome tab, click the Backup Wizard (Advanced) button.

5. If prompted, click No to clear any previously configured backup jobs, then click Next on the Welcome to the Backup Wizard page.

6. On the What to Back Up page, you are given the following options:

   a. *Back Up Everything on This Computer.* This option copies everything on your PC to a backup location.

   b. *Back Up Selected Files, Drives, or Network Data.* This options enables you to choose specific data to be backed up, such as My Documents subfolders and Outlook data.

   c. *Only Back Up the System State Information.* This option is used to protect critical system data.

   Choose Back Up Selected Files, Drives, or Network Data, and then click Next.

7. You'll be presented a window like the one shown in Figure 12-6. Choose specific files and folders to back up. To back up a folder and all of its contents, place a check mark next to it. To choose only specific items within a folder, click the folder (do not check it), and then navigate and select the items you want to back up in the right-hand pane.

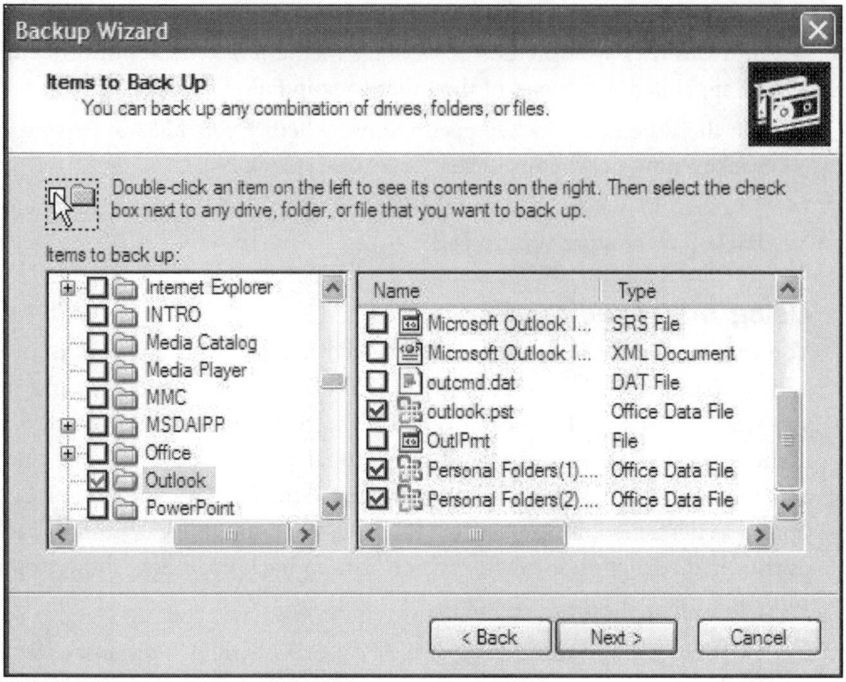

Figure 12-6
Select exactly which files and folders to back up, in this case, Outlook data.

For instance, to back up your Outlook data, double-click My Computer in the left pane. Double-click your hard drive (usually C:), and then navigate to Documents and Settings*username*\\Application Data\\Microsoft. Place a check mark in front of the Outlook folder. Click Next.

8. Choose a backup location and name the backup file, and then click Next.

9. On the Completing the Backup Wizard page, click Finish.

Write Backup Files to a CD or DVD

As the final step in making a backup to CD or DVD, you must write the files to the disc. Follow these steps:

1. Insert a blank CD or DVD in the CD or DVD writer drive.

2. In Windows Explorer, navigate to the location where you saved the backup files on your hard disk.

3. Right-click the latest backup file, and choose Copy from the context menu.

4. In Windows Explorer, navigate to the blank disc, right-click in the right pane of Windows Explorer, and choose Paste from the context menu.

5. Choose Write These Files to CD/DVD, type a name in the CD Name box in the wizard, and click Next.

---

*TIP: Certain add-in backup tools can back up your data and write it directly to a CD or DVD without interacting with you. Search the Office Marketplace (**http:// office.microsoft.com/en-us/marketplace/default.aspx**) and the Internet for free tools that can remove this manual CD- or DVD-writing step from your backup process.*

Use the Save My Settings Wizard

To save your Office-related customizations and preferences, you can use the Save My Settings Wizard in the Microsoft Office Tools folder. This way, in the case of a calamity that requires you to reinstall Office or when you're doing a new installation, you won't have to reconfigure your preferences and degunk the applications (as described in earlier chapters of this book) all over again. The Save My Settings Wizard (called the Profile Wizard in Office 2000) saves your custom templates, customized dictionary files, AutoCorrect lists, and customized program options and preferences, including file save locations, AutoRecover settings, and toolbar configurations, among other things.

Check to see whether the Save My Settings Wizard or the Profile Wizard is installed on your PC by clicking Start and pointing to All Programs, Microsoft Office Tools. If the wizard does not appear in the submenu, you can add it to your PC using Add or Remove Programs or you can download it from the Microsoft Office XP Resource Kit Downloads Web site at **www.microsoft.com/office/orkarchive/ XPddl.htm**. The download file is called Office Resource Kit Tools, or OrkTools.exe, and is 11.5 MB.

To add the Save My Settings Wizard using Add or Remove Programs, follow these steps:

1. Close all Office applications and files.
2. Click Start, and then click Control Panel.
3. Double-click Add or Remove Programs, and then click the Change or Remove Programs button.
4. Click Microsoft XP (or 2003) in the Currently Installed Programs list, and then click the Change button.
5. Select the Add or Remove Features option in the Microsoft Office XP Setup dialog box, and then click Next.
6. In the right pane, in the Features to Install hierarchy, click the plus sign to expand Office Tools.
7. Select Save My Settings Wizard, and then click the down arrow and choose Run All from My Computer as shown in Figure 12-7.
8. Click Update, and then click OK when Setup completes successfully.

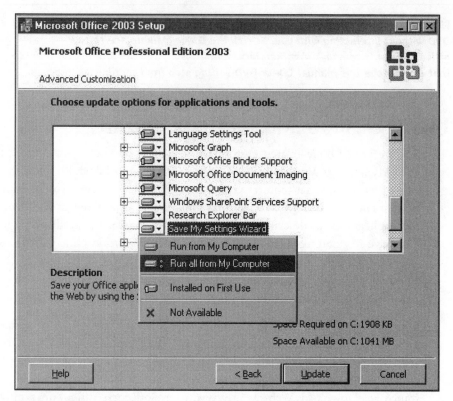

Figure 12-7
Add the Save My Settings Wizard to your PC using Office Setup.

To use the Save My Settings Wizard to make a backup copy of your Office configuration, do the following:

1. Close all Office applications and files.

2. Click Start; point to All Programs, Microsoft Office Tools; and then click Save My Settings Wizard.

3. Click Next on the Welcome to the Save My Settings Wizard page, shown in Figure 12-8.

4. Click Save the Settings from This Machine, and then click Next.

5. Click Browse to navigate to a location to save the settings file. By default, the wizard will offer to save the New Settings File.ops file to C:\Documents and Settings*username*\My Documents. Click Finish.

6. If prompted, click Yes to overwrite a file that already exists. Then click Exit.

Note specifically where you've saved the settings file so that you can include it in future backup jobs.

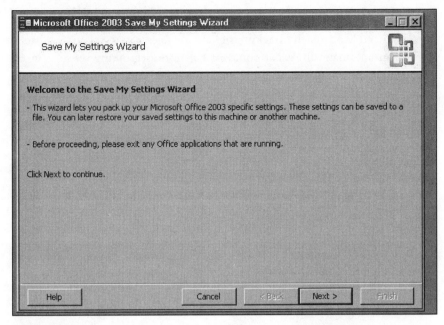

Figure 12-8
Close all Office programs before running the Save My Settings Wizard.

Schedule Your Backups

Basically, there are three ways you can schedule backups: manually, by using the Backup utility, or by using the Scheduled Tasks utility. No matter which method you choose, the main thing is to set up a regular schedule and *stick to it.*

Perform a Manual Backup

You can do a manual backup at any time. It's an especially good idea to perform a manual backup just before you install new software or devices or get caught up in a lot of heavy degunking. (Later in this chapter we discuss how to create a restore point, which can allow your PC to be almost magically restored to a previous running state should something catastrophic occur. However, it's unwise to put all your eggs in that one basket by relying on a restore point as the main method of returning a faulty system to working order.)

Before you download new software, install new hardware, or delete gaggles of files, take a moment to create a backup. Likewise, just after adding new and important data to your system's hard drive and before the next scheduled backup, perform a manual backup to keep everything safe. To perform a backup as a manual job at any time, use the Backup Utility in either Wizard or Advanced Mode or follow the steps given earlier in the section "Create a Manual Backup."

Schedule a Job Using the Backup Utility

Advanced Mode of the Backup tool also enables you to schedule a backup job to run automatically. What could make more degunking sense than that? To schedule a backup, follow these steps:

1. Click Start; point to All Programs, Accessories, System Tools; and click Backup.

2. On the Welcome to the Backup or Restore Wizard page, click the Advanced Mode link.

3. In the Welcome tab, click the Backup Wizard (Advanced) button.

4. In the Schedule Jobs tab, choose a day from the calendar to schedule a backup, as shown in Figure 12-9.

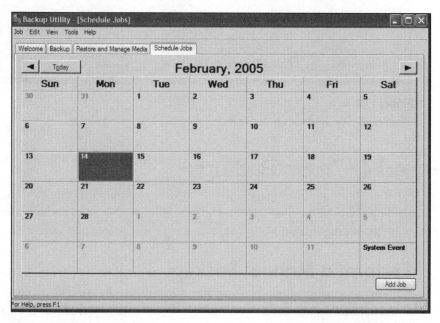

Figure 12-9
Pick a day to schedule a backup.

5. Click Add Job.

6. Click Next on the Welcome to the Backup Wizard page, and then follow the steps outlined in the preceding sections to configure exactly which type of backup you want and where it will be stored.

You can schedule into the future as many backup jobs as you like. And you can customize each job by specifying the type of backup and which data is to be backed up. Remember to leave your PC turned on and storage media available for the scheduled backup time.

Using the Scheduled Tasks Utility

The Scheduled Tasks utility is a Windows tool that enables you to run designated tools and applications at preconfigured times. It's an easy way to set up an automatic backup schedule, among other things. As long as your PC is turned on and the necessary storage media are available, the Scheduled Tasks utility will create your backup with no further instruction from you. You can set the Scheduled Tasks utility to perform a backup (or any other operation, such as running Disk Cleanup or Disk Defragmenter) at a specified time every day if you're a heavy PC user or on a specific day of the week or month. There are three ways you can use the Scheduled Tasks utility: run the Scheduled Tasks Wizard, manually create and configure a task, or drag an item into the Scheduled Tasks window. We discuss using the Scheduled Task Wizard here because it is the easiest and most gunk-free method.

TIP: Before you run the Scheduled Tasks utility, be sure that the date and time on your PC are accurate.

To use the Scheduled Tasks Wizard, follow these steps:

1. Click Start, and then choose Control Panel.
2. Double-click Scheduled Tasks.
3. In the Scheduled Tasks window, double-click Add Scheduled Task.
4. Click Next on the opening page of the wizard, and then choose Backup in the Application list, as shown in Figure 12-10. Click Next.
5. Type a name for this task or accept the default name Backup. Then choose a frequency for the task from the following options: Daily, Weekly, Monthly, One Time Only, When My Computer Starts, When I Log On. Click Next.
6. If you choose Daily, Weekly, Monthly, or One Time Only, the next screen enables you to choose the specific day, time, and start date, as shown in Figure 12-11. Click Next.
7. Many tasks, including Backup, must be scheduled by the administrator. Enter the administrator username and password into the text boxes on the next page. Click Next.
8. Click Finish to add the task to Scheduled Tasks.

Protect Your Backups

The first rule of protecting your backups is to store them somewhere away from your PC. After all, what sense does it make to be diligent about making backups if you're going to store the CDs or the external disk on top of your CPU? Whatever physical mishap befalls your PC will surely damage the backups as well.

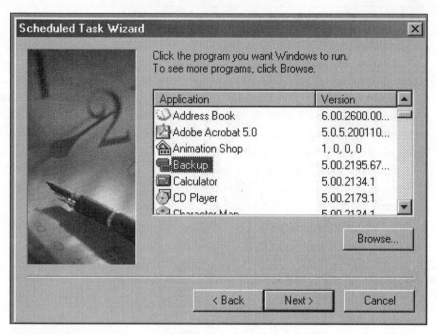

Figure 12-10
Choose Backup in the Scheduled Tasks Wizard to schedule it to run automatically.

Figure 12-11
Schedule the specific date and time to run Backup.

Next, consider making a backup of a backup. You might think this is a bit overzealous, but remember we said to imagine the worst-case scenario and plan to be protected against it? Some data is irreplaceable, and if you keep two copies of it in two separate locations, it's highly unlikely you'll suffer data loss.

Third, keep your backups organized. Lost or misplaced backups might as well be considered nonexistent for all the good they'll do you. Use a consistent naming convention for backups and keep them arranged by date or type. Label CDs, DVDs, and Zip disks clearly and permanently with the date and time of the backup; name files stored on external or Zip drives so that they are listed in order by date or time, taking into consideration the ASCII file-ordering method described in Chapter 4. If you should ever need to restore your data using backups, you'll know just exactly where to go to get the needed information.

If you store highly sensitive or personal information, consider protecting the backup medium with a password or encryption. When you compress files before you back them up, often you can choose to encrypt the files so that only authorized users can later uncompress and view them.

Finally, don't erase or pitch a previous backup until you have made a more recent backup and have verified that necessary data can be restored from it. Keeping previous backups for an amount of time after they've been replaced is a good way to ensure that you haven't deleted or overwritten something you'll want back later.

Restore! Restore!

Alas, there will come a time when you will lose something that you need, whether by natural disaster or user error. If you've been following our recommendations in this chapter, you now have a healthy backup plan in place, and you're about to see whether it works. You can restore information to your PC a couple of different ways using the Backup utility. And you can use the System Restore utility to return your PC to a previous running state if it starts to act wacky.

Restore Using Backup

The Backup utility contains functionality to help you restore files you have previously backed up. You can use the Backup utility Restore Wizard or the options available in the Restore and Manage Media tab of the Backup utility in Advanced Mode. The restore functions enable you to perform the following operations:

√ Restore items to a specific location on your PC without overwriting any files

√ Restore items by overwriting older files

√ Restore items to a separate, single file

As mentioned earlier, you must be an administrator on your PC to run the Backup utility. The key is to already have a backup of the files that you'll want to restore and to know where to locate them. The methods discussed earlier in this chapter can help you work out a usable backup plan.

Restoring information consists of four basic steps:

1. Select the files and folders you want to restore.

2. Select a location to restore the files and folders.

3. Set the restore options.

4. Restore the data.

The Restore Wizard walks you through these steps. To run the Restore Wizard to perform a restore operation, complete the following procedure:

1. Close all applications and files.

2. Click Start; point to All Programs, Accessories, System Tools; and then click Backup.

3. On the Welcome to the Backup or Restore Wizard page, click Advanced Mode.

4. In the Welcome to the Backup Utility Advanced Mode window, click the Restore Wizard button.

5. Click Next on the first page of the wizard.

6. Use the Explorer-type folder hierarchy to navigate to the drive, folder, or file that you want to restore on the What to Restore page. Click Next.

7. Click Advanced on the Completing the Restore Wizard page.

8. On the Where to Restore page, use the Restore Files To drop-down list to choose from the following options:

    a. *Original Location.* Choose this option to restore the data to the location it was in when you backed it up. Then click Next.

    b. *Alternate Location.* Choose this option to restore the data to a specific folder that you designate. The folder structure of the backed-up data will be preserved in the new location. Type the path to the alternate folder location, and then click Next.

    c. *Single Folder.* Choose this option to restore the data to a specific folder that you designate. The folder structure of the backed-up data is not preserved, but all the files and folders will appear in the designated folder. Type the path to the single folder location, and then click Next.

9. On the How to Restore page, choose from the following options:

   a. *Leave Existing Files (Recommended).* This is the safest option. No files will be overwritten. Click Next.

   b. *Replace Existing Files If They Are Older Than the Backup Files.* This option allows existing files to be overwritten only if the restored version contains more recent modifications than the existing file. Click Next.

   c. *Replace Existing Files.* This option allows the Restore Wizard to overwrite existing files. Click Next.

10. On the Advanced Restore Options page, enable the appropriate settings, if necessary, and then click Next.

11. Click Finish on the Completing the Restore Wizard page to begin the restoration process.

12. Click Close in the Restore Progress dialog box.

The Restore and Manage Media tab of the Backup utility in Advanced Mode enables you to complete the same operation.

TIP: *Once you make a backup, it's a good idea to periodically use the preceding steps to check to be sure the backup is viable and all the information you meant to save was saved in usable form.*

Use Windows System Restore

The Windows System Restore utility enables you to step back in time by returning your computer to a previous state, the state it was in when you liked the way it was running. With System Restore, you can undo changes made to your PC and restore it to a time of better performance. System Restore creates *restore points,* which are like snapshots of your system. You can use restore points to track the changes made to your system. Creating restore points and restoring to specific restore points do not change or affect personal data files, such as Outlook data and the files you create using Office applications, because System Restore does not restore files that use common file extensions such as .doc, .xls, or .ppt and it does not restore files contained in the My Documents folder. System Restore continually monitors your PC and automatically creates a restore point every 24 hours that the computer is turned on and in these situations:

√ When a program is enabled

√ When an application is installed

√ When a device driver is installed

√ When Automatic Updates are installed

√ When a restore operation is run

Knowing how to create a restore point manually can help you if you need to return to a time of smooth operation, such as before you installed an add-in or downloaded a piece of software. If you choose to restore to a point before a program was installed using Windows Installer or InstallShield, System Restore can remove the program files and Registry settings made by the new software.

To create a restore point, follow these steps:

1. Close all applications and files.
2. Click Start; point to All Programs, Accessories, System Tools; and then click System Restore.
3. Select the Create a Restore Point option on the Welcome to System Restore page, and then click Next.
4. Type a description in the Restore Point Description box. The current date and time are automatically added to the name you choose. Click Create.
5. Click Finish when the restore point is created.

To restore your computer to a specific restore point, follow these steps:

1. Close all applications and files.
2. Click Start; point to All Programs, Accessories, System Tools; and then click System Restore.
3. Select the Restore My Computer to an Earlier Time option on the Welcome to System Restore page, and then click Next.
4. Use the calendar to pick a day with restore points available. Choose a restore point in the list. System Restore informs you that it will restore your computer to the point before this program was installed, as shown in Figure 12-12. Notice that the restore points are listed in consecutive order; if you choose the restore point at the top of the list, all programs or system changes made subsequent to that point will be restored. Click Next.
5. Close any open programs and save your work in applications before clicking Next on the Confirm Restore Point Selection page because Windows must shut down your system to revert to the restore point.

Summing Up

We can't say it enough: implementing an easy-to-use and comprehensive backup and restore plan is essential to the safety of your data (and your sanity). We must have dispelled any myths lingering in your mind about how impossible, confusing, and time-consuming backing up your important stuff really is. In this

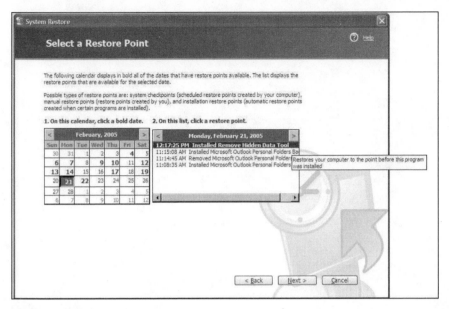

Figure 12-12

Choose a restore point from the list of available restore points.

chapter, we showed you a way to figure out exactly what you should back up, where you should put it, and how often you should do it. Then we explained two easy methods of performing a backup operation and showed you how to do this on a schedule. Finally, we discussed how you can protect your precious backups and how you can use them to restore your data should something go wrong.

Fixing Things That Break in Office

Degunking Checklist:

√ Be aware of the three main types of errors you can encounter.

√ Learn why applications fail and errors occur.

√ Gather information about an error and then take appropriate action to resolve it.

√ Fix broken templates in Word, Excel, and PowerPoint.

√ Troubleshoot poor Office performance.

√ Repair corrupted files or recover data from them.

√ Understand the best practices you can implement to prevent file corruption.

One of the most frustrating things about Office applications is how they just decide to stop working. No warning. No explanation (except that annoying error message). Your application just stops running, or won't load, or freezes for no apparent reason. It's the randomness of these types of problems that's the most perplexing aspect of it all. Why do programs have to crash? There are a variety of reasons, but the short summary is that all computing devices eventually wear down, break, or get fouled by dust, an electrical surge, or an introduced virus or problem file. In this chapter, we'll try to equip you with a variety of troubleshooting tools that should help resolve most problems related to your Office applications.

This is a great time for us to plug the 12-step degunking process again (see Chapter 2). If you take the time to degunk your PC and Office thoroughly as we describe, and do it *before* something goes wrong, you'll ward off a lot of headaches later on. That said, when you do run into trouble while using Office, there are systematic protocols you can use to diagnose and then treat the problem. This is called *troubleshooting,* and all PC users should improve their skills in this area. In this chapter, we'll discuss the various types of errors you're likely to run across and show you how to recognize the symptoms of poor Office performance and data corruption. We'll explain an organized procedure you can use to troubleshoot the problem and then take action to fix it; we do this for Office overall, and for each of the core applications. We'll show you how to fix broken templates and recover corrupted Office files, and finally, we'll give some pointers on how to avoid file corruption in the future.

Understand the Categories of Errors

There are three main types of errors that your PC or a particular application can experience:

√ Exception error

√ Invalid page fault

√ Kernel error

The first type of error, an *exception error,* is when something unexpected occurs in the Microsoft Windows operating system. According to Microsoft, fatal exception errors are codes that are returned by a program because an illegal instruction has been encountered, invalid data or code has been accessed, or the privilege level of an operation is invalid. In short, there's little you can do to prevent an exception error, but you can troubleshoot it as we describe later.

The second type of error, called an *invalid page fault,* occurs when an application performs an illegal procedure, such as incorrectly attempting to access random access memory (RAM). Typically, you'll get a message saying, "Microsoft Word [or Excel or PowerPoint or Outlook] has encountered a problem and needs to close. We're sorry for the inconvenience." This is when you feel like pulling your hair out and hope your AutoRecover setting is optimized.

The third type of error, a *kernel error,* is also considered an invalid page fault. This happens when a problem occurs between the Windows operating system (the kernel) and the application. Again, the application will show you an error message and close automatically.

Why Errors Arise

Specific situations increase the chances of an error occurring, including these:

√ An application attempts to open a corrupted file or a file based on a corrupted template.

√ You try to save a document when system resources are low.

√ A corrupt printer driver or video driver is causing conflicts.

√ A file has been saved to a bad sector, which is a part of the hard disk that is flawed or damaged.

√ A virus has infected the PC, or a macro virus has infiltrated a Microsoft Office file.

√ Your antivirus software is conflicting with Windows or Office.

√ There is a file-sharing conflict between you and another user on a network.

√ A document has been converted from one file type to another too many times.

√ You've tried to save a file with a name that exceeds the maximum number of characters allowed.

√ You don't have the proper permissions to access the file or folder.

In addition, some Office features are inherently prone to cause problems, including master documents, versions, fast saves, the Document Map, nested tables, and the use of a multitude of formats for bulleted or numbered lists in one file. Also, if you try to save to or work from a floppy disk, you'll most likely experience document corruption or other trouble.

What to Do When Errors Arise

The bad news is there isn't much you can do once an error arises. You can, however, do some troubleshooting to prevent the same error from occurring again. We'll next outline the troubleshooting process for Office and the applications Word, Excel, PowerPoint, and Outlook.

Understand the Troubleshooting Process

Troubleshooting is a systematic way of narrowing down the possible causes of a problem and then implementing a procedure to fix it. Basically, you are a detective using the clues left by the application or operating system to trace the trouble to its source. Troubleshooting consists of two main steps:

1. Gathering information
2. Taking action based on the information gathered

In the following sections, we'll discuss the process of gathering information and then offer several ways you can try to fix general problems with Office applications. If these suggestions don't solve your particular dilemma, you can then follow the directions we give later in the chapter for troubleshooting the individual applications and corrupted documents and templates.

TIP: *Microsoft provides an extensive database of documentation that can help you solve problems with Microsoft products. Go to **http://support.microsoft.com** to visit the Microsoft Help and Support Web site where you can search the Knowledge Base and access an Office-specific solution center. Also, use the Help feature on the Start menu to visit the Help and Support Center for the version of Windows you're running on your PC.*

Gather Information

You need to collect as much information as you can about the problem so you can narrow down the cause.

Save the Error Message

When you run into a problem, oftentimes an error message appears on-screen to tell you so. Although it's an unwelcome visitor, you can gather useful information from it. What you should do if this happens is the following:

1. Write down the error message word for word so that you can refer to it later.
2. Click to see the error report.
3. If possible, copy and paste this report into Notepad or a new Word document and save it. The report can provide valuable clues when you begin to research the problem. At the very least, write down the names of the major components or files in the report and make a note of the error number if one is given.
4. Go to **http://support.microsoft.com** to check the Microsoft Knowledge Base to learn more about the issue. Type in the module name or the error number to see whether there is a workaround already specified for it.

Determine When the Error Occurs

Next, you must determine exactly when the problem occurs. Ask yourself five questions:

1. *Is the problem reproducible?* Try to resolve the problem with the information you gained from the Microsoft support sites, and then work the application again to see whether the problem recurs. If the problem continues to plague you, be sure to document the steps you take as you work through the rest of the troubleshooting procedure so you have a clear record of what you have tried and what has not worked so far.

2. *Does the problem occur when you use other programs?* If, for instance, you receive the same error message regardless of which application you're using, the problem is probably with the Windows operating system or with a program running in the background. Use the information given in the section "Start Your PC in Safe Mode" later in this chapter to try to isolate the specific cause or component that's causing the conflict.

3. *Are there specific known issues about the application that describe the problem?* For example, the fast saves feature in PowerPoint is known to cause inexplicable and erratic behavior; this is documented in the Knowledge Base. Also, Microsoft has acknowledged the fact that the Auto Scale feature in Excel charts can cause certain types of problems, as can the XPrint Add-in in versions of Outlook later than 2000. Usually the support documentation will provide a workaround for the problem.

TIP: Check the Microsoft Knowledge Base at http://support.microsoft.com to discover known issues.

---

4. *Does the problem occur only in this file?* Try to rule out factors by looking for similar misbehavior when you access other files or use a different application. Copy the problem file onto removable media and try to access it on another PC. If the problem occurs only in one file, you can move on to the steps to repair the damaged document or extract the usable data from it (see "Troubleshoot Office Problems" later in this chapter). If the problem occurs when you access files all based on the same template, try to repair the template using the information in "Fix Broken Templates" later in this chapter.

5. *Does the problem occur only at certain times?* For example, does Word crash only when you try to save a file? Does PowerPoint refuse to run? Pinpointing the exact time and circumstances under which a problem occurs will help you resolve it.

Take Appropriate Action

Once you've narrowed down the scope of the problem, you can begin to eliminate potential causes one by one and test to see whether the problem recurs. You will need to take appropriate actions, depending on the severity of the problem. Your response to an error will include completing at least one of the following six steps:

1. Start your PC in safe mode.
2. Start both your PC and the problem application in safe mode.
3. Start your PC in safe mode and start the application regularly.
4. Repair the Office application by using the Reinstall or Repair option in the Office Setup Wizard.
5. Remove Office and reinstall it.
6. Reinstall the Windows operating system.

What you are doing in each step is isolating potential problem sources in a systematic fashion so you can either rule them out as a cause or inspect them further. For instance, when you start your PC in *safe mode,* you are preventing add-ins and all but the most basic device drivers from running. Components other than the basic ones needed to start the operating system can cause problems if they are damaged in any way. By running the operating system without them, you can determine whether the operating system or the add-ins are causing the problem. Next, when you start both the PC and the application in safe mode, you can determine whether the problem lies in the operating system, the application, or any of the add-ins and startup files for the application.

CAUTION: It's only when you can't isolate a problem using all the tools available to you that you will need to consider reinstalling Office or Windows. These are the most serious steps, and we want to avoid taking these steps at all costs!

Now let's go through each of the troubleshooting options, one by one.

Start Your PC in Safe Mode

Safe mode can help you diagnose a problem by enabling you to start the computer using only the minimal system files and basic drivers, including those that run the mouse, monitor, keyboard, video display, and any default system services. All other devices and add-ins are disabled in safe mode. If the problem does not recur when you start Windows in safe mode, you know that the Windows operating system is not causing the trouble and that some add-in or item in the Startup folder is. Enable each add-in one by one when you restart your PC to isolate the troublemaker. Then consult the add-in software's manual or the Knowledge Base for directions on how to eliminate the problem.

If the problem does recur when you start in safe mode, you've just learned that one or more basic operating system files or drivers are damaged. To solve this sort of problem, you might be able to use the Recovery Console or you might have to uninstall and then reinstall the Windows operating system. Back up your data before you do anything! And then search the Knowledge Base for a solution to fix the troubled Windows component. If you must reinstall Windows, review the information in Chapter 3, "Performing a Gunk-Free Installation or Upgrade."

TIP: *Make sure the Windows operating system is kept up-to-date with the latest security patches and service packs by visiting http://windowsupdate.microsoft.com/. If you keep up with the latest fixes, quirks in the operating system can be resolved before you have to take action on your own. You can also configure Automatic Updates on your PC to detect and download critical updates automatically. Set up an Automatic Updates schedule by clicking Start, clicking Control Panel, double-clicking Automatic Updates, and configuring the options in the dialog box.*

To start Windows in safe mode, follow these steps:

1. Click Start, and then click Shut Down or Turn Off Computer (depending on your operating system).

2. In the dialog box, choose Restart, and then click OK.

3. Pay attention to the boot process, and when you see the message "Please select the operating system to start" appear on-screen, press F8.

4. On the Windows Advanced Options menu, use the arrow keys on your keyboard to choose Safe Mode, and then press Enter.

Start Both Your PC and the Problem Application in Safe Mode

When you start both the PC and application in safe mode, you are eliminating all add-ins and nonbasic device drivers from the equation. If the problem recurs this time while the app is running in safe mode, you know that some corruption has damaged the Office application files. In this situation, you can try to repair the application or you can choose to uninstall and reinstall Office.

TIP: *Be sure your installation of Office is kept current with the latest free updates that help improve and maintain stability and security and fix known issues. Visit the Office home page at http://office.microsoft.com/, and then click the Check for Updates link to see which updates you can download and install.*

To start the PC and app in safe mode, follow these steps:

1. Click Start, and then click Shut Down or Turn Off Computer (depending on your operating system).

2. In the dialog box, choose Restart, and then click OK.

3. Pay attention to the boot process, and when the message "Please select the operating system to start" appears on-screen, press F8.

4. On the Windows Advanced Options menu, use the arrow keys on your keyboard to choose Safe Mode, and then press Enter.

5. Hold down the Ctrl key as you double-click an Office application icon on the Desktop to start the Office program.

6. If a message appears asking whether you want to start in safe mode, click Yes.

In safe mode, the following restrictions apply:

√ You cannot create or modify templates and save the changes.

√ Menu and toolbar customizations are not loaded, and you cannot save new customizations.

√ You cannot save new AutoCorrect entries.

√ Recovered documents are not automatically displayed.

√ Extra features and add-ins will not be run.

As you can see, you cannot expect to work normally in safe mode—and you certainly cannot expect to degunk anything—it's for diagnostic purposes only. If you can reproduce the problem while running the app in safe mode, your application files may be damaged in some way. Follow the directions given in "Repair the Office Applications by Using the Reinstall or Repair Option in the Office Setup Wizard" if you think your Office application is damaged.

If the problem does not crop up, add back each startup item and add-in, one by one. You can view and then systematically enable each disabled item to figure out which one is causing the problem by following these steps:

1. In safe mode in the application, choose About Microsoft Office *ApplicationName* on the Help menu.

2. In the About Microsoft Office *ApplicationName* dialog box, click the Disabled Items button.

3. Choose an item from the list in the Disabled Items dialog box, and then click Enable.

4. Try to reproduce the error. If the problem does not occur, repeat this procedure to enable another item.

5. Work through the list of disabled items one by one until you isolate the problem.

In later versions of Office, safe mode diagnostics are automated. At startup, the Office app will check itself and disable items that are causing it to malfunction. You can, however, still initiate safe mode using the preceding steps if you think there is a problem item that Office has overlooked.

Start Your PC in Safe Mode and Start the Application Regularly

Now that you've eliminated the possibility that an application-specific add-in or startup item is causing the problem by running the app in safe mode, you need to determine whether a Windows startup item or add-in is conflicting with the Office application as the cause of your troubles. To do so, start your PC in safe mode and start the application by regular means. Try to reproduce the error. If the error does not recur, you know that a Windows startup item or add-in is causing the conflict. One way to eliminate such a problem is simply to isolate and then remove the troublesome item from the Windows Startup folder.

TIP: See Joli Ballew and Jeff Duntemann's book **Degunking Windows** (Paraglyph Press, 2004) to learn how to tweak your Windows Startup folder.

If the problem does recur and you've already systematically tested each application add-in and startup item in each of the Office applications and have determined that none of them is causing the problem, your Office installation might be damaged. Use the procedure given in the following section to repair Office. If that does not work, uninstalling and reinstalling Office can solve the problem.

Repair the Office Application by Using the Reinstall or Repair Option in the Office Setup Wizard

If you've determined that none of the application-specific add-ins, startup items, or device drivers is causing the problem, the Office files may be corrupted. You can attempt to repair the Office installation by following these steps:

1. Close all open applications and files.

2. Click Start, and then click Control Panel.

3. Double-click Add or Remove Programs in Control Panel.

4. Select Microsoft Office in the Currently Installed Programs and Updates list, and then click Change.

5. Choose Reinstall or Repair as shown in Figure 13-1, and then click Next.

6. Choose Detect and Repair Errors in My Office Installation, and then click Next. While Office Setup works to find and fix damaged areas, you might be asked to close running applications if you haven't done so already. Click Install.

7. Click OK when Setup tells you Office has been successfully repaired.

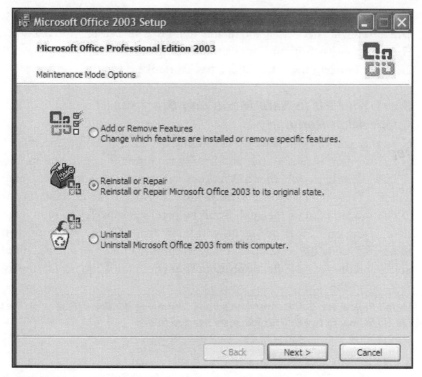

Figure 13-1
Use the Office Setup Wizard to repair damaged Office applications.

Try running the Office application again. Does the error occur? If not, you've solved the problem. If you're still experiencing difficulty, it might be time to try uninstalling and reinstalling Office.

TIP: On the Help menu in each Office application is the Detect and Repair command. Choose this command to perform the same detection and recovery procedure as the Reinstall and Repair option in Windows Setup.

Uninstall Office

Sometimes things can get so fouled up that it's better to wipe the slate clean and start anew. Before you even consider doing this, back up your Office-related data and customizations using the procedures we discuss in Chapter 12, "Backing Up and Restoring Microsoft Office." You'll need to have your original installation CD available for the reinstall process.

To uninstall Office, follow these steps:

1. Close all open applications and files.

2. Click Start, and then click Control Panel.

3. Double-click Add or Remove Programs in Control Panel.

4. Select Microsoft Office in the Currently Installed Programs and Updates list, and then click Remove.

5. Follow the steps of the wizard to remove Office from your system.

Degunk Windows Before Reinstalling Office

Once you've removed Office, it's the perfect time to do a little cleaning up. Use the information given in "Get Windows Ready Before Installing Office" in Chapter 3 and "Delete Unnecessary Files and Folders" in Chapter 4 to help. Also, run the Windows Check Disk utility to check for bad sectors and file system damage on your hard disk. To run Check Disk, follow these steps:

1. Close all open files and applications.

2. Double-click My Computer on the desktop.

3. Right-click the icon for your hard disk, and choose Properties from the context menu.

4. In the Tools tab, click the Check Now button in the Error-Checking section.

5. In the Check Disk dialog box, select both the Automatically Fix File System Errors and Scan For and Attempt Recovery of Bad Sectors options as shown in Figure 13-2. Click Start.

6. If necessary, schedule the disk check operation for the next time you restart your PC. Then restart your PC to perform the disk check.

Reinstall Office

Then it's time to reinstall Office. Insert your installation CD and away you go! Remember to perform a Custom installation so you have maximum control over which files and features are added to your PC without gunking it up.

Now, can you reproduce the error? If so, it's time for a last-ditch effort to set things straight: reinstall Windows.

Reinstall Windows

If none of the preceding steps are able to restore error-free functionality, you might uninstall and reinstall the Windows operating system. Use this as a last resort after all other possibilities are exhausted. It's a big undertaking, so you must consider it carefully. Before you uninstall and reinstall, be completely certain that some small, forgotten application or incompatible device driver is not

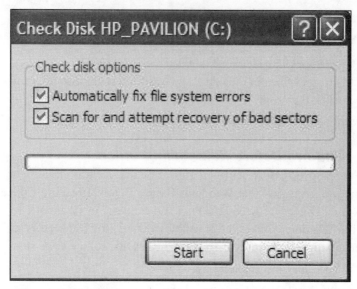

Figure 13-2
Enable the disk check operation to find errors and attempt recovery.

causing the problem. Also, try to use the Repair function in Windows Setup to see whether the problem can be erased before you have to reinstall. When you feel you've run out of options, try using the System Restore utility to restore your PC to an earlier state when it was running smoothly. If you decide that doing a clean install of Windows is your only option, you must have your original installation CD or disks on hand and you should back up all your data as well as any software you've downloaded or purchased.

TIP: Degunking Windows *(Paraglyph Press, 2004) by Joli Ballew and Jeff Duntemann gives detailed instructions on using System Restore and the Repair option to recover from Windows problems. It also discusses how to prepare your system for a clean install of the operating system.*

Troubleshoot Poor Office Performance

At times, although no specific error message appears, you might simply feel Office is not running right. Perhaps you hear the hard disk churning constantly whenever you start Office. Or your mouse pointer moves more slowly than you remember. Maybe menus take longer to open, and the save and file open processes seem to take forever. These are all signs of poor Office performance. You can take the following steps to optimize Office performance:

√   *Degunk your Office installation using the 12-step program!* Need we say more?

√   *Double-check to be sure your PC meets the minimum system requirements for the version of Office you're running.* In Chapter 3, in the section "Prepare for the Installation," we discuss the system requirements for Office 2003 and earlier versions. If your system does not meet the system requirements, certain Office features will be unable to run. If your system just barely meets the system requirements and you often run many applications at once, you might be putting too much of a strain on limited resources. Install more RAM or run only one or two apps at a time.

√   *Turn off speech recognition and handwriting recognition.* These two components use memory and can slow performance. By removing them, you are not deleting them from your computer, but simply preventing them from being loaded into memory when you run Office. This can free up some RAM.

√   *Update your antivirus software.* Most antivirus programs scan files on your computer as you open and save them. Some programs, however, can interfere with smooth performance by preventing you from opening good files that the software somehow misconstrues as infected. By keeping your antivirus software up-to-date with the latest virus signatures, you promote smoother interoperability between virus-scanning operations and Office.

√   *Start your PC in safe mode to disable startup items.* If Office performance improves while Windows runs in safe mode, you know that an add-in or startup item is dragging down performance. Isolate the culprit and remove it from the Startup folder. (For more information, see "Start Your PC in Safe Mode" earlier in this chapter.)

Fix Broken Templates

If during the troubleshooting process you find that the problem crops up when you use a specific file or a group of files based on the same template, the template might be corrupted. It's good practice to keep a backup, macro-free version of all your custom templates so that you can rename and fix them when you run into trouble. Make a copy of each custom template, strip out any macros, and save the template using a file name that indicates it is the "clean" copy of the original template. Then, when you make your regular backups as discussed in Chapter 12, be sure that the Templates folder is backed up along with the rest of your data. This will ensure that you always have a working backup copy of the template should something go wrong.

Repair Normal.dot in Word

If you experience unexplained problems when working in Word, one of the first things you should check is whether the global template Normal.dot is corrupted. All Word documents are automatically based on Normal.dot unless you explicitly attached a custom template instead. Normal.dot contains format settings, global macros, and any other customizations you've added to it. If Word won't open and run or it freezes up as soon as you start it, Normal.dot may be damaged. Also, when certain formatting features are inexplicably unavailable or cause errors when you try to use them, you can suspect Normal.dot of corruption.

An easy way to troubleshoot Normal.dot is to allow Word to re-create it automatically, which it does whenever you run Word and it cannot locate an existing copy of the template. Some installations of Office have more than one legitimate copy of Normal.dot, so to find them all, follow these steps:

1. Close all Office applications and files.

2. Click Start, and then click Search.

3. In the left pane of the Search Results dialog box, click All Files and Folders.

4. Click the More Advanced Options link, and then be sure the Search Hidden Files and Folders option is enabled.

5. In the All or Part of the File Name text box, type **Normal.dot**, and then click Search.

6. In the right pane of the Search Results dialog box, right-click each version of Normal.dot and choose Rename from the context menu. Rename each template file using a name that you will recognize as designating it as a copy of the original (possibly corrupted) file. If you have added customizations to Normal.dot, keeping a copy of the possibly corrupted version instead of deleting it altogether may allow you to copy your customizations over to the new, clean Normal.dot using the Organizer later.

7. Close the Search Results dialog box.

8. Open Word.

When Word looks in C:\Documents and Settings*username*\Application Data\Microsoft\Templates (where Normal.dot is normally stored) and doesn't find a copy of the global template, it will create a new, clean version automatically. If you cannot reproduce the problem, you've solved it by fixing a corrupt Normal.dot file. If you had customized the previous version of Normal.dot and want to resurrect those customizations from the corrupted file, use the Organizer. Choose Templates and Add-Ins on the Tools menu, and then click the Organizer button in the Templates and Add-Ins dialog box. Use the tabs of the Organizer dialog box to copy styles, AutoText, toolbar customizations, and macros from the old, corrupted Normal.dot that you renamed in the preceding steps to the new, clean version of Normal.dot.

If the problem still recurs in Word after you've created a new Normal.dot file, the trouble does not lie in a corrupted global template. Move through the steps of the troubleshooting process given in the section "Take Appropriate Action" earlier in this chapter as well as "Troubleshoot Damaged Word Documents" later.

Troubleshoot Workbook and Worksheet Templates in Excel

Excel differs from Word in that it does not require new workbooks and worksheets to be associated with a global template as Word does. You might have, however, created default book and sheet templates named Book.xlt and Sheet.xlt, which contain customizations that you like applied to all new workbooks and sheets. These templates are stored in the XLStart folder. Sometimes these default templates can become damaged and will cause unexpected behavior in Excel files based on them. If you want to keep the default templates, rename them and move them to the Templates folder for safekeeping while you troubleshoot. To troubleshoot templates in Excel, follow these steps:

1.   Close all Office files and applications.

2.   Right-click Start, and choose Explore.

3.   In Windows Explorer, navigate to C:\Program Files\Microsoft Office\Office11\XLStart.

4.   Locate the Book.xlt and Sheet.xlt files. Right-click each file, and choose Rename from the context menu. Type a new name that you will recognize later as the copy of the default templates.

5.   Hold down the Ctrl key as you click both renamed files, right-click the selected files, and then choose Cut from the context menu.

6.   Navigate to C:\Documents and Settings*username*\Application Data\Microsoft\Templates (where *username* is your logon name), right-click in the right pane of Explorer, and choose Paste from the context menu.

7.   Restart Excel and try to re-create the problem.

If the problem does not recur, you have solved it by removing corrupted workbook and sheet default templates. You will have to manually re-create new default templates if you wish to have default templates available. If the trouble does crop up again, the default templates were not the problem, so you can put them back into the XLStart folder for use. To restore Book.xlt and Sheet.xlt, do the preceding process in reverse: rename the default templates in the Templates folder as Book.xlt and Sheet.xlt and move them back to the XLStart folder. Follow the steps given in "Take Appropriate Action" earlier in this chapter and "Troubleshoot Damaged Excel Files" later to continue troubleshooting the issue.

TIP: *Sometimes an Excel file you name using the .xlt file extension cannot be accessed or applied to new Excel workbooks and sheets as a template. In Excel, not only must you save a template file using the .xlt extension as part of the file name, you must save it as a template. In the Save As dialog box, choose Template from the Save as Type drop-down menu to save a file as a template. Remember to store templates in the Templates folder for easy access.*

Troubleshoot Templates in PowerPoint

Myriad design templates are available for use in any PowerPoint presentation, including built-in templates, customized templates you've created, and templates you've downloaded from the Internet. If your presentation begins to act wacky and you suspect that a template is causing the problem, you must first determine which templates are used in the presentation and then narrow down the field to which one is causing the problem. To troubleshoot templates in PowerPoint, follow these steps:

1. Save a copy of your presentation.

2. Open the copy of the presentation, click the downward-pointing arrow in the task pane area, and choose Slide Design.

3. Note which design templates are listed in the Used in This Presentation section of the Slide Design task pane.

4. At the bottom of the Slides tab, click the Slide Sorter button to view all slides.

5. Hold down the Ctrl key as you click to select all slides based on the same template. (You can tell which template is applied to a slide by selecting the slide and noting which design template becomes highlighted in the Used in This Presentation section of the Slide Design task pane.)

6. Click the downward-pointing arrow for the Default Design template in the Available for Use section of the Slide Design task pane, and choose Apply to Selected Slides.

7. Try to reproduce the error. If you cannot reproduce the error, the design template you just replaced is the culprit. Search your system for that template file and delete it. You'll have to create a new template with those customizations if you care to use that design in the future. Remember to reformat the slides based on this corrupt template in the original copy of your presentation before you go before an audience.

8. If you can reproduce the error, repeat steps 4 through 7 until you find the damaged design template.

9. Close the copy of the presentation, and then delete it.

10. Open the original version of the presentation, make the editing and design changes needed to clean up the slides that were previously based on the corrupted template, and then save your changes.

If after eliminating each design template systematically you still encounter the original error, run through the remaining steps of the troubleshooting process given in "Take Appropriate Action" earlier in this chapter and the section "Troubleshoot PowerPoint Problems" later.

Troubleshoot Office Problems

In the following sections, we'll discuss the factors that might cause otherwise inexplicable problems that the general troubleshooting procedure did not solve. Also, we mention some built-in Office tools that can help detect and repair problems with Office files, including the Document Recovery, Application Recovery, and Open and Repair tools. Then we'll show you how to troubleshoot according to the idiosyncrasies of each Office application.

Confounding Factors

The issues discussed in these sections can cause trouble when you run Office applications. Keep these in mind so you can be sure to test for them and then eliminate them from the equation while you are troubleshooting.

Antivirus Software Conflicts

Antivirus software that monitors your system continuously can mistakenly identify one of your Office files as an infected file and prevent it from working properly. Also, sometimes the virus-monitoring process interrupts the file save or file open process and can cause an error. Be sure to use a virus-scanning program that is guaranteed to interoperate with Microsoft Office, and make sure that you keep it up-to-date. (If your antivirus program continues to give you problems, contact the manufacturer or switch to another product if the manufacturer isn't helpful.)

Restricted User Permissions

Sometimes you might not have adequate permissions to open a file or save a file to a specific folder. If you cannot open an Office file, can open only a read-only copy, are prevented from using some editing features, or cannot turn off Track Changes, for instance, the document creator may have encrypted the document with a password or used protection features to increase security for the file. To open, edit, and save a file, you must have Read, Write, Rename, and Delete permissions on the file and the file save location folder.

File Sharing Conflicts

If you work in a networked environment and you sporadically encounter problems saving files, you might be experiencing a file sharing conflict. Office cannot save changes made to multiple instances (multiple open copies) of a document at the same time. For example, if you try to save your changes to an Excel file at the same time another user attempts to save an instance of that file, Office will experience an error.

File Naming Violations

Office file names can contain up to 256 characters. If you exceed this limit or use illegal characters in the name (such as / \ √ ? " < > | :), you'll experience an error when you attempt to save the file.

Use Office Document and Application Recovery

The Office Application Recovery feature (called Document Recovery in earlier versions of Office) can help you manage Office applications that are not responding and recover your work during an application failure. Click Start, point to Microsoft Office, point to Microsoft Office Tools, and then click Microsoft Office Application Recovery. Click the Restart Application button in the Application Recovery dialog box to close the frozen application; you'll lose any changes made to the open document.

To make Office repair the application and recover your work, click the Recover Application button in the Application Recovery dialog box. Office will close and repair the selected application and then restart the application with the Document Recovery pane open. (Earlier versions of Office simply open the original and recovered documents in separate windows.) If Office was able to recover the file you were working on at the time of the application failure, that file will be listed in the Document Recovery pane as *FileName* [Recovered], where *FileName* is the name of the original file. The original file will also be listed in the Document Recovery pane as *FileName* [Original]. Recovered files usually contain more recent changes than originals (how recent the saved changes are depends on the AutoRecover time interval setting you specify in the Options dialog box for each application). Choose whether you want to open and view, save, close, or view the repairs made for each file listed. If you close the file without saving first, any changes will be lost.

The Application Recovery feature is a useful tool to use when you need to force Document Recovery to start when an application is unable to start it automatically.

Use the Open and Repair Command

Sometimes you can repair troubled Office files by using the Open and Repair command. This tool is located in the Open dialog box (from the File menu in an Office app) in the Open button drop-down menu as shown in Figure 13-3. You can have the Office application attempt to detect and correct any corruptions it finds as it opens the selected document. Or you can choose to simply have the application extract the usable information from the file if it was previously unable to repair the damage.

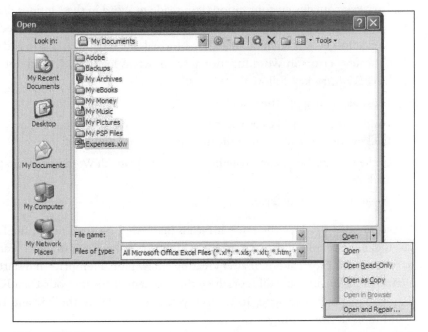

Figure 13-3

Use the Open and Repair command to try to repair problematic Office files.

Troubleshoot Damaged Word Documents

If you've gone through the basic troubleshooting procedure and have been unable to fix the problem, your Word document may be damaged or corrupted. To determine just which component is causing the trouble, you'll complete these steps:

1. Start Word in safe mode.
2. Clear add-ins from the Startup folder.
3. Start Word without the custom dictionary.
4. Start Word without the AutoCorrect file.

5. Start Word without the Spelling and Grammar tool loaded.

6. Check whether a font or fonts are damaged.

By completing this process, you can determine which component is the problem.

Start Word in Safe Mode

Both the Normal.dot global template and the Word Data Registry key are loaded upon Word startup. As you know, Normal.dot is the global template applied to every new Word document unless you specify otherwise. The Data Registry key contains customizations you made to Word in the Options dialog box, such as the number of files listed in the File menu Most Recently Used list and the AutoRecover interval. If either Normal.dot or the Data key is damaged, it causes errors in Word functionality. To bypass loading Normal.dot and the Data Registry key, follow these steps:

1. Close all open applications and files.

2. Hold down the Ctrl key as you double-click the Word shortcut on the Desktop or select Word from the Start menu.

3. In the message box asking whether you want to launch Word in safe mode, click Yes.

4. Try to reproduce the error.

If you cannot reproduce the error, it means that either Normal.dot or the Data key is damaged. Follow the steps given in "Repair Normal.dot in Word" earlier to try to repair Normal.dot. If after creating a new global template and starting Word normally you can still reproduce the problem, it means your Data Registry key might be damaged. To fix this, you need to delete the key and reset Word to its default settings.

WARNING! *This procedure involves editing the Registry using the Registry Editor utility. You can do serious damage to your PC if you do not edit the Registry correctly. Consult the Microsoft Knowledge Base for more information and follow the directions exactly to avoid complications.*

To reset the Word Data Registry key, complete these steps:

1. Close all open applications and files.

2. Click Start, and then click Run.

3. In the Run dialog box, type **regedit** in the Open text box, and click OK.

4. Expand the following Registry key:
   HKEY_CURRENT_USER\Software\Microsoft\Office\11.0\Word\Data.

5. In the left pane, click the Data folder, and then press Delete to delete the Data Registry key.

6. When you see the "Are you sure you want to delete this key" message, click Yes.

7. Click Exit on the Registry menu.

8. Restart Word normally and try to reproduce the error.

If you cannot reproduce the error, you just found and fixed the problem, which was a corrupted Registry key. After this procedure, you will have to re-create the customizations you made to Word using the Options dialog box (see Chapter 6, "Degunking Microsoft Word," for more information).

TIP: *You can download the Word 2002 Support Template from* **www.microsoft.com/** **downloads/details.aspx?FamilyID=efb7219f-aaf5-4858-8abe-** **0b08aeb69664&DisplayLang=en**. *If you are running Word 2002 or earlier, this template will help you troubleshoot Word documents, including deleting the Data Registry key and starting Word in safe mode.*

If you can reproduce the error, you need to test whether an add-in or item in the Word Startup folder is causing a conflict.

Clear Add-Ins from the Startup Folder

Test to see whether an add-in or startup items are bugging Word. To start Word cleanly, follow these steps:

1. Close all open applications and files.

2. Right-click Start, and choose Explore.

3. Navigate to C:\Program Files\Microsoft Office\Office11\Startup (which is the Office Startup folder), select all the items in the folder by holding down the Shift key as you click them, and then drag the group to the Desktop for safekeeping during the rest of the procedure.

4. Navigate to C:\Documents and Settings*username*\Application Data\Microsoft\Word\Startup (which is the Word Startup folder), select all the items in the folder, and drag the group to the Desktop.

5. Restart Word normally and try to reproduce the error.

If you cannot reproduce the error, it means one of the startup items or add-ins is causing the problem. Add the items back to their respective folders one by one, restart Word normally, and try to reproduce the error until you find the culprit. Once you know which is the troublesome file, you can avoid storing it in the Startup folder to restore proper functionality to any of the Office applications.

If the error crops up again, proceed with the troubleshooting tips given in the following sections.

Start Word without the Custom Dictionary

Whenever you type a space, type a word, or press Enter, the Word Spelling and Grammar tool attempts to check the spelling and grammar of the entered data. If you've added words to the dictionary as you spell-checked documents in the past, these words were inserted into a custom dictionary file. Sometimes custom dictionary files that you've created, or ones that you've installed separately, can become corrupted and can wreak havoc whenever you type in a Word document. To test whether a custom dictionary file is damaged, open Word without loading the file by following these steps:

1. Close all open applications and files.
2. Click Start, and then click Search.
3. In the Search Results dialog box, click All Files or Folders, click More Advanced Options, and be sure the Search Hidden Files and Folders option is enabled.
4. In the All or Part of the File Name box, type ***.dic** to search for all dictionary files. Click Search.
5. The default custom dictionary file name is Custom.dic. However, you might have renamed this file or added other dictionary files to Word. For each custom or customized dictionary file that appears in the right pane of the Search Results dialog box, right-click the file and choose Rename from the context menu. Rename each file with a name you will recognize later.
6. Close the Search Results dialog box.
7. Restart Word regularly and try to reproduce the problem.

If, after you restart Word with the custom dictionary disabled, you still encounter the problem, keep on troubleshooting.

If, however, you cannot reproduce the problem once you start Word again, you just solved the mystery: a dictionary file was corrupted. If you renamed more than one dictionary file in the preceding procedure, make them accessible to Word one by one by renaming them to their original names, restart Word, and attempt to reproduce the problem to see which file was damaged. Rename the damaged file as specified earlier, and then add the custom entries it contains to the new default dictionary that Word creates. Follow these steps:

1. Right-click Start, and choose Explorer.
2. Navigate to where the dictionary file is stored. The default custom dictionary normally can be found at C:\Documents and Settings*username*\Application Data\Microsoft\Proof.

3. Double-click the file to open it in Notepad.

4. Select all the words listed, choose Copy from the Edit menu, and paste the list into a new Word document.

5. Choose Spelling and Grammar from the Tools menu, and as the tool picks up each word, click Add to Dictionary.

Start Word without the AutoCorrect File

When the AutoCorrect file (which uses the .acl file extension) is damaged, it can create unusual behavior in Word. To determine whether it is causing your trouble, start Word without it by following these steps:

1. Close all open applications and files.

2. Click Start, and then click Search.

3. In the Search Results dialog box, click All Files or Folders, click More Advanced Options, and be sure the Search Hidden Files and Folders option is enabled.

4. In the All or Part of the File Name box, type ★.acl, and then click Search. A list of ACL files appears in the right pane of the Search results dialog box.

CAUTION: *There are three files named Mso1033.acl, Mso2057.acl, and Mso3081.acl, which are important Office files. Do not rename these files as discussed in this procedure.*

---

5. Right-click an ACL file (not Mso1033.acl, Mso2057.acl, or Mso3081.acl), and choose Rename from the context menu. Type .old at the end of the file name.

6. Restart Word normally and try to reproduce the error. If you can reproduce the error, repeat step 5 for each of the ACL files listed in the Search results pane (except for Mso1033.acl, Mso2057.acl, and Mso3081.acl) until you find the culprit.

If you cannot find the culprit using this method, continue to troubleshoot Word.

Start Word without the Spelling and Grammar Tool

Each time you type a space, type a word, or press Enter in a Word document, the Spelling and Grammar tool attempts to check the spelling and grammar. If the files for this tool are damaged in any way, they can cause an error when you work in Word documents. Try to determine whether the Spelling and Grammar tool is the problem by starting Word without it:

1. Open the afflicted document.

2. Before you do anything else, choose Options on the Tools menu.

3. In the Spelling & Grammar tab, clear the Check Spelling As You Type, Check Grammar As You Type, and Check Grammar with Spelling options as shown in Figure 13-4. Click OK.

4. Try to reproduce the problem.

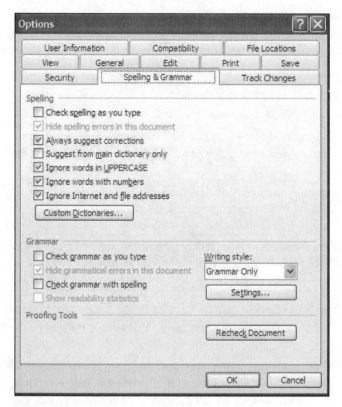

Figure 13-4

Disable spelling and grammar checking in the Options dialog box.

If you cannot reproduce the problem, you have just determined that either the spelling or grammar checking files are damaged. To resolve the problem, choose Detect and Repair on the Help menu. After the repair operation has completed successfully, enable spelling and grammar checking again using the Options dialog box.

If you still get an error after this procedure, try to determine whether any of your fonts are corrupted, as discussed next.

Check Whether a Font or Fonts Are Damaged

If a font file is damaged, it can cause Word to lock up while you work in a document. Try to determine which fonts are used in the file, and then use the following procedure to remove that font from your system. Tahoma is the font that Office uses in dialog boxes and on-screen messages. Damage to the Tahoma font can be an insidious and deceptive troublemaker! If you've downloaded fonts or installed them from another source, you might have to reinstall them using the original media if you remove them. Follow these steps to recover from font problems:

1. Determine which fonts are used in a problem application.

2. Close all open applications and files.

3. Click Start, and then choose Control Panel.

4. Double-click the Fonts icon.

5. Select the font files that are used in the problem document and drag them to your desktop to remove them. Office will substitute another font in any document that was using the removed fonts.

6. Restart Word normally and try to reproduce the error.

If you cannot reproduce the error, you might have discovered that a font was damaged. To resolve the problem, choose Detect and Repair on the Help menu. If you removed a font installed from another source, reinstall that font.

If the error persists, your document itself may be damaged.

Repair Damaged Word Documents

At some point, you might just have to face the fact that the problem lies within the document itself. Before you give up hope completely, you can try to repair damaged documents using the following methods:

√ *Save the file in another format.* Choose Save As on the File menu and choose another file format from the Save as Type drop-down menu. Usually, saving a Word doc as a Web page can help filter out corruptions—it also loses some of the document formatting, however. Then open the new version of the file, and convert it back into a Word document that uses the .doc file extension. Sometimes converting a file between types can strip out problematic formatting that causes errors, but be careful not to do this too many times to the same document or else you'll most likely introduce new errors.

√ *Copy everything but the last paragraph mark to a new document.* The paragraph marks and section break markers in Word store formatting. If the associated formatting is causing a conflict, it can make a file behave erratically. In the open document, click the Show/Hide icon on the Standard toolbar, and copy and paste everything but the section breaks and the last paragraph mark to a new Word document to strip out problematic formatting.

√   *Copy the undamaged portions of the document to a new document.* If none of the troubleshooting tips given so far help correct the problem, your best bet is to recover as much usable data as possible from the damaged file, delete the damaged file, and re-create the missing parts in the new file. Remember, having good and frequent backups can save you from having to re-create too much work because you might be able to restore a previous version of the file or use it to cobble together a new complete version.

For Files That Will Not Open

If you cannot get a particular Word document to open, you can take several steps to force open the file or at least extract the usable data from it:

√   *Open the document in draft format.* Sometimes formatting causes errors and if you can, you should open the document without its formatting. Follow these steps:

1. In Word, choose Normal on the View menu.

2. Choose Options from the Tools menu.

3. In the View tab, select the Draft Font and Picture Placeholders options as shown in Figure 13-5.

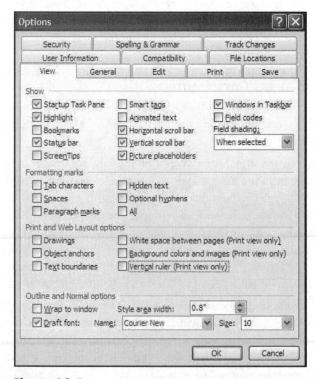

Figure 13-5
Try to open a document using draft formatting.

4. In the General tab, clear the Update Automatic Links at Open option, and then click OK.

√ *Insert the document as a file in a new document.* Open a new Word document, and choose File on the Insert menu. Use the Insert File dialog box to navigate to the problem file, select it, and then click Insert. This is how you copy all data except the last paragraph mark into a new document when you can't open the problem file to copy and paste manually. Be sure to save the new file.

√ *Open the file in WordPad.* If you cannot open the file by any other method, you might be able to recover the data in the file (devoid of the original formatting) by opening the file in WordPad, saving it, and then resaving that file as a Word doc. Follow these steps:

1. Click Start, point to Programs, point to Accessories, and then click WordPad.

2. Choose Open on the File menu, select the damaged file, and then click Open.

3. Choose Save As on the File menu, name the file and append the .doc file extension to the name, and then click Save. Note the location where you saved the file.

4. Close WordPad.

5. Restart Word and open the file you just saved in WordPad. If there are binary figures at the beginning or end of the document, you can delete them. Reformat the data as necessary.

6. Choose Save As on the File menu, and choose Word Document (*.doc) from the Save as Type list, and then click Save.

Use the Microsoft support services at **http://support.microsoft.com** to look for more ways to pry open damaged documents if none of these methods work.

Troubleshoot Damaged Excel Files

Use the general troubleshooting procedures to determine the scope of the problem. If you conclude that your Excel file is damaged, you can use a few tricks to try to save it.

For Excel Files That Will Not Open

Try these methods to force an uncooperative workbook to open:

√ *Set the Recalculation option to manual.* Follow these steps:

1. Open a blank workbook.

2. Choose Options on the Tools menu.

3. In the Calculation tab, choose the Manual option, and then click OK.

4. Try to open the problem file.

√   *Open the damaged file in Word or WordPad.* You might be able to extract some usable information if the file will open in Word or WordPad. You won't recover anything but the results of the cell formulas, though.

√   *Open the file using Excel Viewer.* You might be able to open the problem workbook in Excel Viewer; then you can copy the cells and paste them into a new workbook. Again, by using this method you will only be able to recover the contents of the cells, not the cell formulas or charts or macros used in the file. (If you don't have Excel Viewer installed, you can download it from the Microsoft Downloads site at **www.microsoft.com/downloads/details.aspx?FamilyId=C8378BF4-996C-4569-B547-75EDBD03AAF0&displaylang=en**.)

Extract Usable Data from Excel Files

You can try the following four methods to extract the usable data from an otherwise unusable Excel file:

√   *Save the file to a new location.* Sometimes saving a file to a new location clears up a mystery.

√   *Move the original worksheets to a new workbook.* You must leave at least one sheet, a filler sheet, in all workbooks, so to move the target worksheets to a new location, you must first supply a filler sheet. Follow these steps:

1. In the original file, choose Worksheet on the Insert menu.

2. Click one of the target sheets and then choose Move or Copy Sheet on the Edit menu.

3. In the Move or Copy dialog box, choose (New Book) from the To Book list, and then click OK.

4. Repeat steps 2 and 3 for each target sheet you want to move. Be sure to leave at least the filler sheet in the original workbook file.

√   *Save the file as a different Excel file type.* Choose Save As on the File menu, and then choose another Excel file format from the Save as Type drop-down menu.

√   *Save the file in HTML format.* Sometimes saving a workbook in Hypertext Markup Language format can strip out error-prone formatting and leave you with a working file. Resave the HTM file as an XLS file when you recover the data. You might have some reformatting to do.

Troubleshoot PowerPoint Problems

By now you know you have to determine the scope of the problem first. If you've concluded that a presentation is damaged, you can try the following procedures to reconstruct the presentation or extract as much usable information from it as possible.

√ *Insert the slides into a new presentation.* Follow these steps:

1. Open a blank presentation file.
2. Choose Slides from Files on the Insert menu.
3. In the Find Presentations tab of the Slide Finder dialog box, click the Browse button.
4. Navigate to and select the damaged presentation file, and click Open.
5. Click the Insert All button to insert all the slides into the new blank presentation, and then click Close.
6. Save the new presentation.

√ *Paste the slides into a new presentation file.* Copy all the slides from the damaged presentation, open a new file, and paste the slides. Sometimes only one corrupted slide can cause a whole presentation to act funny. You might want to copy and paste slides into the new presentation file one by one to be certain you catch the troublemaker, if there is one.

√ *Save the presentation as a Rich Text File format file.* In the damaged presentation, choose Save As from the File menu, and select Outline/RTF (*.rtf) from the Save as Type drop-down menu. Then to use the RTF file, in PowerPoint choose Open on the File menu, click All Files (*.*) on the Files of Type drop-down menu, and select the RTF file. You can then try to resave the file as a PowerPoint presentation (PPT) file.

For Presentations That Will Not Open

If you cannot get a presentation to open, several methods may help you access the data it contains.

√ *Drag the presentation file to the PowerPoint program file icon.* In Windows Explorer, drag the problem file onto the PowerPoint program icon—use either the PowerPoint shortcut on your Desktop or the executable file stored in C:\Program Files\Microsoft Office\Office11. This can sometimes allow you to open a difficult file.

√ *Try to open the latest temporary file for the presentation.* As you work in a presentation file, PowerPoint creates a temporary file to which it saves the changes you make before it writes them to disk at the end of the editing session. Depending on how PowerPoint ended the last editing session for this file, a temporary file might be hanging around still. We normally try to degunk these lost souls, but in this case, attempting to open the latest version of the temp file might enable you to access the data in the damaged presentation. Check the folder where the damaged file is stored, and open any temp files you find there to see if you can find the right one. When you do find the right one, rename it and change the .tmp file extension to .ppt, then try to open it in PowerPoint.

√ *Open the file in PowerPoint Viewer.* If you don't have a copy of PowerPoint Viewer on your PC, you can download it from the Microsoft Downloads Web site. If you get the problem presentation open, try to resave it, or copy the slides into another PowerPoint file.

√ *Save the file to a different location.* Sometimes just saving to another folder can enable you to open and work normally in a presentation file.

Troubleshoot Outlook Problems

Outlook troubles can be some of the most frustrating, possibly because more than from any other application, we expect instantaneous action when we use Outlook: instant communication, instant results. If the Outlook application itself fails or generates errors, start Outlook in safe mode to see whether an add-in or startup item is causing the difficulty. To do so, follow these steps:

1. Close all open applications and files.

2. Hold down the Ctrl key as you open Outlook.

3. Choose Options form the Tools menu, and in the Other tab, click Advanced Options.

4. In the Advanced Options dialog box, click the COM Add-Ins button, and then remove all of the add-ins listed.

5. Click OK twice.

6. Restart Outlook normally and try to reproduce the error.

If you cannot reproduce the error, one of the add-ins was causing the conflict. Add them back to Outlook one by one to isolate the troubled file, and then disable that add-in.

The majority of problems users encounter while using Outlook are related to trouble sending and receiving e-mail. There are a few things you can do to promote smooth e-mail operation:

√ Be sure that your e-mail account settings, including your username, password, incoming and outgoing mail server names, and e-mail address, match the information supplied by your Internet service provider (ISP). Check this information in the E-mail Accounts dialog box by choosing E-mail Accounts on the Tools menu.

√ If you use a dial-up connection, be sure that you are using the correct phone number to connect to a local server, and that you have a dial tone when you try to connect. Ensure that the dialing properties are set correctly.

√ Increase the time that Outlook tries to connect to the outgoing server so that you forestall server time-outs, which occur when the time interval in which Outlook must connect with the server expires before Outlook makes the connection to upload a message. Follow these steps:

1. Choose Options on the Tools menu.

2. In the Mail Setup tab, click the E-mail Accounts button.

3. Choose View or Change Existing E-mail Accounts, and then click Next.

4. Select your e-mail account from the list, and then click Change.

5. In the E-mail Accounts dialog box, click More Settings.

6. In the Advanced tab of the Internet E-Mail Settings dialog box, use the slider to increase the amount of time available for server time-outs, as shown in Figure 13-6. For a high-speed Internet connection, a setting of about 1 minute is usually adequate. For a dial-up account, a setting of about 3 minutes usually works. Click OK.

7. Click Next, click Finish, and then click OK.

If it seems as if the send/receive process takes an enormously long time, consider a few things.

√ You might be sending or receiving a large message.

√ The time it takes to transmit depends on the speed of your Internet connection.

√ If you use Word as your e-mail editor, you should have at least 128 megabytes of RAM available.

√ If you're running other applications at the same time as Outlook, you might be straining the available resources on your PC.

√ Virus-scanning programs that run in the background can be slowing down the transmission process.

If messages stay in your Outbox after you click the Send button, there could be a few reasons:

√ You might have specified that outgoing messages not be sent until the next scheduled send/receive. Choose Options on the Tools menu, and in the Mail Setup tab, be sure the Send Immediately When Connected option is enabled.

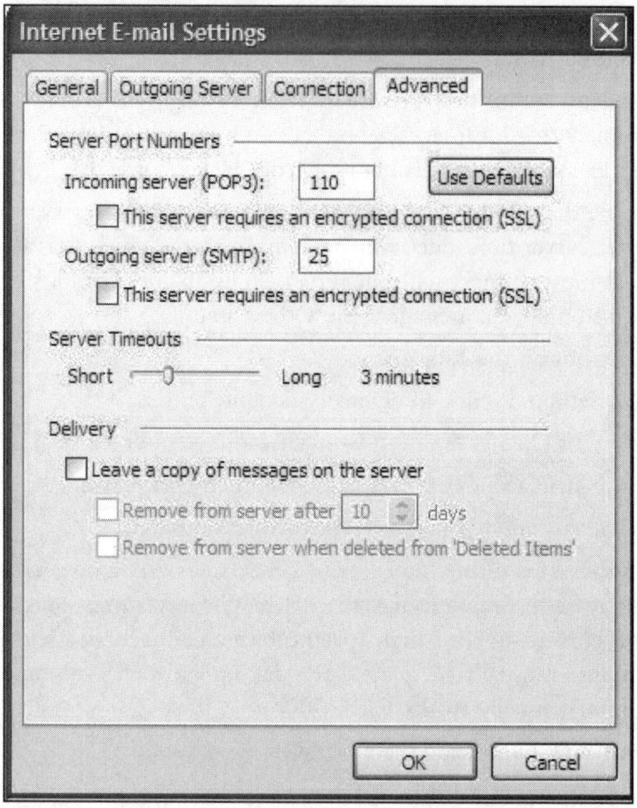

Figure 13-6

Increase the time allowed for server time-outs in the Advanced tab of the Internet E-Mail Settings dialog box.

√   If you've opened or edited a message in the Outbox, that message will not be sent until you again click the Send button.

√   Your mail server might not be available for some reason. Wait until a little later to try to resend the message.

√   If you are having trouble sending (or receiving) pictures, the files may be too large for your mail server or the recipient's mailbox to handle. Check with your ISP to see what your mailbox size is. Then check to be sure attachments do not exceed the file size allowed by your ISP.

Finally, if you cannot see any messages in your Inbox or in another mail folder—you did a really good job degunking! Actually, a few different things may be happening:

√   A filter might be applied to the current view. If so, the words *Filter Applied* will appear in the status bar at the bottom of the Outlook window. You can remove the filter by choosing Arrange By on the View menu, pointing to Current View, pointing to Customize Current View, and then clicking the Filter button in the Customize View: Messages dialog box. Click Clear All, and then click OK twice.

√ If you're using Outlook 2003, the groups might be collapsed in the Folder List. Click the + button beside the name of a group to expand it.

√ If you have enabled AutoArchive like a good GunkBuster, AutoArchive might have moved messages over a certain age to an archive folder. Check in the archive folders to find older messages.

√ You might have accessed your e-mail account from another computer and the mail messages were downloaded there.

Prevent File Corruption

Troubleshooting is an involved process that requires an extreme amount of patience and intestinal fortitude. So that you can avoid it as much as possible, implement the following best practices to prevent Office file corruption:

√ Make sure your PC meets the minimum system requirements to run Office.

√ Make sure there is a constant power supply to your PC and that you've protected your processor, peripheral devices, and phone or cable lines with a high-quality surge protector.

√ Work in a clean and dry environment and prevent dust from building up in and around your PC and electronic devices.

√ Move sources of electromagnetic radiation, such as speakers, radios, fax machines, or anything that runs using electricity, away from your PC.

√ Do not store floppy disks near your PC, which is a source of electromagnetic radiation that can corrupt the data stored on the disk.

√ Keep storage media such as floppies, CDs, and Zip disks in a closed container to prevent dust buildup and scratches.

√ Back up your work regularly! (See Chapter 12 for more information.)

√ Keep Windows and Office current with the latest security patches and updates to maintain stability and improve security and usability.

√ Try to work locally rather than over a network if possible.

√ Maintain hard disk health, first by keeping your PC and Office gunk free and second by running Disk Scan once a week.

√ Log off of Windows before you shut down or restart your PC.

√ Regularly scan for viruses.

Summing Up

In this chapter, we discussed the reasons applications fail and how to troubleshoot to find the cause of a problem. We showed you how to improve poor Office performance, as well as how to fix broken templates and repair or recover corrupted data files in each of the Office applications. Finally, we provided a list of best practices that will help you prevent data corruption and errors in the future. Word, Excel, and PowerPoint all have similar structure, but the reasons that they fail are often different. With this chapter, you should now have a fairly in-depth resource on how to solve just about any Office application gunk problem.

Appendix A

Enhancing Office with Add-ins and Third-Party Tools

This appendix is designed to help you use some of the useful tools, called add-ins, so that you can automate some of the degunking processes, such as creating backups, detecting spyware, and cleaning up documents for review. Add-ins can be downloaded for free or for a nominal cost. They can help you extend Office's standard feature and option set. We recommend backing up your system prior to downloading and installing a third-party add-in, as well as setting a Windows restore point that will enable you to restore your system should the add-in not work properly (see Chapter 12 "Backing Up and Restoring Office").

Microsoft supplies heaps of free add-ins for Office programs that you can download from the Internet. Third-party tools also can be downloaded from the Internet. Some third-party programs are free, others allow you to try them for free before you buy them, and others can be purchased for a reasonable cost.

About Add-ins

Add-ins are supplementary programs that can extend the capabilities of Office applications by adding specialized commands and custom features. Usually, add-in files are small and modular and may insert new commands on application menus and toolbars so you can access their features easily. Add-ins use memory when they are loaded, so it's usually a good idea to unload add-ins that you don't use very often to conserve resources and improve Office performance. You'll also find yourself unloading or disabling add-ins when you are troubleshooting a problem in an application. When you unload an add-in, it is not removed entirely from your PC, but is simply disabled and can be reloaded again later. There are two basic types of add-ins:

√ *COM add-ins.* Component Object Model (COM) add-ins use the .dll file extension (which stands for dynamic-link library) or .exe file extension (which stands for executable) and can run in one or more Office applications.

√ *Application-specific add-ins.* These supplemental programs are sometimes available when you install Office. For instance, Excel comes with a group of add-ins, including the Analysis ToolPak, Conditional Sum Wizard, and Solver Add-in, among others, that you can choose to load when you run Excel. You can also download application-specific add-ins from Microsoft or third-party vendors.

You must install add-ins on your PC and then load them into the appropriate application to be able to use them. After you download them from the Internet, add-ins are usually stored in one or more of the following locations on your PC:

√ C:\Documents and Settings*username*\Application Data\Microsoft\AddIns

√ C:\Program Files\Microsoft Office\Office11\Library

√ C:\Program Files\Microsoft Office\Office11\Startup

√ C:\Program Files\Microsoft Office\Office11\XLStart

√ C:\Documents and Settings*username*\Application Data\Microsoft\Excel\XLStart

√ C:\Documents and Settings*username*\Application Data\Microsoft\Word\Startup

Some add-ins install themselves directly in the application's startup folder and are already loaded the next time you open the application. If you must load the add-in manually, you can use one of the following methods:

√ In Word, choose Templates and Add-Ins on the Tools menu, click the Add button, and then choose All Files (*.*) or Word Add-ins (*.wll) from the File of Type drop-down menu. Navigate to where the add-in is stored, select it, and then click OK.

√ In Excel, choose Add-Ins on the Tools menu, and either choose an available add-in from the list or click the Browse button to navigate to a specific file.

√ In PowerPoint, choose Add-Ins on the Tools menu, choose one from the available list, and then click Load. Or click the Add New button to navigate to a specific file to load it.

√ In Outlook, choose Options on the Tools menu. In the Other tab, click the Advanced Options button, and then click the COM Add-Ins button. Choose an add-in from the list or click the Add New button to navigate to a specific file and load it.

When you load it manually, an add-in is available only for the current work session. You can, however, move the add-in into the Microsoft Windows, Office, or application-specific startup folder to ensure the add-in is loaded automatically.

Add-In Resources

As a service to its customers, Microsoft Corporation creates and makes available a slew of add-on tools to support its products. Check out the Office Marketplace at **http://office.microsoft.com/en-us/marketplace/default.aspx** to search for Office services, add-ins, and other products that can enhance Office. For products and services that can add functionality to the version of Windows you are running, go to the Windows Marketplace at **www.windowsmarketplace.com**.

If you search the Internet for Office add-ins and feel overwhelmed by the plethora of tools available, find a reputable software publication site, such as PCWorld (**www.pcworld.com**) or CNET (**www.cnet.com**), and read the reviews or editors' picks.

If you run Windows XP and later, another neat Microsoft feature that can help you separate the wheat from the chaff while researching third-party add-ins is the Designed for Windows Logo Program. The logo, shown in Figure A-1, is displayed on products that work well with Windows XP and later. To display the logo on their products, software developers must apply to Microsoft and be certain their product meets specific Microsoft design criteria.

Add-Ins from Microsoft

Let's look at four add-ins that you can download for free from the Microsoft Download Center. One tool helps you remove malware from your system, one blocks spyware, the other helps you create backups of your Outlook Personal Folders files, and the last makes it easier to remove hidden data from your Office files.

TIP: To find an add-in at the Microsoft Download Center, go to **www.microsoft.com/ downloads**, type the name of the add-in in the Search for a Download box, and then click Go.

Figure A-1

The Designed for
Windows Logo Program
logo can help you
identify products that
interoperate well with
Windows and Office.

Malicious Software Removal Tool

File Name	Windows-KB890830-V1.1-ENU.exe
Source	Microsoft Download Center (www.microsoft.com/downloads)
Operating System	Windows 2000, Windows XP, Windows Server 2003
Size	256 KB
Price/Terms	Free

Microsoft has created the Malicious Software Removal Tool add-in to help you keep your system free of known, prevalent malicious programs, or malware. It works in tandem with your antivirus software to provide a deeper line of defense against specific known threats such as MyDoom, DoomJuice, and Sasser.

When you download or run the tool, it immediately scans your system for *active* malware and stops the malicious processes found. Because it does not perform a full hard disk scan to detect inactive malware lodged in hidden nooks and crannies, you must use the Malicious Software Removal Tool in combination with up-to-date virus-scanning software for higher security.

The tool creates a log file of the system scan and then automatically reports back to Microsoft any malware found and the context of the situation, including the version of the operating system running, the processor architecture, and the results of the removal process. No personal identifying information about you is included in this report back to Microsoft. If you're lucky, after the tool runs you'll receive a message telling you no malicious software was found.

If the tool detects malware on your system, it will either remove it or present you with steps to take to complete the removal process. You then might have to restart your computer. But breathe easier: you just added another arrow to your quiver of security tools.

Microsoft Windows AntiSpyware

File Name	MicrosoftAntiSpywareInstall.exe
Source	Microsoft Download Center (www.microsoft.com/downloads)
Operating System	Windows 2000, Windows XP
Size	6374 KB
Price/Terms	Free

As of this writing, the Microsoft Windows AntiSpyware tool is in beta, which means that it's ready to be released to the public for testing in real-world situations. This tool is meant to help protect your system from spyware, which includes aggressive advertising tactics that install secret programs on your system to spy on your Internet browsing habits, steal your personal information, or hijack your PC.

Although Microsoft provides no technical support for the beta version of this tool, you can usually find the help you need by posting to the related newsgroups at **http://communities.microsoft.com/newsgroups/ default.asp?ICP=spyware&sLCID=us**. Keep your eyes open for the time when this tool is released in its final form so you can update.

Microsoft Outlook Personal Folders Backup

File Name	pfbackup.exe
Source	Microsoft Download Center (www.microsoft.com/downloads/)
Operating System	Windows 2000 Service Pack 3, Windows 98 Second Edition, Windows Millennium Edition (Me), Windows XP
Application Version	Outlook 2000, Outlook 2002, Outlook 2003
Size	160 KB
Price/Terms	Free

This tool helps you make regular, comprehensive backups of those pesky Outlook Personal Folders files that always seem to be overlooked during regular

Office backups. You can use the Personal Folders Backup tool to protect the contents of your Inbox, mail folders, calendars, contacts list, and archived folders.

After installation, open Outlook, choose Options on the Tools menu, and click the Advanced Options button in the Other tab. Click the COM Add-ins button to verify that the Outlook Backup Add-in has been added to the list of available add-ins. The tool is designated to run upon Outlook startup and the Backup command is added to the File menu.

Choose Backup on the File menu to run the add-in. Use the Options button in the Outlook Personal Folders Backup dialog box to enable the Remind Me to Backup Every option, and choose the number of days between reminders. Then choose which Personal Folders files you'd like to back up. Choose a destination where backup files will be saved, such as a removable hard disk, a CD-RW drive, or a folder on your hard drive, by typing in the path name or using the Browse button.

When you're ready to perform the backup, Outlook will tell you it must close before creating the backup. You can also use this tool to access previous backups. Choose Backup on the File menu, and click the Open Backup button to see a previous backup file.

Microsoft Office Remove Hidden Data

File Name	rhdtool.exe
Source	Microsoft Download Center (www.microsoft.com/downloads/)
Operating System	Windows 2000 Service Pack 4, Windows XP Service Pack 1
Application Version	Excel 2003, PowerPoint 2003, Word 2003, Excel 2002, PowerPoint 2002, Word 2002
Size	260 KB
Price/Terms	Free

In Chapter 11, "Securing Office," we discuss a quick and easy method to secure your Office files before you distribute or share them. The Microsoft Office Remove Hidden Data add-in makes the process even *quicker* and *easier*. You can use this tool to prepare your Word, Excel, and PowerPoint files for review by finding and removing hidden, personal, and collaboration data.

You can choose to run the add-in in individual files or on a group of files. You should only use the Remove Hidden Data tool when editing is complete and you are ready to share the document; otherwise, the tool removes data that is needed for collaboration, such as Track Changes information and comments. Also, it's a good idea to save the "clean" file under a new file name, so that you can keep the original file with all of its data intact until you are sure you will no longer need it (then degunk it from your system!).

After you run the tool, you'll receive a report that documents exactly which information was removed from the file. The Remove Hidden Data tool cannot work when information rights management is enabled in a document; neither can it remove information from protected documents, shared workbooks, or digitally signed files. It is, however, a wonderful tool for making certain inappropriate information is completely removed from an Office file before distribution.

Third-Party Tools

In this section, we've compiled short descriptions of some useful third-party add-ins and tools that you can use to degunk Office. Included are tools to help you back up your Office-related files, manage add-ins, and detect hidden files or Outlook attachments.

Genie Backup Manager

File Name	Genie Backup Manager Home v 5.0 (GBMProV5_Setup.exe)
Source	Genie Soft (www.genie-soft.com/products/gbm/default.html?AfID=13778)
Operating System	Windows 98 Standard Edition, Windows Millennium Edition (Me), Windows XP Professional and Home Editions, Windows 2000 Professional, Windows NT Workstation 4.0
Size	7.45 MB
Price/Terms	Free trial $74.95

Use the Genie Backup Manager to automate and customize the backup process. Let the Genie Backup Manager wizard guide you through the process of specifying which files should be backed up, how often, and to what media. The tool works quickly and can automate backups of the following items:

√ Microsoft Outlook (2000/2002/2003)

√ Address Book

√ Internet Explorer Settings and Favorites

√ Windows Settings (Dialup, Appearance, Mouse, Cursors, Console, etc...)

√ Windows Registry

√ Fonts

√ Desktop

√ Any file or folder

What makes Genie especially useful is the fact that you can just click an option box to enable an item to be backed up without having to navigate your file system to find specific files—Genie Backup Manager does that for you. Lots of options are available to customize your backups in almost limitless ways. The Backup Manager can create a backup and save it to an online location or removable media.

A neat feature is that you can choose to save the backup as a self-executable file, which means that you can use this file to restore from even on PCs where the Genie Backup Manager is not installed. Backups are compressed as regular ZIP files and can be scheduled for automatic execution. You can create differential, incremental, or full backups of unlimited size and then test your backup files for integrity. The Genie Backup Manager offers comprehensive restore options as well.

OfficeIns

File Name	OfficeIns.zip
Source	Nir Sofer (www.nirsoft.net/utils/officeins.html)
Application	Microsoft Office
Size	36.4 KB
Price/Terms	Free

OfficeIns is a useful little utility to help you manage your Office add-ins. This can be an indispensable service when you are troubleshooting or simply trying to minimize the number of add-ins running to conserve resources. OfficeIns displays a list of all installed add-ins for Microsoft Office products, including Word, Excel, PowerPoint, and Outlook.

Hidden File Detector

File Name	HiddenFileDetector.exe
Source	Bill Coan (www.wordsite.com/downloads/hfdty.htm)
Application	Word 97, Word 2000, Word 2002 (XP)
Size	127 KB
Price/Terms	Free

Sometimes regular Word documents can harbor unwelcome visitors in the form of spyware or space-hogging embedded image files. You can use the free Hidden File Detector add-in to identify these culprits and help you liberate your Word documents of unnecessary and secret payloads. The tool adds the Detect Hidden Files command to the Tools menu so you can access detection features from within any Word document. After you run the tool, it will report all the hidden fields and graphics it finds in the file, plus detail the possible malicious uses to which such items can be put.

Outlook Attachment Sniffer

File Name	OASniffer41_eng.zip
Source	Ralph Brooks (www.rsbr.de/Software/OASniffer/index_eng.htm)
Operating System	Windows 95, Windows 98, Windows Millennium Edition (Me), Windows NT, Windows 2000, Windows XP
Application	Outlook 2000 or later
Size	1.85 MB
Price/Terms	Free 30-day trial $15 to buy

The Outlook Attachment Sniffer enables you to do more than just extract Outlook attachments from your mail folders. You can use this tool to automatically process incoming e-mail messages and sort them into appropriate folders, export messages to disk, as well as extract attachments from some or all of your messages. This can help enormously when you wish to degunk your Outlook mail folders and flush them of extraneous attachments that are cluttering up the place.

DocRepair

File Name	DocRepair2.exe
Source	Liang Ren (www.softpedia.com/progDownload/DocRepair-Download-1878.html)
System	Windows NT 4.0, Windows Millennium Edition (Me), Windows 95, Windows 98, Windows 2000, Windows XP
Application	Word 6.0, Word95/97, Word 2000, Word XP
Size	.69 MB
Price/Terms	Free 30-day trial $79 to buy

Use this tool to help you rescue corrupted Word documents, even if they will not open. DocRepair can help you deal with error messages such as "The document name or file path is not valid" and work around application freeze-ups. The tool's wizard guides you through the steps of using the various features. Just select the corrupted file, choose the recover options, and go! DocRepair reports the status of the recovery operation as it works. When it's finished analyzing the documents and its corruptions, it allows you to see a copy of the recovered file.

Appendix B

Automate Office Using Macros

If you've ever wished you had your own personal robot to do all your boring or tedious work, Microsoft Office macros will interest you. A *macro* is a series of Office commands and actions you group together into one super command that can run without further intervention from you. Macros are used to automate repeated tasks in Office. They are coded in the Microsoft Visual Basic for Applications language, but don't let this scare you—Office provides an easy way for you to create a macro, and you don't need to be a programming expert to do so. In fact, recording a macro using the tools provided in Office is very easy. So, the next time you find yourself repetitively executing the same set of keystrokes, mouse clicks, or commands, save time by creating a macro to do the dirty work for you. In this appendix, we'll show you how.

There are two ways to create a macro:

√   Use the macro recorder to "tape-record" a set of keystrokes and mouse clicks.

√   Use the Visual Basic Editor to write new VBA code.

The macro recorder is simple to use and turns your keyboard and mouse actions into Visual Basic for Applications (VBA) code automatically. You needn't know anything about VBA to use the recorder. On the other hand, by using the Visual Basic Editor, which is found on the Macro submenu on the Tools menu, you can create much more powerful and customized macros coding directly in VBA. You can include instructions that you cannot capture simply by using the macro recorder. Although the Visual Basic Editor is designed for use by beginners and is replete with online help features and a tool set to help you debug your code, it is beyond the scope of this tiny introduction to macros. After you become more familiar with macros, we encourage you to check out the editor more fully—it's tremendously useful when you want to edit or troubleshoot macros. In this appendix, we'll show you how to use the macro recorder.

Create a Macro

Creating a macro consists of four basic steps:

1. Plan the macro.
2. Record the macro.
3. Run the macro.
4. Edit the macro.

Macros work in any Office application.

Plan Your Macro

Before you even think about recording anything, you need to plan the macro carefully because, like in life, if you make a mistake, the tape keeps on rolling. The macro recorder records everything—even the wrong things—until you turn it off. Plan the keys you will press and the commands you will run and the order of each action. You might even find it useful to practice the sequence to uncover potential snags, as well as warm up your fingers.

Next, consider whether you want to make the macro even more accessible by creating a toolbar button, menu item, or keyboard shortcut for it. If you plan to use this macro frequently, having it right at your fingertips can be more convenient than running it from the Macros dialog box.

Think about a name to assign to the macro. Macro names can't have any spaces and must start with a letter. Use PascalCase or insert an underscore between words, as in Macro_Name, to create longer and more descriptive names. If you plan to run the macro in Excel, be sure the macro does not use the same name as a cell reference or named range, or you'll get an error. Also, if you assign a macro a name that is the same as a built-in Office command, the macro will supersede the original command and the macro will be run when that command is called. If this is not as you intend, simply delete the macro and re-record using a different name. The Office command will resume normal functioning.

Plan where you will store the macro. You can store it in a single document or in a template so that it's available to many files. Macros stored in individual documents are saved as macro projects; they can be copied to other documents. By default, Word saves macros you record in it to the Normal.dot global template.

Finally, decide how you will deal with security. If the macro security level is set to High on your PC, you will not be able to run macros you create or download unless they are digitally signed (see Chapter 11, "Securing Office," for more information on digital signatures and macro security levels). To self-sign a macro you create, you can obtain a digital certificate from an official certification authority, such as VeriSign, on the Internet or from your IT manager. If the macro security level is set to Medium, the Office application will display a warning when you try to run unsigned macros. If you're sure the macro is virus- free, such as one you created yourself on a clean PC, you can choose to enable the macro to run.

Record the Macro

Once the planning is finished, all the hard decisions have been made already—recording the macro is straightforward! It will be easier to follow along if we use an example. In this appendix, we'll create a simple macro in Excel that opens a new workbook and formats the first row and first column of Sheet 1 to be text labels. Follow these steps to record the macro:

1. In Excel, close any open workbooks.

2. Choose Macro on the Tools menu, and click Record New Macro.

3. In the Record Macro dialog box, type a name for the macro, assign a shortcut key, choose a storage location, and type a short description. In this example, we call the macro NewBookFormatting, as shown in Figure B-1. Click OK to start the recorder.

4. Open a new workbook, select row 1, and perform the following actions:

   a. Choose Cells on the Format menu.

   b. In the Number tab, choose Text.

   c. In the Alignment tab, choose Center from the Horizontal Text drop-down menu in the Text Alignment section.

   d. In the Font tab, select Bold for Font Style.

   e. In the Patterns tab, choose light orange, and then click OK.

5. Select column 1, and then repeat steps a through e.

6. Choose Macro on the Tools menu, and click Stop Recording.

That's all there is to it!

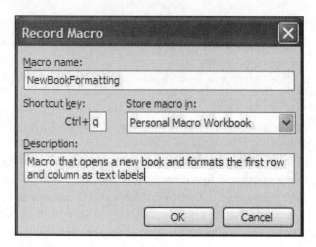

Figure B-1
Name and describe the macro.

Run the Macro

It's now time to test the macro. Choose Macro on the Tools menu, and then click Macros. Choose the macro from the list in the Macro dialog box, and click Run. Verify the macro performs as you expect. If not, move on to the next step.

Edit the Macro

To edit a macro—to remove unwanted steps or to figure out where it takes a misstep—you have to use the Visual Basic Editor. Choose Macro on the Tools menu, and then click Macros. Select the macro from the list, and then click Edit in the Macro dialog box. The Visual Basic Editor will open, enabling you to step into the program or debug it. Many excellent resources on VBA are available to help you. Check the Visual Basic Editor Help files and MSDN, the Microsoft Developer Network at **http://msdn.microsoft.com**. To take the simple route, you can always re-record the macro, paying special attention to keeping the sequence simple and straightforward.

Index

A

Active cell indicator, 140
Active cells, 140
Active sheet, 140
Add-ins
    conflicts caused by, troubleshooting, 326–329
    disabling, 326–329
    in Word, disabling, 341–342
Allow Fast Saves option
    disabling, 265
    enabling and disabling, 115
    saving documents with, 264
Always Create Backup Copy option
    disabling, 115
    enabling, 113–115
American Standard Code for Information Interchange (ASCII), alphabetization scheme, 66
Animations
    avoiding complicated, 184
    number of, reducing, 184
    using, 191–192
Antivirus software
    conflicts with, 337
    installing and running, importance of, 260
    macro viruses, detecting and removing, 280, 287–289
    scanning for viruses with, 39
    updating, 333
Application failures
    causes of, 322–323
    recovering files and documents after, 110
    troubleshooting, 323. *See also* Troubleshooting; Troubleshooting process
    types of, 322–323

Application files, troubleshooting damage in, 328
Application Recovery feature, 338
Applications. *See also* Excel; Outlook; PowerPoint; Word
    activating and registering, 46–47
    application files, repairing, 329–330
    application files, storing, 6
    closing during installation, 42
    configuration changes in, 109
    crashes and freeze-ups of, 322. *See also* Application failures; Errors
    default views in, setting up, 75–86
    Detect and Repair command, 330, 344
    file-saving schemes of, 6–8
    gunk in, eliminating, 20–21
    interoperability of, 20. *See also* Interoperability
    macro autodetection, 285–287
    macro warning dialog box, 286
    Open and Repair command, 339
    performance, free disk space and, 179–180
    performance, RAM and, 179
    performance, troubleshooting, 332–333
    personalized menus in, enabling and disabling, 87–88
    printing in, degunking, 99–104
    restarting, 338
    safe mode, starting in, 327–329
    safe mode diagnostics, 329
    transferring data between, 232–243
    troubleshooting. *See* Troubleshooting; Troubleshooting process
Appointments, color-coding in Outlook, 203–204
Auto Scale feature, problems with, 325
AutoArchive
    default aging periods for, 199

W

X

Z

Degunking Your Email, Spam, and Viruses

By Jeff Duntemann
ISBN 19321193-X
340 pages
Available Now!
$24.99 U.S.

Overwhelmed by spam?

Plagued by pop-ups? Ever been hit by a virus or Trojan horse? Wasting time sorting through your huge pile of email? If so, *Degunking Your Email, Spam, and Viruses* is the book for you! Jeff Duntemann, co-author of the best-selling book *Degunking Windows,* shows you how to keep annoying email clutter at bay, how to quickly organize your email so you can find what you need, how to eradicate and prevent spam and pop-ups, how to protect yourself from Internet scams, hackers, and dangerous viruses, and much more. A great book for anyone who needs help keeping their PC safe and free of spam and email clutter.

Degunking Windows

By Joli Ballew and Jeff Duntemann
ISBN 1-93211-84-0
320 pages
Available Now!
$24.99 U.S.
Bestseller!

Featured in Parade Magazine

Clean up and speed up your sluggish PC!

This is the book that Windows XP users all around the world have been talking about. It covers the basics to help you quickly get your PC back to top performance. It's organized according to the special "cleaning" process that will improve the performance of your computer. Shortcut and time calculation charts are provided at the beginning of the book to help you determine how much time is required to perform different degunking tasks. Topics covered include the basics of degunking ("Why is my computer all gunked up in the first place?"), cleaning files, hard drives, and making space, uninstalling programs you don't need, fixing your desktop and start menus, improving and cleaning the registry, hardware stuff to help with degunking, and much more.

Degunking Your Mac

By Joli Ballew
ISBN 1-93211-94-8
280 pages
Available Now!
$24.99 U.S.

Make your Mac run faster and better than ever!

Degunking Your Mac covers the latest operating system (OS X Panther) and earlier versions, including OS 9. It provides the essential tips and tricks to help you bring your Mac up to top performance. All of the crucial degunking tips and tricks are in the book, including how to degunk Macs that run dual operating systems, how to better manage hard drives that get gunked up with all types of media files, how to properly optimize the desktop, how to manage fonts properly and get rid of unneeded "font gunk," how to properly get rid of the extra stuff that OS X installs, and much more.

Degunking Your PC

By Joli Ballew
ISBN 1-933097-03-5
340 pages
Available: March 2005
$24.99 U.S.

Are all the connections to your PC and peripherals all gunked up?

Are you tripping over a viper's nest of cords and cables at every turn? Do you have printer drivers installed that date back to the Eisenhower administration? Is it impossible to vacuum under your desk? Still using dial up? Having trouble syncing your PDA with your PC's address book? If so, you have PC gunk! *Degunking Your PC* will show you the way to get out of the rat's maze of cables and old plug-and-play devices and onto the road of clean and neat PC organization. Joli Ballew, the co-author of the bestselling book Degunking Windows, will show you simple, fast, and effective ways to manage your PC hardware so that everything works seamlessly and efficiently. Degunk your PC and get rid of those cables once and for all!